Modernist Literature

D1420038

Modernist Literature
An Introduction

Mary Ann Gillies and Aurelea Mahood

Edinburgh University Press

Edinburgh University Press Ltd
22 George Square, Edinburgh

Edited and typeset by the authors.

Printed and bound in Great Britain by
Cromwell Press, Trowbridge, Wilts

A CIP record for this title is available from the British Library

ISBN 978 0 7486 2763 9 (hardback)
ISBN 978 0 7486 2764 6 (paperback)

CONTENTS

ACKNOWLEDGMENTS

No book is ever written without support and encouragement. We would like to thank the following people for providing us with just that and so much more.

John Whatley, who suggested that we embark on this project in the first place.

Jackie Jones, our wonderful editor at Edinburgh University Press, whose belief in this book meant that it saw the light of day.

The many professionals at Edinburgh University Press who assisted in the transition of the manuscript to finished book, especially James Dale, Ian Davidson, Máiréad McElligott, Stuart Midgley, and Esmé Watson.

Dania Sheldon, who compiled the index.

Bev Neufeld, for assisting us with various formatting issues at a crucial moment.

Sheila Roberts, who graciously agreed to proofread a penultimate draft of the book at very short notice.

John Pierce, Diane Gibson, Peggy Lacasse, and Mary Ann's other colleagues in the Dean of Arts and Social Sciences Office at Simon Fraser University whose ongoing support of her research, despite the fact that it takes time away from faculty business, is invaluable.

Andrew Klobucar and Rick Appel, for listening when Aurelea was working through the many stages of revision.

Denise and Brent Mahood and Anneliesa Bush, who reminded Aurelea to go outside during the rewrites.

Finally, we would like to thank our students, at Simon Fraser University and elsewhere, whose love of modernist literature continues to inspire us. We dedicate this book to them.

INTRODUCTION

AFTER VICTORIA

As Lucy Tantamount dryly observes to Walter Bidlake in Aldous Huxley's *Point Counter Point* (1928), 'Living modernly's living quickly.'[1] The scene is not simply an example of disaffected banter between a pair of lovers; it is a skirmish between opposing viewpoints. In Lucy's estimation, Walter is anything but up-to-date. She is of the opinion that Walter thinks in 'an absurdly unmodern way about everything.'[2] He does not understand that

> [y]ou can't cart a wagon-load of ideals and romanticisms with you these days. When you travel by aeroplane, you must leave your heavy baggage behind. The good old-fashioned soul was all right when we lived slowly. But it's too ponderous nowadays. There's no room for it in the aeroplane.[3]

With its attention to speed and rejection of the past, Lucy's jeering declaration is striking for at least two reasons. First, it suggests the highly self-conscious perception of time and space characteristic of twentieth-century literature and culture. Second, it captures the sense that speed—in particular, the speed with which change takes place—is a fundamental characteristic of modern life. Or as Lucy puts it while also extending the aeroplane metaphor, 'If you like speed, if you want to cover the ground, you can't have luggage. The thing is to know what you want and to be ready to pay for it. I know exactly what I want; so I sacrifice the luggage.'[4] She is prepared to sacrifice the weight of past conventions in order to explore new ground. These glib remarks made by one of Huxley's characters on the subjects of technology, fashion, and change are but one example of the early twentieth century's preoccupation and fascination with the aesthetics of change and the art of modern living.

That said, however, any attempt to determine what distinguishes the literature of the early twentieth century from other eras cannot of course limit itself to a review of dialogue in a select sample of the period's novels. In its examination of the first four decades of the twentieth century, this textbook combines Lucy's commitment to 'living modernly' and 'living quickly.' It assesses the delicate interplay between the aesthetic and material conditions of literary production over a forty-year span as further transfigured by evolving literary and cultural values. Each chapter looks at a different genre and maps the expression of the modern in the given genre while simultaneously attending to matters of relevance to both form and content.

As the twentieth century progressed, the drive to embrace the modern note signalled in Pound's succinct call to 'make it new' embedded itself in ever increasingly formalized definitions of modernism. Indeed, modernism's revolutionary impulses continued to be privileged in critical circles decades after the publication of *Make It New* in 1934. In 1976, for example, British critics Malcolm Bradbury and James McFarlane published *Modernism, 1890–1930*. This influential collection of essays opens with Bradbury and McFarlane's oft-quoted entry 'The Name and Nature of Modernism.' This essay shows how previous decades of literary criticism devoted to cataloguing modernist aesthetic conventions had come to be distilled within an Anglo-American critical tradition. It identifies five key modernist tendencies: the movement away from representational realism towards abstract and autotelic art forms; a high degree of aesthetic self-consciousness; an aesthetic of radical innovation, fragmentation, and shock; the breaking of familiar formal and linguistic conventions; and the use of paradox.[5] Likewise, in the much earlier *A Glossary of Literary Terms* (1957), well-known American critic M.H. Abrams wrote:

> the specific features signified by 'modernism' vary with the
> user, but most critics agree that it involves a deliberate and
> radical break with some of the traditional bases both of Western
> culture and of Western art. . . . A prominent feature of modern-
> ism is the phenomenon of an avant-garde . . . that is, a small,
> self-conscious group of artists and authors who undertake, in
> Ezra Pound's phrase, to 'make it new.' By violating accepted
> conventions and decorums, they undertake to create ever-new
> artistic forms and styles and to introduce hitherto neglected, and
> sometimes forbidden, subject matters.[6]

Both definitions emphasize the centrality of a conscious break with the past to all variants of modernism. In similar fashion, the most recent edition of J.A. Cuddon's widely-used *Penguin Dictionary of Literary Terms and Literary Theory* (2004) describes literary modernism as 'a breaking away from established rules, traditions and conventions' which reveals 'fresh ways of looking at man's position and function in the universe and many (in some cases remarkable) experiments in form and style. It is particularly concerned with language and how to use it (representationally or otherwise) and with *writing itself*.'[7] For readers of modernist texts at the beginning of the twenty-first century, as all three definitions suggest, modernism is synonymous with a rejection of the past and an embrace of aesthetic innovation. It is synonymous with diverse movements in art, architecture, and literature characterized by deliberate breaks with classical and traditional forms or methods of expression. It is synonymous with the opening four decades of the twentieth century. With their emphasis on inter-disciplinarity and diversity, these definitions discourage readings of modernism inclined to dismiss it as an esoteric literary movement produced by loosely affiliated iconoclasts. Subtle variations aside, in all instances modernism emerges as a complex response across continents and disciplines to a changing world. As such, all four chapters will examine the genre under consideration with reference to Anglo-American modernism and literary history. In doing so, how the literature of the new century both differed and drew upon the past will be explored.

From the vantage point of the twentieth-first century, it is readily apparent that the world did not change irrevocably with the end of the nineteenth century. It is, however, evident that during the final decades of the century clusters of seemingly unrelated ideas were 'in the air' inflecting contemporary thought and artistic production—ideas that only gained increased force as they entered into the cultural mainstream and found expression in art and everyday exchanges. Questions of concern to men and women at the end of the nineteenth century gradually became commonplaces in the twentieth century. In 1889, publisher and writer Grant Allen remarked, 'everybody nowadays talks about evolution. Like electricity, the cholera, women's rights, the great mining boom, and the Eastern question, it is "in the air".'[8] Social and scientific progress and questions relating to gender, race, and national politics continued to be 'in the air' for decades to come. Over thirty years later, 'Feminism, Jazz, Prohibition, Cubism, the League of Nations, *Vers Libres*, [and] Motorbicycles' were declared enthusiasms of the new century in an unsigned 1924 editorial published in British *Vogue*.[9] The *Vogue* editorial—'Fashions of the Mind'—identifies the ongoing concern surrounding technology and progress—whether aesthetic, sexual, or political—characteristic of twentieth-century literature and history.

In short, although Queen Victoria did not die until 22 January 1901, the force of the nineteenth century and the Victorian Age had waned well before the end of the century and the monarch's death. Traditional beliefs and stabilities had been undercut by forces in the nineteenth century that continued to be of relevance in the twentieth century. Twentieth-century literature registers the impact of nineteenth-century revolutions in science, political economy, and psychology, the cumulative effect of educational reforms, the changing position of women, and rising nationalist movements both at home and in the colonies.[10] The sense of a loss of moorings was pervasive, and perhaps inevitable. In response, modern writers—many of whom had been born in the final decades of the nineteenth century—began to dispense with the frames of reference provided by the past. The stylistic experiments now associated with modernism were fuelled by artists' responses to paradigm shifts in the nation's scientific and intellectual communities.

Men and women in a broad range of disciplines widely viewed themselves as working in a period of intense change and uncertainty. Indeed, a transformation so profound had taken place that almost everyone—in the most everyday of situations—was comfortable referring to themselves as modern. Rather than attempting to catalogue the impact of contemporary views on change in a generalized sense, each chapter in this book charts the expression of a dominant theme characteristic of a specific decade and genre. It is important to emphasize that the theme, or tendency, taken up in a given chapter is by no means the only question or concern 'in the air' at the time. The theme should be conceived as but one possible direction of investigation that has been selected because it facilitates an analysis of the special strength of a specific genre during a ten-year period.

THE 1900S:
THE SHORT STORY AND THE NEW WOMAN

The changing social position of women was a powerful and potent force of relevance to the public and writers alike at the beginning of the twentieth century. Throughout the nineteenth century parliament passed a series of acts that helped slowly transform the status of women in Britain. The Custody Act 1839, the Divorce and Matrimonial Causes Act 1857, and the Married Women's Property Acts 1870 and 1882, in combination with the gradual admission of women to universities, represented a restrained rejection of prescribed and limited roles for women. Highly public calls for change continued into the twentieth century with a particular emphasis on the demand for universal suffrage. Committed reformer Emmeline Pankhurst founded the Women's Social and Political Union (WSPU) in 1903, after which instances of public agitation and protest by British suffragettes continued to increase.

Although women were not granted the right to vote until 1918 and there were limited legal changes of consequence to women passed in the first decade of the century, turn-of-the-century writing was not similarly belated in acknowledging and addressing changing gender relations. Virginia Woolf's attitudes towards change and gender in the opening decade of the new century are expressed subtly in her essay 'Mr Bennett and Mrs Brown.' Critics conventionally explore Virginia Woolf's declaration: 'on or about December 1910, human character changed,' with reference to the First Post-Impressionist exhibition at the Grafton Gallery in London and the death of Edward VII. It is, however, worth noting that Woolf continues with the observation that

> [t]he change was not sudden and definite . . . . But a change
> there was, nevertheless; and, since one must be arbitrary, let us
> date it about the year 1910. The first signs of it are recorded in
> the books of Samuel Butler, in *The Way of All Flesh* in particu-
> lar; the plays of Bernard Shaw continue to record it. In life one
> can see the change, if I may use a homely illustration, in the
> character of one's cook. The Victorian cook lived like a le-

viathan in the lower depths, formidable, silent, obscure, inscrutable; the Georgian cook is a creature of sunshine and fresh air; in and out of the drawing-room, now to borrow the *Daily Herald*, and now to ask advice about a hat. . . . All human relations have shifted—those between masters and servants, husbands and wives, parents and children. And when human relations change there is at the same time a change in religion, conduct, politics and literature.[11]

This passage warrants scrutiny for several reasons. First, although Woolf arbitrarily declares 1910 an instant of momentous change, bowing to the ingrained convention of assigning dates to history, the instances of change that she cites are decidedly late nineteenth century in origin. Samuel Butler's *The Way of All Flesh* (completed in 1884 and posthumously published in 1903) is a bitter indictment of Victorian life. The novel savagely attacks Victorian conceptions of the family, education, and religion. In turn, one of Butler's greatest admirers, the young Bernard Shaw, was among the most strident voices in a growing chorus that called Victorian assumptions into question. Shaw's plays challenged complacent audiences, teasing and disturbing them with one provocative paradox after another. *Mrs Warren's Profession* (1893), *Arms and the Man* (1894), and *Candida* (1896) are but among the better known Shaw plays written and performed before the end of the century. As her references to Butler and then Shaw suggest, Woolf is well aware of the intimate and subtle connection between contemporary examples of change and the past. Second, the reference to the *Daily Herald*, a progressive paper originally published by striking London printers in December 1910, can be interpreted as an acknowledgment of the role played by newspapers and magazines in forming public opinion *and* registering changes in public opinion.[12] Finally, Woolf concludes her commentary on change with the assertion that shifts in human relations do not occur in isolation. If human relations change so too must all the institutions and forums in which men and women are implicated. Literature is but one arena in which change can be registered and examined.

The earliest version of 'Mr Bennett and Mrs Brown' was first published in 1923—five years after the end of World War I. The force and importance of the changing human relations catalogued by Woolf were of such significance to her that 1910 remained a compelling marker of a growing division between the nineteenth and twentieth centuries even after the horrors of World War I. The fictional treatment of shifting human relations—in particular, those between women and men—at the beginning of the twentieth century lies at the heart of her second novel *Night and Day* (1919), which explores the truth of feelings—especially the nature of love—and poses crucial questions about gender, intellectual freedom, and marriage. As Chapter 1 demonstrates, Woolf was by no means alone in her intense preoccupation with such matters. Acknowledged masters of the modern short story such as James Joyce, D.H. Lawrence, and Katherine Mansfield all wrote stories exploring gender in relation to family, marriage, politics, and freedom long before Woolf wrote 'Mr Bennett and Mrs Brown.'

In addition to reading the opening decade of the twentieth century against short stories by Joyce, Lawrence, and Mansfield with an emphasis on the 'woman question,' Chapter 1 examines the short fiction of E.O. Somerville and Martin Ross. Somerville and Ross are best known for their deceptively light comic short stories that offer unexpectedly sly and biting commentary on matters related to questions concerning gender, class, and nationality. Edith Somerville and Violet Martin—second cousins and later companions—began writing together in the late 1880s. Their first book, *An Irish Cousin*, appeared in 1889. By the time Martin died in 1915, they had published fourteen titles together, including *The Real Charlotte* (1894), *Some Experiences of an Irish R.M.* (1899), and *In Mr Knox's Country* (1915).

The chapter's analysis of the short story also assesses the match between the genre and the topics discussed in the chapter. In *Katherine Mansfield and the Origins of Modernist Fiction* (1991), Sydney Kaplan argues that the novel presented Mansfield with 'narrative conventions she found troubling and limiting, especially in their encodings of concepts about women's roles.'[13] In turn, Kaplan concludes her chapter assessing Mansfield's failure to write a novel and her choice of the short story as her preferred genre with the suggestion that 'by rejecting the conventions of the [novel], its plot-generated structure, she also rejected its implications about women's possibilities.'[14] While this argument does not hold true in relation to Somerville and Ross, Joyce, and Lawrence, all of whom were comfortable writing in more than one genre, it does suggest a particular strength of the short story—its fitness in recording the experience of outsiders—and falls in line with existing though limited criticism on the modern short story. Numerous critics have argued that the short story thrives best in a fragmented society. With this fragmentation, the matter of perspective—the angle of vision—becomes most important in the short story, 'which does not present a world to enter, as does the novel, but a vignette to contemplate.'[15] By this token, Mansfield's short stories offered a perspective which rejected the marriage-plot so dominant in nineteenth-century novels, and instead explored feminine desire from often hitherto unexplored angles. All of the short story writers in this chapter isolate individuals—on account of gender, class, and or nationality—so much so that the genre comes to seem 'the natural vehicle for the presentation of the outsider, but also for the moment whose intensity makes it seem outside the ordinary stream of time . . . or outside our ordinary range of experience.'[16]

THE 1910s:
POETRY, TECHNOLOGY, AND THE WAR

The second decade of the new century marked the end of the short-lived Edwardian period. After the death of his father, Edward VII, George V acceded to the throne in 1910. The 1910s were anything but untroubled. The decade was violently interrupted by the 'war to end all wars.' The Great War broke out one year after the end of the Balkans War and just weeks after the assassination of Archduke Franz Ferdinand of Austria-Hungary.[17] The assassination helped propel a continent of nations beholden to one another through complex systems of military alliances and secret treaties into a protracted, bloody war in which millions of lives were lost.

It was a war of technological and mechanical firsts; modern machinery accelerated the ease and speed with which men could be killed. Deaths among combatants and civilians alike were unprecedented—more soldiers died in World War I than in all European wars fought during the nineteenth century combined. April 1915: the first poison gas attack. January 1915: the first airship raid on England (East Anglia). September 1916: the first use of tanks in battle. February 1917: the advent of unrestricted submarine warfare. May 1917: the first air raids by planes on London. The conflict did not end for four years. A general armistice was declared on 11 November 1918, and the Treaty of Versailles was signed by the Allies and Germany the following year. The impossible task of monitoring the postwar world with the hope of maintaining a lasting peace fell to the League of Nations, and so ended a decade of violent initiation into the realities of modern warfare.[18]

Chapter 2 assesses the impact of modern technology on the stylistic revolutions associated with poetry written during the 1910s. Poetry—with its tendency towards brevity and its comparative speed of composition, as well as publication, which frequently outpaces that of fiction—was the perfect literary medium through which to respond to the Great War. As with the shifts in human relations catalogued by Woolf in 'Mr Bennett and Mrs Brown,' the poetic revolutions of formal and stylistic importance to the development of Anglo-American poetry during the conflict began well in advance of World War I.

Arguably, the modernization of English-language poetry began with the start of a poetic revolution heavily influenced by the work of French Symbolist poets in the late nineteenth century and by T.E. Hulme, English poet and philosopher.[19] Hulme's insistence on clear, hard, precise images was celebrated and promoted enthusiastically by the American poet Ezra Pound who had settled in London in 1908. In 1912, the movement received a name—Imagism—which Pound first applied to the work of Richard Aldington, Hilda Dolittle (H.D.), and T.E. Hulme.[20] According to Pound, the first published use of the word

7

'Imagiste' was in his note to T.E. Hulme's five poems printed at the end of his 'Ripostes' in the autumn of 1912. Pound's two best-known commentaries on Imagism—'A Few Don'ts' and 'A Retrospect'—appeared in the March 1913 issue of *Poetry* and in the 1918 essay collection *Pavannes and Divagations*. As articulated by Pound, three primary principles epitomized Imagism: the direct treatment of the 'thing,' whether subjective or objective; the rejection of any words that do not contribute to the presentation [of the image]; and composition in the sequence of a musical phrase, not in the sequence of a metronome.[21] In adhering to these three propositions, an Imagist poem captures

> an intellectual and emotional complex in an instant of time . . . .
> It is the presentation of such a 'complex' instantaneously which
> gives that sense of sudden liberation; that sense of freedom
> from time limits and space limits; that sense of sudden growth,
> which we experience in the presence of the greatest works of
> art.[22]

Peter Nicholls' comments on Pound and Imagism in *Modernisms: A Literary Guide* (1995) are instructive when seeking to determine the literary implications of Pound's directives. In Chapter 8, Nicholls remarks that Pound 'regarded art as the means by which to give structure and value to an otherwise formless modernity; and the way to do this was always in some measure to restore a context to the chaotic "reality of the moment," to disclose those cultural mediations which a mere impressionism would efface.'[23]

While Nicholls does not explicitly examine the new poetics with specific reference to World War I, his suggestion that Pound's aim for Imagism was that it 'in some measure . . . restore a context to the chaotic "reality of the moment"' is compelling when considered in relation to Robert Graves' views on poetry. He formulated these views after direct combat experience in the trenches and woods of France. Graves—like so many of the war poets—was compelled to write poetry that set out to capture the reality of modern warfare rather than deferring to the clichéd, outmoded language of earlier poetry devoted to the battlefields of Europe. In *Good-bye to All That* (1929), Graves recalls the November 1915 meeting between himself and Siegfried Sassoon—an encounter in which conversation quickly turned to poetry:

> We went to the cake-shop and ate cream buns. At this time I
> was getting my first book of poems, *Over the Brazier*, ready for
> the press; I had one or two drafts in my pocket-book and
> showed them to Siegfried. He frowned and said that war should
> not be written about in such a realistic way. In return, he
> showed me some of his own poems. One of them began:
>
> Return to greet me, colours that were my joy,
> Not in the woeful crimson of men slain . . .

Siegfried had not yet been in the trenches. I told him, in my old-soldier manner, that he would soon change his style.[24]

Graves was right. Sassoon and fellow war poets fashioned a body of work that now stands as a profound and haunting record of the brutality and horror of World War I.

The machine-made terrors of modern warfare demanded a new kind of poetry: a poetry that did away with outdated concepts of valour and honour; a poetry that responded to the immediate sensation of the experience and forged images and rhythms appropriate to the scenes and experiences treated in the poem. The body of writing composed in direct response to the war is a devastating example of an instance in which an aesthetic revolution and the material conditions of production converge to generate a body of work that definitively breaks with the past. The dynamic interplay between poetry and war, such as was evident during World War I and directly after, powerfully illustrates the impossibility of assessing literary history without reference to socio-political history.

THE 1920S:
THE NOVEL AND MODERN FASHIONS

The end of the Great War was accompanied by a sense of physical and moral exhaustion. Writers were faced with the monumental task of creating literature with 'new and appropriate values for modern culture, and a style appropriate to those values.'[25] Writers strove to produce stories whose tone and method were suited to a world in which the Great War was felt to have irrevocably shattered any remaining hope in the old certainties about faith, history, and knowledge. While seeking new methods and alternatives to the old beliefs and systems, modern writers strove to be true to the new scepticisms and hesitations. Novelists, in particular, proved particularly adept at capturing the ethos of the postwar world; the 1920s produced many of the most highly regarded English-language novels of the twentieth century—modern masterpieces like James Joyce's *Ulysses* (1922), E.M. Forster's *A Passage to India* (1924), Virginia Woolf's *To the Lighthouse* (1927), and Aldous Huxley's *Point Counter Point* (1928). The novels of the period are characterized by a personal and textual inwardness as the writers looked inward in an effort to capture new personal realities.

Almost a century later, the modernist novel is now profoundly associated with its repeated explorations of its characters' interior lives—a primary characteristic foreshadowed in Joseph Conrad's 1901 novella *Heart of Darkness*.[26] In retrospect, Marlow—the story's central narrator—with his rhetoric of the invisible, inaudible, impossible, unintelligible, and the unspeakable now appears foundational in relation to the history of modernist prose. Within two decades after the publication of *Heart of Darkness*, Woolf called for writers and readers alike to 'look within' and examine 'an ordinary mind on an ordinary day.'[27] By the 1920s, the injunction to capture the 'incessant shower of innumerable atoms . . . as they fall, [and] as they shape themselves into the life of Monday or Tuesday' had become a commonplace in English literary culture.[28] Writers had rapidly refined the technical means by which to record and explore the 'myriad impressions' a mind receives in the course of a day—'trivial, fantastic, evanescent, or engraved with the sharpness of steel.'[29] To do so required writers to 'record the atoms as they fall upon the mind in the order in which they fall, [and] trace the pattern, however disconnected and incoherent in appearance, which each sight or incident scores upon the consciousness.'[30] Free indirect discourse and stream-of-consciousness were two of the most important modernist techniques for gaining access to a character's mind.

Joyce's landmark novel *Ulysses,* frequently hailed as the most important novel of the twentieth century, makes skilled use of both techniques. Unsurprisingly, Woolf described Joyce as

> concerned at all costs to reveal the flickerings of that innermost
> flame which flashes its messages through the brain, and in order
> to preserve it he disregards with complete courage whatever
> seems to him adventitious, whether it be probability, or coher-
> ence, or any other of these signposts which for generations have
> served to support the imagination of a reader when called upon
> to imagine what he can neither touch nor see.[31]

Not only did Joyce reject the confident Victorian naturalism inherited by the Edwardians but he ably demonstrated that writers (and readers) must 'not take it for granted that life exists more fully in what is commonly thought big than in what is commonly thought small.'[32] While the mythic template against which the novel is set recalls Homer's Odysseus, Leopold Bloom navigates altogether modern and domestic dangers as he wends his way home—returns to his Penelope and Ithaca. The effect is two-fold: first, everyman—as opposed to a Greek hero—is the subject of the novel and, second, by way of the double story, in spite of all its revolutionary pyrotechnics, *Ulysses* exposes a continuous parallel between contemporaneity and antiquity — between the past and the present. The impetus for revolutions—stylistic or political—is rooted in the evolving relationship between the past and the present; the past, in turn, whether rejected or rewritten, necessarily becomes an integral component of the most experimental of tales—the most modern of novels.

In short, two primary characteristics of modernist novels are affirmed with the publication of *Ulysses*. First, it showcases a profound interest in the inner workings of the ordinary mind. Second, it presents an intense interest in that mind's response to the contemporary moment as filtered through the weight of history whether personal, familial, religious or national. The techniques and themes of *Ulysses* were variously reconfigured and deployed by a diverse cross-section of British writers throughout the inter-war years. Not only were many of these works successes in a technical sense but they were also acclaimed by readers and critics alike. Aided by book reviews (in magazines and newspapers) and literary essays, modernism entered into the literary mainstream during the 1920s. Literary fashion and what was fashionable among readers of mainstream magazines and the country's broadsheets had converged.

As Chapter 3 shows through re-readings of *A Passage to India* and Elizabeth Bowen's *The Last September* (1929), both novels offer intense psychological portraits of women and men experiencing different forms of dislocation—geographic, generational, spiritual, and psychic. The forces of history come to bear on individuals—on private lives—in both novels; in turn the novels record the impressions and emotions to which our consciousness can variously fall prey. The novels are symptomatic of a literature that expresses sympathy with a wide range of characters and is increasingly multi-perspectival with regard to narrative structure. The modern imperative to attend to the individual and interiority transfigures the literary landscape and adds to the range and subtlety of experiences represented in contemporary fiction. The diversity of voices and styles that is so rich a component of late twentieth-century writing is firmly rooted in the literary fashions popularized nearly a century ago.

THE 1930S:

DOCUMENTING THE POLITICS OF ENGAGEMENT

In contrast to the 1920s, the 1930s are only too full of events now burned upon our collective memory of the twentieth century: 1933, Hitler becomes Chancellor of Germany; 1935, Germany reoccupies the Saar, Italy invades Abyssinia, and the League of Nations fails to take adequate action to restrain the aggressors; 1936, the Spanish Civil War begins; 1939, World War II begins. With the ascendancy of Spain's Franco, Italy's Mussolini, and Germany's Hitler, Fascism followed the economic depression and staggering unemployment that characterized the early 1930s. The threat of another war that had haunted the 1920s became increasingly real as the decade progressed. Writers who came of age during this period shared an acute awareness of the pressures and political problems of their times. This awareness has, in part, contributed to the clichéd view of the 1930s as a decade in which writers returned to social realism and a range of documentary endeavours while rejecting the reputed apolitical solipsism of high modernism.

To refer to the above perception of the 1930s as a cliché is not to suggest that writers like W.H. Auden, Cecil Day Lewis, Louis MacNeice, Stephen Spender, Graham Greene, Christopher Isherwood, and George Orwell were not politically engaged authors with a profound interest in the function of art during times of crisis. Unquestionably, a renewed sense of urgency with regard to the imperative of communicating with one's audience infuses the work of these and other poets, novelists, and playwrights alike. It is, however, to contend that how we view modernist innovation in relation to political engagement can be reconfigured if we do not proceed as though experiments with style were a thing of the past in the 1930s. The politics of style is a fundamental component of the 1930s art. In addition to providing an opportunity to explore the politics of style and engagement, there is yet another advantage associated with the insistence on examining the political implications of the genres in which writers choose to work. Drawing attention to political engagement in terms of a communicative act with an audience highlights the performative axis of the literary arts.

Documentary forms emerged as important, and innovative, means of protecting artistic integrity while permitting the artist a platform from which to explore political and social beliefs. Cinema was one of the most important documentary forms in the 1930s, with documentary film units such as the publicly funded General Post Office (GPO) Film Unit and the privately funded Shell Oil's Film Unit feeding the public's desire for documentaries. The roots of British documentary film can be traced, in part, to the advent of newsreels in 1910 and in part to the work of Russian filmmakers such as Sergei Eisenstein whose depictions of life in Soviet Russia and use of a dialectical story structure strongly impressed filmmakers such as John Grierson of the GPO Unit. However, British audiences were most familiar with newsreels; indeed newsreels were hugely popular in the 1920s and '30s.[33] These short films—routinely about five minutes in length—presented a number of the week's current events and in the process created an audience demand for films that depicted the world around them in a seemingly objective and realistic manner.[34] In fact, newsreels and documentary films were carefully crafted, and frequently used for propaganda purposes—notoriously in this period in Leni Riefenstahl's *Triumph of Will* (1934), for example, which chronicles the Nazi Party Congress in Nuremberg. As documentary films continued to flourish, artists working in other media began to adopt and adapt the filmmakers' techniques. Literature, in particular, began to import documentary elements into genres where they seemed a natural fit—drama and non-fiction prose such as travel writing—and in those where they seemed less so—such as poetry and fiction. Chapter 4 focuses on two specific genres in which elements of documentary form became crucial: drama and prose fiction.

Studies of twentieth-century British drama all too often emphasize postwar developments limiting the pre-1945 references to a passing mention of the wartime verse plays commissioned by the BBC and written for radio by T.S. Eliot, Louis MacNeice, and other poets. An impoverished history of drama emerges wherein it seems as though nothing of importance took place between the staging of plays by Wilde or Shaw early in the century and then those of Beckett after the 1940s. In addition to Eliot and MacNeice, another important writer of verse plays during the 1930s was W.H. Auden who co-wrote three plays with Christoper Isherwood before the outbreak of World War II. Collaborations between Auden and Isherwood include *The Dog Beneath the Skin* (1935), *The Ascent of F6* (1936), and *On the Frontier* (1938).

Auden wrote *On the Frontier* with Isherwood ten years after establishing himself as the leading voice of the new generation with the publication of his first book of verse in 1928. From the outset, critics admired Auden for his technical virtuosity and an ability to write poems in a variety of verse forms energized with references to popular culture, current events, and vernacular speech. These same qualities animate his plays. In particular, the verse plays that Auden wrote with Isherwood are a complex interweaving of popular culture, current events, and the vernacular effectively deployed as a commentary on stagnation, moral paralysis, and the need for action. Their third and final collaboration, *On the Frontier*—which was first performed in Cambridge at the Group Theatre the year before war broke out—depicts a situation in which two countries move towards conflict despite the fact that no one character within the play wills that movement. The theatre critic in the *Manchester Guardian* declared the first performance of the show, on 14 November 1938, an 'indisputable success.'[35] Auden's biographer, Humphrey Carpenter, described the play as an 'unsteady beginning of a real revolution in English drama.'[36]

MacNeice's opening night review declared that the effect of watching *On the Frontier* was akin to viewing 'a series of melodramatic cartoons . . . [it is] like a number of escaped posters and photographs blown by the wind in one's face.'[37] As the observation suggests, the play borrows techniques from other forms of media culture—it does not limit itself to exclusively literary allusions. The kinship to documentary film is evident throughout *On the Frontier* because of its insistence in presenting a seemingly realistic portrait of two societies rushing blindly to war—playing on the very real fears of a British public who were informed via newsreels of the rise of Germany and the spectre of another world war—and then undercutting that realism by the techniques used to depict those societies. For example, an offstage reading of newspaper clippings symbolizing a range of political perspectives precedes the final scene; five men read

> contrapuntally from five newspapers of different political posi-
> tions, each with its own view of the chaos of Europe. They are
> mutually contradictory as to causes, but agreed to conse-
> quences—a world war. It is the apocalypse, as reported in the
> press.[38]

The disembodied voices recall radio broadcasts and compel the audi-ence to contemplate the complex and often cacophonic interplay be-tween public and private, news and history, fact and fiction, art and action. The sounds of civilization and chaos become perilously inter-changeable, exposing the thin line between civility and barbarity.

Novelists were also experimenting with documentary form. Stream-of-consciousness technique had revolutionized the novel form in the 1920s, but its focus on the interior life of characters meant that the social world in which the character lived was frequently pushed to the side. Writers such as Woolf and Joyce entered the 1930s as masters of stream-of-consciousness fiction, but both attempted to move beyond the interiority of focus by incorporating other elements into their fic-tion. Woolf experimented, unsuccessfully, with alternating social commentary essays with prose fiction in the novel that eventually be-came two distinct works: a novel, *The Years* (1937), and her famous feminist polemic, *Three Guineas* (1938). However, her final novel—the posthumously published *Between the Acts* (1941)—balanced so-cial concerns within a fictional world far more successfully. Joyce's *Finnegans Wake* (1939) is a bravura performance blending elements from many genres, including documentary. Yet the novelists who were more successful in their incorporation of documentary tech-niques into their fiction tended to focus more fully on the society around them.

One novelist whose work is almost synonymous with 1930s social documentaries is George Orwell. Orwell's first major success was *Down and Out in Paris and London* (1932), which recounted his ex-perience of living in poverty in both cities. In early 1936, Victor Gollancz, of the Left Book Club, commissioned Orwell to write an-other documentary novel that would chronicle the lives of those living in the depressed North Eastern part of England. The result was *The Road to Wigan Pier* (1937), which combined a vivid depiction of pov-erty amongst the coal miners of Lancashire and Yorkshire with Or-well's searing critique of what he saw as the irresponsible elements of the left. Both books blended fact and fiction, and used a mixture of reportage and narrative to render portraits of lives ground down by poverty. *Homage to Catalonia* (1938), Orwell's account of his experi-ences in Spain during the Spanish Civil War, is perhaps his best-known documentary novel. It combines a journalistic account of life at the front with strong social commentary that revealed the factionalism within the left wing groups that undermined their war efforts and left Orwell politically disillusioned. Orwell's clear, direct prose stood out in contrast to the allusiveness of much contemporary fiction, making the worlds presented in his novels seem all the more real. In many ways, then, Orwell's work epitomizes the documentary form that came of age in the 1930s.

THE 1940s:
A LITERARY CODA—IN THE MIDST OF WAR

If Orwell and the documentary come of age in the 1930s, then Virginia Woolf, H.D., and T.S. Eliot mastered the forms which best allowed for the mature expression of their creative vision during World War II. By way of offering a conclusion, the Coda returns to three writers whose careers very nearly span the entire period under examination and, in doing so, it examines three examples of established modernist writers responding to the return to war—a war anticipated long before it ever began. In moving away from the second-generation modernists foregrounded in Chapter 4, the Coda is interested in reinforcing a view of modernism which is far more complex than a reading that privileges 1922 as the movement's high water mark, after which there is simply aesthetic decline and degradation.

The very possibility of entertaining such a reading—a reading where Woolf is not simply the author of *Mrs Dalloway*, where H.D. is not exclusively an Imagist poet, where Eliot is not simply the author of *The Waste Land*—is rooted in the history of modernist scholarship. That said, the Coda has the further objective of providing an overview of key tendencies in modernist scholarship since the 1930s. This snapshot of scholarly developments in the latter half of the twentieth century will emphasize the exciting role that literary criticism has played in expanding our sense of the rich diversity inherent in modernist writing.

For now, however, it is literature which is the focus. Differences in genre aside, Woolf's novel and the poetry of H.D. and T.S. Eliot are likewise characterized by lyrically complex explorations of history, conflict, and reconciliation, renewal, redemption. In *Between the Acts*, Woolf's final novel, pleasure and violence commingle as characters repeatedly struggle to make sense of each other's words and actions. The residue of the past and the force of contemporary events weigh heavily upon the characters, shaping and limiting their actions—their responses—to one another. Through her inclusion of a historical pageant and exploration of the audience's reactions, 'Woolf is able to achieve a cross-grained play between acts, acting, and the "unacted part".'[39] The novel's complex structure with its admixture of styles and conventions in combination with a self-conscious evocation of artists and audiences offers an opportunity to reflect on concerns central to literary culture as it approached the mid-century mark amongst yet more violence and uncertainty as to the future.

Set during the war itself, H.D.'s epic poem *Trilogy* is redolent with the scenes of destruction and violence haunting *Between the Acts*. While Woolf invites her reader to take on the role of audience member, H.D.'s highly effective use of the first person plural and second person pronouns lends a powerful intimacy to an otherwise dauntingly complex interrogation of the artist's role during a period of conflict. The visionary responsibilities of the war poet lie at the centre of *Trilogy*'s three books. Likewise, as we encounter Woolf continuing to experiment with the formal limits and capabilities of the novel, H.D. is formally engaged in the recuperation of the epic to accommodate a feminine vision. As the genre should, this epic will tell a story of cultural and national significance; it will not, however, do so by focusing exclusively on heroes and gods. H.D.'s cast will be far more inclusive.

Eliot, like H.D., chooses to respond to World War II through poetry. In what will prove to be his final poem, *Four Quartets*—written between 1935 and 1942—Eliot's late masterpiece emerges as a consolidation of his poetic experimentation wed to the spiritual and intellectual fruits of his 1927 conversion to Anglo-Catholicism. The poem explores religious and aesthetic themes while simultaneously serving a social and political function. Admittedly a highly personal poem, *Four Quartets* nevertheless points out how one 'might survive the compulsions of history, might reconcile freedom and necessity in dangerous times.'[40] The poem emerges as an elegant and emotionally powerful examination of paradox, acceptance, and humility—three words which can apply equally well to the works of H.D. and Woolf here set in conversation with Eliot's *Four Quartets*.

CRITICAL MANOEUVRES

It is important to reiterate that this book does not seek to redefine modernism. In light of how it proposes to explore the evolving temper of the period, *Modernism: An Introduction* asks how appraisals of twentieth-century British literature—specifically, texts written before 1945—can be refined by a three-pronged investigation into the dynamic relationship between the era's pre-eminent literary movement and its shifting thematic and socio-cultural concerns. In short, if we assess the interplay between evolving aesthetic concerns, the material conditions of literary production, and generic differences what becomes apparent about the evolving preoccupations of modern literature?

The ability to identify that which is modern or up-to-date in art and literature is dependent on an awareness of the aesthetic and material contexts which shape its production. The insistence on examining the material and aesthetic forces which shape literary production and literary movements is grounded in a belief that literature is simultaneously an historical and cultural phenomenon. Nevertheless, this insistence is tempered by Michael Bell's observation that literature 'undeniably reflects in some sense the life and thought of its time but to determine how it does so is the delicate and continuing function of criticism':

> It may address itself to 'life' in a greater or lesser degree but its value as literature is not in any simple sense contingent on such a criterion. The vitality or meaningfulness of literature hinges on its internal intensity rather than the quality of historical information in a factual sense that it may include. It is a delicate matter, therefore, to mediate pertinently between literary experience and its putative context; to discuss 'influences' and preoccupations without collapsing the tension of this vital heterogeneity.[41]

Proceeding cautiously with an awareness of this risk, each chapter will treat literature as a product of the vital tension between the contemporary moment and the artist's imagination. In other words, although the literary critical movements dominant in the final decades of the twentieth century unquestionably undercut the conception of the modernist text as an inviolable, purely aesthetic artefact, it nevertheless still behoves readers to be fully aware of both the limitations *and* the value of an historical and materialist approach to the study of literature.

We invoke terms such as historical and materialist with the intention of signalling an affiliation with three inter-related critical schools: Marxist criticism, New Historicism, and reception theory. When applied to the study of literature, Marxist theory focuses on the material conditions in which a text is produced, disseminated, and received. Marxist—or 'materialist'—critics are concerned with issues of class and labour both as they appear in the texts themselves and as they become manifest in the production of the books themselves. This concern emerges from the insistence on the primacy of the material circumstances of our lives over our ideas—a critical perspective grounded in the work of nineteenth-century political economist Karl Marx. The Marxist critic assumes that the relationship between art and society is organic and indivisible—that a work of art is not only a reflection but also a product of its social and historical milieu.[42]

In turn, New Historicism pays especial attention to the historical context in which a literary text was produced, with the conviction that the time and place of composition are integral parts of the text itself. New Historicism argues that we cannot separate texts and history— they are irrevocably entwined. From the perspective of a New Historicist, literary history is a record and analysis of the production, distribution, and consumption of a cultural product. Indebted to Marxist materialism, the New Historicist critic believes that criticism must 'strip away the "censorship" imposed by differing historical and cultural perspectives and by the very nature of language to reveal the way the social system inevitably imposes itself upon that experience.'[43]

As do Marxist and New Historicist critics, adherents of reception theory explore the literary text as a historically-situated artefact. Reception theory—as the name suggests—focuses on the reception of a text; however, unlike reader-response theory, it is not interested in the response of a single reader at a given time. It is interested in the changing responses—interpretive and evaluative—of the general reading public as well as the evolving historical tradition of critical interpretations and evaluations of a given literary work. Based in the work of German critic Hans Robert Jauss during the early 1970s, reception theory conceives of tradition as a dialectic or dialogue between a text and generations of successive readers. There are two components to this dialogue:

> As a *reception-aesthetic*, [reception theory] serves to 'define' the meaning and aesthetic character of any individual work of literature as a set of semantic and aesthetic 'potentialities,' which make themselves manifest only as they are realized by the cumulative responses of readers over a course of time. In its other aspect as a *reception-history*, this mode of study also transforms the history of literature—traditionally conceived as an account of the successive production of a variety of works with fixed meanings and values—by making it instead the history of changing but cumulative ways that selected texts are interpreted and assessed, as the horizons of its successive readers alter with the passage of time.[44]

A desire to expand the record of the changing ways in which modernism has been and continues to be constructed firmly informs the theoretical orientation taken throughout this book. This, of course, is a story that will continue to alter with each passing decade of the twenty-first century and with the accompanying shifts in critical orientation. For now, however, the story to be told is that of the literature of the opening decades of the last century and the genres that defined it.

NOTES

1 Aldous Huxley, *Point Counter Point* (1928; London: Flamingo, 1994) 205.

2 Huxley 205.

3 Huxley 205.

4 Huxley 206.

5 Malcolm Bradbury and James McFarlane, *Modernism, 1890–1930* (1976; London: Penguin, 1983) 19–53.

6 M.H. Abrams, *A Glossary of Literary Terms* (1957; New York: Holt, Rinehart, and Winston, 1988) 108–9.

7 J.A. Cuddon, *Dictionary of Literary Terms and Literary Theory*, 4th ed. (London: Penguin, 2004) 516.

8 Grant Allen, *Falling in Love, with other Essays on More Exact Branches of Science* (London: Smith, Elder, & Co, 1889) 31.

9 'Fashions of the Mind,' *Vogue* Early February 1924: 49.

10 Seminal works that helped contribute to significant paradigm shifts in science, psychology, and political published before 1901 include: Charles Darwin, *On the Origin of Species* (1859); Sigmund Freud, *The Interpretation of Dreams* (1900); Karl Marx, *The Communist Manifesto* (1848); and Friedrich Nietzsche, *Beyond Good and Evil* (1886).

11 Virginia Woolf, 'Mr Bennett and Mrs Brown,' *A Woman's Essays*, Rachel Bowlby (ed.) (London: Penguin, 1992) 70.

12 In December 1910, London printers were locked out in response to their demand for a forty-eight-hour work week. In an attempt to communicate their side of the story, the printers produced a strike sheet called *The World*. The following month it was renamed the *Daily Herald*. The first issue of 13,000 copies sold out; there were further increases in circulation when the strike continued into the following year. When the strike ended in April 1911, the printers stopped publishing their newspaper. However, the striking printers had shown that there was a market for a left-wing newspaper, and several leaders of the labour movement joined together to raise the necessary funds to establish such a paper. The *Daily Herald* reappeared on 15 April 1912. Within a few weeks, sales of the *Daily Herald* reached 230,000 a day. In addition to encouraging workers to take industrial action, it was the only national newspaper that fully supported the suffragettes.

13 Sydney Kaplan, *Katherine Mansfield and the Origins of Modernist Fiction* (Cornell: Cornell University Press, 1991) 84.

14 Kaplan 102.

15 Charles May, *The Short Story: The Reality of Artifice* (Toronto: Macmillan, 1995) 13.

16 Wendell Harris, 'Vision and Form: The English Novel and the Emergence of the Short Story,' *Victorian Newsletter* 47 (1975) 11.

17 Gavrilo Princip—a Serbian nationalist affiliated with the Black Hand, a secret society with more than 2,500 members in 1914—on 28 June 1914 assassinated the Archduke who was on a state trip to Sarajevo with his wife, Duchess Sophie von Chotkovato.

18 A primary responsibility of the League of Nations was supposed to be the enforcement of treaty provisions. However, as the 1920s progressed, it became increasingly apparent that the League was unable to effectively enforce the provisions of the many treaties signed between the combatants at the end of the war.

19 French symbolist poets believed that evocativeness and suggestiveness could best be obtained by verse forms that were not too rigid, and so *vers libérés* and *vers libres* were the forms of choice. Arthur Rimbaud and Stéphane Mallarmé were among the chief figures experimenting with these forms. The movement's definitive manifesto was published in a September 1886 issue of *Le Figaro* by Jean Moréas. In the *Figaro* article, Moréas contended that romanticism and naturalism were over and henceforth symbolic poetry *'cherche à vêtir l'idée*

d'une forme sensible.' Poets most indebted to symbolist movement outside of France include W.B. Yeats, T.E. Hulme, Ezra Pound, and T.S. Eliot.

20 Richard Aldington, for example, published a volume of verse entitled *Images of War* one year after the war; it was, however, a full decade before he completed and published his war novel and best-known work, *The Death of Hero* (1929), a psychological study of a young officer transformed by the war.

21 Ezra Pound, 'A Retrospect,' *Literary Essays of Ezra Pound*, T.S. Eliot (ed.) (London: Faber, 1954) 3.

22 Pound 4.

23 Peter Nicholls, *Modernisms: A Literary Guide* (London: Macmillan, 1995) 173.

24 Robert Graves, *Good-bye to All That* (1929, New York: Anchor, 1998) 174–5.

25 Kevin Dettmar and Jennifer Wicke (eds), *The Twentieth Century*. vol. 2c. *The Longman Anthology of British Literature*, David Damrosch (ed.) (New York: Longman, 2003) 1996.

26 Conrad's story was first published serially in *Blackwood's Edinburgh Magazine* in 1899. It appeared in volume form in 1901.

27 Virginia Woolf, 'Modern Fiction,' *The Crowded Dance of Modern Life*, Rachel Bowlby (ed.), (London: Penguin, 1993) 8.

28 Woolf 8.

29 Woolf 8. With reference to ongoing explorations of interiority, in a 1926 review Elizabeth Drew matter-of-factly observed, 'It is obvious that the novel has followed a signpost marked "Psychology," and that it is still busy exploring this pathway. It seems as if civilized mankind has developed a self-consciousness and a critical attitude towards its general and human environment to a degree never before experienced, and the main problem of modern literary communication has been how to adapt the technique of novel writing to this enlarged and sharpened vision; how to present the intricacies of human rela-tionships, how to accent the element of the unseen and the unexpressed in the affairs of life.' According to Drew, this problem had been tackled so effectively that 'the modern frankness of thought . . . is now freely expressed not only by and for the sophisticated intellectual public' (*Time and Tide* 29 January 1926: 104).

30 Woolf 9.

31 Woolf 9.

32 Woolf 9.

33 The first newsreel, the weekly *Pathe's Animated Gazette* was issued in June 1910. Over the next two decades, newsreels became an entrenched feature of British cinema. An excellent history of British newsreels has been created by the British Universities Newsreel Database, URL: http://www.bufvc.ac.uk/databases/newsreels/

34 It is interesting to note that though the newsreels purported to show events as they were unfolding, it was not uncommon for the film footage that appeared in newsreels to be staged after the events had occurred.

35 As quoted in Humphry Carpenter, *W.H. Auden: A Biography* (London: George, Allen & Unwin, 1981) 247.

36 Carpenter 247.

37 Louis MacNeice, 'The Theatre,' *The Spectator* 18 November 1938: 858.

38 Samuel Hynes, *The Auden Generation* (London: Faber, 1979) 309.

Queen Victoria's death in 1901 drew to a close a remarkable reign during which Great Britain had become one of the most important Imperial powers in the world. Her death came at a time when her country was on the brink of enormous change, much of it related to challenges to its entrenched socio-political systems and beliefs. British Imperial might was being contested in South Africa where the British Army was fighting a losing battle against the Afrikaners. The Irish Question continued to resist solution and would simmer throughout the first decade of the new century. England's great cities—London and Manchester, in particular—were crumbling, their infrastructure unable to keep pace with the rapid urbanization of the late nineteenth century. The traditional ruling parties—the Conservatives and the Liberals—were confronted by a new political movement that sought to represent the newly enfranchised working class, and by 1906, the Labour party occupied twenty-nine seats in the House of Commons. Women continued to agitate for legislative reform that would not only extend the vote to them, but would also safeguard their rights in other areas. Clearly, Britons who mourned the passing of their Queen did so with a growing awareness that the continuity and stability of the British Empire, which she had come to symbolize by virtue of her long reign, was also passing away.

The tumult of this period is similarly evident in literary culture. The 1880s and '90s had witnessed an astonishing growth in the literary marketplace in part due to the lower costs of producing printed matter and in part because of a greater demand from the reading public. One of the more interesting consequences of the expansion of literary culture was the increasing complexity of the marketplace itself. A growing divide between popular and avant-garde literature emerged, though it would be oversimplifying the realities of the marketplace to say that writers and readers chose one side and remained on it. In practice, most writers hoped to gain both financial and critical success. Yet a divide did exist and we find the seeds of literary modernism evident principally amongst the work of the avant-garde writers of this period.

A variety of literary and artistic movements emerged in the 1880s and '90s—Impressionism, Aestheticism, Decadence, Naturalism, and Symbolism, to name the most prominent—and each was associated with one or more key avant-garde literary figure.[1] Oscar Wilde remains the best-known avant-garde figure from this period. He was known not only for his witty dramas such as *Lady Windermere's Fan* (1892) and *The Importance of Being Earnest* (1895) but also for his prose—*The Picture of Dorian Gray* (1891)—and poetry—*The Ballad of Reading Gaol* (1898). Wilde's adoption of the aesthete's credo 'art for art's sake' drew attention to the formal qualities of literature, contested what was seen as the over reliance of Victorian literature on

23

realism, and challenged his contemporaries and successors to pay close attention to the art of writing. While he was pilloried in the press and jailed because of his homosexuality, there is little doubt of the significant influence that Wilde exerted on the literary scene of the '90s.

The 1890s also witnessed the first steps of writers whom we now associate with modernism: Joseph Conrad, Thomas Hardy, and W.B. Yeats. Joseph Conrad began to write the novels and short stories that were to bring him such acclaim, publishing *Almayer's Folly* (1895) and *The Nigger of the 'Narcissus'* (1897). His short story *Heart of Darkness*, first serialized in *Blackwood's Edinburgh Magazine* in 1899, sounded a warning clarion not only to those who had become complacent about the power and reach of the British Empire, but also to those who had become complacent about the form and function of literature. Conrad took one of the most popular literary forms of the 1890s—an adventure tale set in an exotic locale—and transformed it into a major literary work. The texture of the story is created by its layers of symbols and the counterpoint between the white man's experience of the Congo and the black man's experience of his own country. He adds to that a lush language that evokes an emotional response from the reader. To this base, he injects a political commentary on the wrongs perpetrated in Africa in the name of Imperialism. In the process of creating this masterpiece, Conrad was taking part in the transformation of literature that was occurring at the turn of the twentieth century. Hardy turned full time to poetry after the controversy surrounding the publication of *Jude the Obscure* in 1895, publishing *Wessex Poems* in 1898. His poetry is more often thought of as modernist than Victorian, a judgement rightly deserved given the poetry's experimentation with form and language. Yeats had begun to make a name for himself as a poet, publishing three volumes of poems in the 1890s—*Poems* (1895), *The Secret Rose* (1897), and *Wind Among the Reeds* (1899). In them, he employed the techniques of symbolism, blending them with Celtic myth and occultism, to establish his credentials as a gifted new poetic voice. By the end of the decade, Yeats had returned home to Ireland, where he took an active role in the Irish Literary Revival. Throughout the first decade of the twentieth century he wrote plays for the Abbey Theatre, including *Cathleen Ni Houlihan* (1902), and continued to write the poetry that placed him at the heart of the modernist movement.

George Bernard Shaw, another Irishman, is now regarded as one of the foremost British dramatists of the twentieth century, but in the 1890s, he was just beginning to explore drama as a viable outlet for social commentary. Like most writers of his period, he wrote in a variety of genres. He was a noted journalist, writing art, music and drama criticism for a variety of periodicals. He wrote political pamphlets and turned his hand to novel writing. For Shaw, who founded the Fabian Society in 1884 with Beatrice and Sydney Webb,[2] drama was a means of disseminating Fabian beliefs. Yet Shaw's skills as a dramatist were such that when Harley Granville Barker took over management of the Court Theatre in London's West End and wanted to use it to mount experimental plays, it was to Shaw that he turned. From 1904 onwards, Barker produced no fewer than ten of Shaw's plays. Shaw grew wealthy from the royalties he earned from the productions, but at the same time, his socialist ideals reached a wide audience, while plays such as *John Bull's Other Island* (1904), *Major Barbara* (1905), and perhaps his most famous and successful play *Pygmalion* (1913), filled the theatre.

It is clear, then, that the 1890s were a vibrant decade for literature; novels, poetry, drama, and journalism, indeed most genres, flourished. However, one genre in particular emerged as central to not only the 1890s, but also the 1900s: the short story. The short story became important for a number of reasons: the demise of the triple-decker novel and the end to the monopoly on fiction held by lending libraries such as Mudie's is one reason for the rise of shorter fiction.[3] The fact that a short story could be published in one issue of a periodical and read at one sitting made it attractive to publisher and reader alike. Publishers liked the short story because it reduced the difficulties inherent in marketing stories that were published serially, and it also caused fewer difficulties with writers who were often less than reliable in adhering to delivery schedules for multi-part serials. Readers enjoyed short stories because they presented a complete story—no longer did they have to wait a week, a month, or longer to find out the hero's fate. Audience demand for shorter pieces of fiction also pushed writers in the direction of the short story, with the result that writers could frequently earn as much, and often more, for two or three short stories as they had been earning for full novels. Writers also found the short story provided an outlet for aesthetic experimentation: its relatively short history and short length permitted them greater freedom to experiment with form and themes. And, as the rest of this chapter will demonstrate, the short story also played an important role in the rise of modernism.

THE NEW WOMAN, THE *YELLOW BOOK*
AND THE SHORT STORY

Sarah Grand, the English author of the best-seller *Heavenly Twins* (1893), published an essay entitled 'The New Aspect of the Woman Question' in the March 1894 issue of the *North American Review*.[4] According to Grand, the 'new woman' had 'solved the problem and proclaimed for herself what was wrong with Home-is-the-Woman's-Sphere, and prescribed the remedy.'[5] A tendentious claim such as this did not go unnoticed and within a matter of months the phrase 'New Woman' had become ubiquitous on both sides of the Atlantic. Not only had the phrase become a commonplace, but so too had the image of the cigarette-smoking, Girton-educated, bicycle-riding New Woman in rational dress demanding emancipation.[6]

Irrespective of stereotypes, the New Woman rejected the dominant ideology that insisted men and women were meant to occupy different spheres—public and private respectively—according to their bio-logical sex. She insisted that the separate spheres ideology was a so-cietal construct as opposed to a biological imperative, and demanded women be given the same opportunities and choices as men. The New Woman's dogged resolve in drawing attention to naturalized gender roles and her willingness to transgress societal constraints served to align the New Women with the Aesthetic Movement and with writers like Oscar Wilde, Ernest Dowson, and Aubrey Beardsley who cri-tiqued supposedly natural standards of sexual behaviour. Little distin-guished the general public's response to both groups: 'the fear of de-viance that was created by the perception that both groups were crossing gender lines and reject[ing] what was supposedly natural cre-ated an anxiety that is obvious in the many articles that appeared in periodicals during the 1890s.'[7] Essays and short stories alike—whether for or against the 'New Woman'—voiced concerns about a wide range of issues related to marriage, education, female sexuality, and impediments to economic independence.

The *Yellow Book*, a literary periodical started by Elkin Matthews and John Lane in 1894, closely associated with the Aesthetic Movement, was favourably disposed towards progressive female writ-ers. The first issue included stories by George Egerton and Ella D'Arcy—two important writers of New Woman fiction. In the *Yellow Book* work by women writers appeared alongside stories by well-es-tablished male writers such as Henry James, Arthur Symons, and George Moore. In addition to providing a forum for New Woman fic-tion, with its interest in Continental writers such as the French Symbolists, the *Yellow Book* helped modernize the English short story. Henry James saw the advent of the *Yellow Book* as an opportu-nity for the short story to 'assume' and 'shamelessly parade in, its own organic form.'[8] James's own career had begun almost thirty years ear-lier in 1865 with the publication of 'The Story of a Year' in the *Atlantic Monthly*. A writer of novels and short fiction, James was an important exponent of the modern short story. He was inspired by the form's power to combine richness with concision—its power 'to do the complicated thing with a strong brevity and lucidity.'[9] James did not see any limits to 'the effects and tones that could be achieved, or to the subjects that could be treated, in an art form which was free to explore depths and complexities precisely because it was restricted in length.'[10] For James, the genre's strength was directly linked to the 'science of control' by way of the writer's conscious manipulation of form and content.[11]

Yellow Book contributor George Egerton perceived a similar connection between form and content. She recognized the necessity of experimenting with narrative techniques in order to provide a more complete representation of women's inner lives. In Egerton's work, we have an early English example of the complex interplay between experimentation and transgression closely associated with literary modernism and the modern short story. This view of Egerton is in harmony with the arguments advanced by Dominic Head in *The Modernist Short Story* (1992), where he explores the interplay between 'the generic capacities of the [modern] short story and the way in which writers have depicted their social world.'[12] Head emphasizes the means by which the genre is particularly well-suited to aesthetic engagements with the modern world. Egerton's experiments with form, for example, were the primary means by which she sought to capture the vicissitudes of women's experiences. Throughout her career, she subordinated

> plot to focus instead on impressions, moments of time, and psy-
> chological states. She create[d] ambiguities in her stories
> through the use of ellipses and ambiguous pronoun references.
> Egerton [was] interested in revealing women's ambitions, de-
> sires and dreams, and she [did] that by deliberately sacrificing
> the narrative line of a tightly plotted story.[13]

Egerton's *Keynotes* collection, published by Matthews and Lane in 1894, is an eloquent and forceful example of work by a woman from the late nineteenth century who strives to write openly and honestly about female desire and sexuality. As were so many of the writers who came after her, she was acutely aware that male–female relations were not simply determined by the needs and wishes of individuals but by societal and institutional expectations. Her stories portray women attempting to escape inherited expectations and roles.

As even a brief discussion of the critical views held by James and Egerton suggests, the 1880s and 1890s were marked by the birth of a new kind of short story. Short story writers forged a powerful connection between the formal properties of the genre and the innovative means of representing a social world. The short story with its stress on artifice and control emerged as a dynamic site of modernist innovation as befits the movement's preoccupation with form. Dominic Head makes even wider claims for the genre; he suggests that the 'short story encapsulates the essence of literary modernism, and has an enduring ability to capture the episodic nature of twentieth-century experiences.'[14] In similar fashion, Valerie Shaw argues that the 'twentieth-century short story arises precisely out of a sense that life

can only be rendered in fragments and compressed subjective episodes.'[15] This observation is of interest for at least two reasons. First,
it draws attention to the perceived suitability of the genre and its formal limits to literary treatments of the modern world. Second, it affirms the value of the genre in and of itself rather than simply viewing
it as the novel's impoverished sister. Shaw's verdict affirms that 'the
short story, like the stage, has its own conventions.'[16]

To date criticism has been heavily influenced by the work of Edgar
Allan Poe who was among the first writers to comment on the aesthetic principles characteristic of short prose narratives. By way of
commentaries from French writers who enthusiastically responded to
his work mid-way through the nineteenth century, Poe's writing has
had a significant impact on contemporary definitions of the modern
short story. According to Poe, a short story is distinguished from other
prose genres by its unity of effect and length; Poe believed that it
should be possible to read a short story in a single sitting. As a result,
deliberate artistry is paramount in writing a successful short story. If a
writer's first sentence

> tends not to the outbringing of this effect then he has failed in
> his first step. In the whole composition there should be no word
> written of which the tendency, direct or indirect, is not the one
> of pre-established design.[17]

Every word must contribute to the 'single effect' and

> by such means, with such care and skill, a picture is at length
> painted which leaves in the mind of him who contemplates it
> with kindred art, a sense of the fullest satisfaction. The idea of
> the tale has been presented unblemished, because undisturbed;
> and this is an end unattainable in the novel.[18]

Poe repeatedly drew attention to the importance of careful contrivance
to the fashioning of a short story in order to leave a unified impression. The modern short story—in Poe's terms—can then be described
as deliberately fashioned prose that leaves a unified impression.

It is, however, important to assert the following qualification: to
stress the importance of a 'unified impression' to the craft of story
telling is not to suggest or insist that the modern short story presents a
unified world view. More often than not, the modern short story draws
attention to the 'disruptive literary gesture as an instance of relative
autonomy; as something which is simultaneously conditioned by, yet
critical of its ideological context.'[19] Modernist stories are frequently
highly critical of the very societies that they take as their subject, and
how the story is presented—or the form that the story takes—becomes
the basis of a critique of art and society. The stories disrupt the possibility of easily unified visions of modern life. The disjunction between
desires and reality—disorder and disruption—are productive forces in
the modernist short story.

This chapter explores the means by which the modern short story's tendency towards formal dissonance produces stories that are simultaneously disruptive and critical of the society from which they emerge. The ensuing discussions of short stories by Somerville and Ross, Joyce, Lawrence, and Mansfield assess the different ways in which these writers challenged conventional wisdom with regard to gender, class, and nationality. Every one of these writers explores the tension between outer and inner reality, paralysis and change, past and present, as these themes relate to the construction of personal identity. What follows will point to the means by which the short story emerges as an effective vehicle through which writers (and readers) can sidestep prevailing conventions and beliefs to move beyond 'our ordinary range of experience.'[20] Not only did the writers we are examining challenge prevailing expectations regarding appropriate subject matter for a short story, but they frequently wrote from the position of outsider whether on account of sex, class, or nationality. We will begin with a series of stories written by a pair of Irish women who caught the attention of English publishers, critics, and readers.

SOMERVILLE AND ROSS

In 1898, the first *Irish R.M.* story by Edith Somerville and Violet Martin (who wrote as Martin Ross) appeared in London's *Badminton Magazine,* a late Victorian equivalent to *Field and Stream.* The immediate success of 'Great-Uncle McCarthy' and the stories that followed encouraged Longmans and Green, the magazine's publishers, to commission a collection of stories. *Some Experiences of an Irish R.M.* (1899) was published the next year. *Further Experiences of an Irish R.M.* appeared in 1908, bringing the saga of Major Yeates, Resident Magistrate, into the twentieth century. Although the stories have been a longstanding success with readers, critics have proved less able to appreciate the merits of the *Irish R.M.* stories, which are too often dismissed as 'stage-Irish' tales or rousing hunting yarns.[21] In contrast, James Cahalan convincingly argues for the merits of examining Somerville and Ross as the authors of stories that intermix 'nostalgia for a dying way of life [with] subversively gendered portrait[s] of strong, vital women.'[22] Cahalan has suggested that the male characters are 'outmatched by *women,* who really control the Big House,' which is 'parallel to [Somerville and Ross'] portrayal of the Ascendancy, in the person of Yeates, as rather hopelessly powerless in the face of the lower class.'[23] In story after story, gender and class relations emerge as anything but fixed; the expectations of Major Yeates and the reader are repeatedly subverted and undermined. The stories expose a society in flux, a society in which the roles of men and women are in question and societal values are being challenged on domestic and political fronts.

For instance, while Major Yeates is the latest Resident Magistrate—
newly arrived in Ireland as representative of Her Majesty's government—he is not a figure of unquestionable authority. Although a
member of the Anglo-Irish Ascendancy by blood, Major Yeates has
come to Ireland by way of England and, as such, he is the uninitiated
outsider who must learn the ways of the county to which he has been
appointed. The opening scenes of 'Great-Uncle McCarthy,' the first
story in the collection, reveal a somewhat hapless Major Yeates
caught between two women: his absent fiancée, who is present as the
acknowledged future inhabitant of his new home Shreelane, and his
housekeeper, Mrs Cadogan, who ministers to him in a duplicitous
manner. The story ends with the discovery that, with Mrs Cadogan's
help, relations of the landlord Mr Flurry Knox squat in the Shreelane
loft. The house is under Major Yeates' control only in name. The
whims of Mrs Cadogan and the anticipated needs of Major Yeates'
new wife determine what takes place at Shreelane.

This is not the only secret being kept from Major Yeates. Not only
was he the sole member of the household unaware of the squatters, but
also with the assistance of Tim Connor—the Shreelane gamekeeper—
the McCarthy Gannons were catching and selling the property's foxes
under the aegis of Major Yeates' name. As a result, nearly everyone in
the neighbourhood—with the exception of Yeates—knew about the
comings and goings of the Shreelane foxes. It takes the boycotting of
a shoot which Major Yeates attempts to host early in his tenancy and
an anonymous letter alerting him that his 'unsportsmanlike conduct
has been discovered. You have been suspected this good while of
shooting the Shreelane foxes, it is known now you do worse' before
Yeates becomes aware of the goings on under his very nose.[24] Everything is resolved in humorous and melodramatic fashion when the
hounds from the local hunt led by none other than Major Yeates'
landlord and the local chimney sweep converge upon the McCarthy
Gannons, Tim Conner, and a fox secreted away in the loft at the back
of the house.

The ensuing mayhem and indignant words highlight the skill with
which Somerville and Ross handle the dialogue in all the *Irish R.M.*
stories. This is a comedy of contrasts in which different registers of
language are caught on the same page—the humour neither elevates
nor romanticizes any one group. All of the stories are filled with a
similarly diverse cross-section of characters. As a result, misadventures on account of misunderstandings and secrets dividing characters
generate much of the collection's humour. These are funny stories
with a serious point. Keeping that in mind, Cahalan's work on
Somerville and Ross draws attention to the work of Regina Barreca
who has argued that 'Comedy is a way women writers can reflect the
absurdity of the dominant ideology while undermining the very basis

for its discourse.'[25] Frequently, it is the characters who advocate the dominant ideology or assert their superiority that come out worse for it in the *Irish R.M.* stories, whether they are mothers who are adamant and unbending about whom their daughters should marry, or private secretaries who have come from England to 'collect impressions of Irish life.'[26] In short, the humour in Somerville and Ross's stories does not depend on stereotypes or caricatures of drunken Irish and country bumpkins. Much of the humour emerges from the reversal of expectations or a character's response to seemingly absurd situations.

In many instances, Major Yeates' ignorance on account of being a newcomer and his fear that he, an administrator of the law, might be found guilty of breaking the very law he is sworn to uphold works well to create comedy. In 'Trinket's Colt,' for example, he finds himself in just such a predicament when by asking for help buying a horse on behalf of a friend in England, he sets off an unexpected chain of events. Throughout these stories, the Anglo-Irish Ascendancy is struggling to remain in control of their estates and land. In particular, Mrs Knox, who is the collection's most compelling female character, is in firm control of her tongue, the Knox family, and the big house named Aussolas. The reader's first encounter with Mrs Knox is her off-stage tongue-lashing of Mrs McDonald, the proprietress of the tea-shop in which Flurry and Yeates are sitting while discussing horses. While Mrs McDonald attempts to take on Mrs Knox, Major Yeates is of the view her voice is so commanding that it 'would have made [him] clean forty pig-sties had she desired [him] to do.'[27]

Flurry shows more resolve. He is as willing to take on his grand-mother as he is willing to draw an unsuspecting Major Yeates into a plot designed to secure a horse from his grandmother. Yeates later describes himself as 'an exceptional ass . . . to have been beguiled into an enterprise that involved hiding with Slipper from the Royal Irish Constabulary.'[28] Flurry may well show more resolve because he has nothing to lose. He believes that he is no longer his grandmother's 'pet' and, as she has yet to give him the horse that she promised him, why not take matters into his own hands? His status—or perhaps more accurately his lack of status—affords him the opportunity to take risks as there is little to lose.

Once Flurry has taken the colt from his grandmother without her permission, Somerville and Ross continue to manipulate contrasting social positions to comic effect in the latter half of the story. Mrs Knox, unlike Major Yeates, cannot be easily 'beguiled' and, suspecting her grandson's involvement in the disappearance of the colt, she sends the police to investigate. She also drops by Flurry's stable block personally, much to the dismay of the visiting Major Yeates. After ordering Major Yeates to take cover, Flurry rises to the occasion with the 'economy of truth that the situation require[s]' and attempts to

outwit his grandmother.[29] Major Yeates' response is much less dignified:

> I may as well confess that at the mere sight of Mrs Knox's pur-
> ple bonnet my heart had turned to water. In that moment I knew
> what it would be like to tell her how I, having eaten her salmon,
> and capped her quotations, and drunk her best port, had gone
> forth and helped steal her horse. I abandoned my dignity, my
> sense of honour, I took the furze prickles to my breast and wal-
> lowed in them.[30]

It is incongruous and humorous to have Major Yeates worrying about
social propriety while lying among the furze bushes in a posture that is
anything but dignified and suitable to a man of his position. When
Mrs Knox's dog gives away Major Yeates and she finally notices the
buried colt, Yeates reports that she 'gazed speechlessly at me, and
then, to her eternal honour, fell into wild cackles of laughter . . .
Overwhelming laughter held us all three, disintegrating our very
souls.'[31] The laughter has an equalizing effect as all three characters
acknowledge the absurdity of the situation and Flurry's ingenious
plan—an idea for which his grandmother would 'give a guinea to have
thought of [herself].'[32] Flurry gets the horse and regains his grandmother's approval. Her lack of interest in punitive measures and
pleasure in her grandson's resourcefulness suggest a willingness to
adapt to new circumstances. While she runs her property with care,
Mrs Knox cares little about the impressions of others or the status quo.
She may not always approve of the actions of other characters, but she
is willing to accept the necessity of doing things differently. Within
the humour for which the *Irish R.M.* stories are most frequently remembered, there is a quiet and accommodating acceptance of the inevitability of change in domestic and political life.

JAMES JOYCE

In 1904, George Russell, editor of *The Irish Homestead*, offered
James Joyce £1 each for some stories with an Irish background.[33]
Three submissions—'The Sisters,' 'Eveline,' and 'After the Race'—
appeared in *The Irish Homestead* under the pseudonym Stephen
Daedalus before it was decided that Joyce's work was ill-suited to an
agricultural paper.[34] This edict did not deter Joyce, and he continued
writing his Dublin stories after eloping to the Continent with Nora
Barnacle in October 1904. When he approached the London publisher
Grant Richards in October 1905, he had written twelve stories—in-
cluding the three stories that had already appeared in *The Irish
Homestead* between 13 August and 17 December 1904.

After some wrangling, Joyce and Richards reached a publication
agreement by early 1906 that called for a thirteenth story from Joyce.
The stipulation that Joyce provide a thirteenth story proved unlucky.

When Richards sent the thirteenth story, 'Two Gallants,' to his printers, they declared it too obscene to print. The now alarmed Richards responded by asking Joyce to make changes to 'Two Gallants,' 'Counterparts,' and 'An Encounter.' Over the course of the summer, negotiations went on between the writer and publisher. In the end, Joyce was unwilling to make concessions and the manuscript was returned to Joyce on 26 October 1906. Three years later, seemingly hopeful discussions with the Dublin firm Maunsel on the subject of publishing *Dubliners*, which now included 'The Dead,' took a turn for the worse when one of the firm's directors, George Roberts, raised concerns over references to Edward VII in 'Ivy Day in the Committee Room.' Shortly thereafter the frustrated Joyce wrote an open letter 'A Curious History' to the Irish press bemoaning his difficulties in publishing the collection.[35] The letter left Roberts so terrified of legal action that he refused point blank to publish the book.

Joyce's luck improved in 1914, when *The Egoist* began to serialize his first novel *A Portrait of the Artist as a Young Man*. Encouraged by its reception, Joyce re-approached Grant Richards and offered him the *Dubliners* manuscript a second time. Limited complications aside, the book was finally made available to readers on 15 June 1914, on the same terms as the original 1906 contract with the added provision that Joyce take 120 copies himself at trade price.[36] The timing could not have been worse. Weeks later, tensions in Europe escalated and the Continent was plunged into war by the end of the summer. For all practical purposes, the publication of *Dubliners* went largely unnoticed. Nevertheless, decades later, the collection is regarded as an outstanding example of the modern short story.

Influenced in part by Joyce's use of complex networks of mythological and symbolic allusions in his later works such as *Ulysses*, innumerable critics have attempted to analyze the stories in *Dubliners* with reference to larger patterns. Joyce himself, however, offers one of the most useful templates against which to read the stories. In 1907, he said that he was trying to present Dublin in four of its aspects: childhood, adolescence, maturity, and public life. The stories assess how men and women—at various stages of their lives—define themselves with reference to one another with especial attention paid to the role that social conventions and expectations play in these relations. Joyce also investigates the ways in which we interpret our lives, and the ways in which the version of events we privilege can serve to preserve the personal fictions by which we live. The stories seek to expose the complex machinations and forces—internal and external—which motivate an individual's actions.

All of the stories utilize a similar structure: each moves deceptively towards a climax and each creates expectations of a readily identifiable revelation which is dispelled on account of the complexity of the story's actual epiphany. In doing so, the stories subvert the unifying convention on which they pivot. Throughout the collection, a character's inability to respond to a situation in a manner that brings change is not simply indicative of paralysis on the part of the character. It is indicative of the force of the social network in which peoples are enmeshed. When striving to make sense of the repeated failures to escape, Dominic Head counsels readers not to look for 'unifying effects but for signs of the contradictions (historically determined) which produced them and which appear as unevenly resolved conflicts in the text.'[37] The unevenly resolved conflicts are a fundamental component of Joycean character development. A character's static or irresolute response to an epiphany is a conscious aspect of Joyce's method as opposed to an accidental, symptomatic feature of the stories detected in historical hindsight. The (modern) city itself emerges as a further unnamed factor which each of the stories has in common. The collection is a portrait of a city and its citizens who struggle to escape into a fuller and more meaningful existence.

'Eveline' is the tale of a young woman's inability to reconcile competing versions of herself: daughter, sister, and sweetheart. Eveline surrenders an opportunity to escape when she proves unable to imagine anything beyond the limits of her experience. The impossibility of escape is woven into the story's blunt opening paragraph that makes plain her state of mind: 'She sat at the window watching the evening invade the avenue. Her head leaned against the window curtains and in her nostril was the odour of dusty cretonne. She was tired.'[38] In spite of her youth, Eveline is unable to respond to her environment. She is trapped inside, weighed down by her exhaustion and the dust invading her unchanging life. Eveline is no longer a child. Her mother has died and she has adult responsibilities —a job, the care of her home, and younger siblings—but she is no more aware of the world than when she was a child:

> [D]uring all [these] years she had never found out the name of the priest whose yellowing photograph hung on the wall above the broken harmonium beside the coloured print of the promises made to Blessed Mary Alacoque.[39]

Eveline remains seated at the window as she surveys the room and her life. She recollects childhood, her mother's death, scenes from work, and her courtship—none of which can rouse her from her stupor: 'Her time was running out but she continued to sit by the window, leaning her head against the window curtain, inhaling the odour of dusty cretonne.'[40] Her body remains immobile in spite of what she has been thinking about—nothing less than a means of rejecting the dust (and moving to Buenos Aires). However, the longer she remains immobile and sits inhaling the dust of the past, the more inevitable her entrapment becomes. Her inability to move does not surprise the careful reader; nor does her ultimate failure to join Frank beyond the iron railing at the docks.

Not only is Eveline associated with immobility, she is voiceless. Throughout the story, impersonal facts and the reported speech of other people predominate. There is no distinctive tone or cadence that we come to associate with the title character. If anything, a child-like imprecision characterizes her recollections of the past with which the story opens:

> One time there used to be a field there in which they used to play every evening with other people's children. Then a man from Belfast bought the field and built houses in it—not like their little brown houses but bright brick houses with shining roofs.[41]

It is as though she has failed to find an effective voice with which to replace her childhood self. That this should be the case is arguably unsurprising given how others speak to her. Miss Gavan, for example, does not offer her any words of encouragement that would foster confidence and self-possession:

> – Miss Hill, don't you see these ladies are waiting?
> – Look lively, Miss Hill, please.
> She would not cry many tears at leaving the stores.[42]

Her father's words are even more damaging. They offer no succour. His accusations are simply repeated time and time again:

> He said she used to squander that money, that she had no head, that he wasn't going to give her his hard earned money to throw around on the streets and much more for he was usually fairly bad of a Saturday night.[43]

With the death of her mother, Eveline has inherited the role of subjugated female of the family. Nevertheless, her father's decline since her mother's death holds powerful sway over her; and, in spite of her desire for protection and safety, not even the language of courtship can undercut the hold her domestic circumstances have upon her.

The paragraph devoted exclusively to Frank and their courtship is curiously impersonal. The trajectory of their courtship is set out within twelve short sentences. It is a shadowy affair that was initially driven by Eveline's simple pleasure in having a sweetheart. Eveline knows little about Frank beyond the barest of details:

> He was awfully fond of music and sang a little. . . . He used to call her Poppens out of fun. . . . He had tales of distant countries. He had started as a deck boy at a pound a month on a ship of the Allan Line going out to Canada. He told her the names of the ships he had been on and the names of the different services.[44]

She nonetheless creates a fantasy of life as a means of escaping the squalor of her life in the slums of Dublin. The language of romance fiction is employed to describe the dockside scene with which the story concludes. However, instead of using the swooning prose of romance to describe the moment of liberation and happiness towards which the story apparently builds, it is used to describe the very moment in which she freezes and cannot escape her father and Dublin:

> A bell clanged upon her heart. She felt him seize her hand:
> – Come!
> All the seas of the world tumbled about her heart. He was
> drawing her into them: he would drown her. She gripped with
> both hands at the iron railing.
> – Come!
> No! No! No! It was impossible. Her hands clutched the iron in
> frenzy. Amid the seas she sent a cry of anguish.[45]

The prospect of living with Frank has become synonymous with the violence of submersion—a deathly choice in that Eveline cannot imagine a fate other than the one she has witnessed in her own home. The emotions that overwhelm Eveline at the railing embody the impossibility of escaping. She can do nothing less than freeze: 'She set her white face to him, passive, like a helpless animal. Her eyes gave him no sign of love or farewell or recognition.'[46] Eveline never speaks her refusal. Tongue-tied and helpless, the story ends with her clutching the rail unable to leave with Frank because she does not and cannot believe her own story.

In 'The Boarding House,' silence and unspoken desires throw into motion a chain of events that will irrevocably transform Bob Doran's life. The story pivots on an unholy trinity of a 'perverse Madonna,' a suitor, and her mother.[47] While on first reading, the story, which takes place in the moments before the mother leaves for Sunday mass, appears to revolve around the manipulation of one man by two women, the degree to which Polly's behaviour is encouraged and prescribed by her mother should not be underestimated. In large part, Mrs Mooney's intentions have guided her daughter's actions, which since 'Polly was very lively' were to give her daughter 'the run of the young men.'[48] When a liaison develops between Polly and one of the boarders, Mrs Mooney simply watches the pair and keeps 'her own counsel.'[49] Polly, in turn, knows she is being watched and does not misunderstand her mother's 'persistent silence.'[50] The intention is to have Polly married. Under the firm guidance of her mother—a woman well accustomed to handling her own problems—Polly becomes entangled in a situation that will in all probability lead to marriage.

As in 'Eveline,' there is almost no dialogue. Insights into the characters' personalities and their responses to the unfolding drama are relayed through her series of three reveries that dominate the narrative structure as the story moves toward the fateful moment at which Polly is called down to speak with Bob Doran. Each one is shorter than the last. Polly's reverie, with which the story concludes, is the shortest. It is simultaneously the least and the most revealing of the three interior monologues. It is the least revealing reverie in that Polly has assumed an almost passive posture by the time Bob descends to speak with her mother. Her actions have taken place outside the framework of the story. The pivotal events that have led to the morning conference between Mrs Mooney and Bob Doran are divulged through their remembrances. It is the most revealing reverie in that she has so completely played her part and transferred her trust to her mother that she forgets her perturbation and leaves behind memories of the past for 'hopes and visions of the future.'[51]

Mrs Mooney and Bob Doran can do no such thing; they are not given the luxury of forgetting their immediate concerns. The story opens with Mrs Mooney who views Polly's future as a speculative enterprise akin to a business venture. Mrs Mooney has gambled her reputation as well as that of her daughter and now that her daughter is pregnant she must secure nothing less than reparation: 'For her only one reparation could make up for the loss of her daughter's honour: marriage.'[52] Her daughter must marry in order to safeguard Mrs Mooney's reputation and that of her establishment—a tenuous reputation at best given that this is a boarding house wherein the proprietress is referred to as *the Madam*.

She is sure she will win. She will do no less than use morality and 'the weight of social opinion' to secure the result that she seeks. Indeed, it is noted that '[s]he dealt with moral problems as a cleaver deals with meat: and in this case she had made up her mind.'[53] As the cleaver image tidily suggests, for Mrs Mooney the church, morality, and social opinion are little more than systems to manipulate in order to ensure that the outcomes that she desires can be realized in economic fashion. More balance sheet than reverie, hers is a practical meditation dispatched in calculatingly dispassionate fashion. In that regard, it is fitting that she is acutely aware of the time and that she aims to 'catch [the] short twelve at Marlborough Street' after having the matter out with Mr Doran.[54] Mrs Mooney is all about calculating the odds. Her indifference to the emotional cost of personal transactions is convincing in a woman who has managed for herself ever since the night she left her cleaver-wielding husband. The story turns to her quarry when she realizes that she has a mere thirty minutes in which to dispatch her business and leave for mass. Attending church is essential because without cultivating allegiances such as this she is powerless to draw on the weight of social opinion.

Unlike Mrs Mooney, Bob Doran is not in fighting trim. He bears little resemblance to the 'satisfied' Mrs Mooney awaiting him, confident that she is quite unlike 'some mothers she knew who could not get their daughters off their hands.'[55] Where Mrs Mooney banks on using social opinion to her advantage, Bob Doran worries about social opinion. He worries about the consequences of trying to brazen out the affair. He frets about the implications of marrying Polly. To brazen out the affair would be to risk losing his job whereas to marry Polly is to risk social censure from his family who will be of the opinion that he has married beneath himself. He is trapped by the undesirability of both outcomes, and so he sits 'helplessly on the side of the bed' where the misadventures that brought him to this dilemma took place. Pleasure and distress commingle as he recalls the courtship which found its beginning in Polly's insidious but desirable presence in the boarding house. He cannot move.

He cannot respond to the 'instinct [that] urged him to remain free, not to marry.'[56] As he descends the stairs to the parlour, he longs to ascend

> through the roof and fly away to another country where he
> could never hear again of his trouble and yet a force pushed him
> downstairs step by step. The implacable faces of his employers
> and of the Madam stared upon his discomfiture.[57]

The force that pushes him downstairs is no less than the weight of society. The city's economic and moral values, as expressed through the expectations of appropriate male–female relations, bear down upon him. The impossibility of entering into any future other than that which the Madam—Mrs Mooney—has mapped out for him is made irretrievably apparent when he recoils from the hint of possible violence that non-compliance might bring:

> Suddenly he remembered the night when one of the musichall
> *artistes*, a little blond Londoner, had made a rather free allusion
> to Polly. The reunion had been almost broken up on account of
> Jack's violence. Everyone tried to quieten him. The musichall
> *artiste*, a little paler than usual, kept smiling and saying that
> there was no harm meant but Jack kept shouting at him that if
> any fellow tried that sort of fame on with *his* sister he'd bloody
> well put his teeth down his throat, so he would.[58]

Bob Doran swallows his fears and enters the sitting room to accept his fate. His acceptance of his assigned role makes Mrs Mooney's objective—a husband for her perverse child Madonna—viable. 'The Boarding House' is yet another portrait of a Dubliner who turns away from 'the chance of escape and self-fulfilment by allowing lack of will and material considerations to ensnare him.'[59]

Over and over, the stories examine paralysis and indecision. In this regard, 'The Dead' is no different from any other story in the collection. It moves towards an epiphany—the consequences of which lie outside the narrative. The word 'epiphany' means revelation. Joyce used the term to denote a sudden spiritual manifestation whether triggered by a phrase, a gesture, or a memorable phase of the mind itself.

Joyce's art seeks to reveal the essential truth found in and through the everyday; in Joyce the landscape of the everyday is endowed with the power more conventionally ascribed to sacred objects. The short stories draw attention to everyday symbols and the scenes in which our lives come into sharp though sometimes fleeting focus. Throughout *Dubliners*, epiphanies are moments when 'the themes of the story find their exact focus, when the implications of the narrative suddenly manifest themselves.'[60] In many instances, the characters experience what might be called 'dead-end' epiphanies. Often there is a notable absence of illumination and or inability to respond to the moment of realization. As the discussions of the previous two stories suggest, it is important to pay close attention to tone, register, and state of mind when assessing a character's response to a story's climax. The failure to escape or respond becomes the primary means by which Joyce critiques contemporary society and, in particular, Ireland. This holds true for 'The Dead.' What remains to be decided, however, is whether Gabriel's vision of a universal snowstorm represents the ultimate inconsequentiality of his life and those of other Dubliners or is a moment of illumination that will help him to reinterpret and reconstruct his life. This judgment lies with the individual readers who must assess how Joyce has shaped his material and decide for themselves.

For our purposes, while Gabriel's political and cultural views loom large throughout the story, it is his relationships with women that have a particular interest. The story draws attention to the impossibility of understanding any one individual without reference to a range of social relations and forces. The exchanges between men and women draw attention to the politics of gender relations and highlight the impact of shifting power dynamics upon both sexes. The relationships that bind the two sexes accentuate the ways in which they limit and define one another. Gabriel's innumerable anxieties are heightened in his dealings with women. He is defined in part by the language he uses to speak with everyone from the servant girl Lily to his wife Gretta:

> A characteristic pattern of behaviour divulges itself in his awkward reaction to Lily the caretaker's daughter, and repeats itself in his response to Gretta's teasing about galoshes, to the imagined reception of his speech, to Miss Ivors' criticism, and finally to his wife's revelation about her youthful admirer.[61]

He is painfully self-aware and unable to act spontaneously as his endless rehearsing of his speech suggests. Gabriel lives at a distance from his feelings and unfailingly doubts himself—he repeatedly feels 'as if . . . he had made a mistake.'[62] Unsurprisingly then, Gabriel frequently yearns to escape into the snow and repeatedly overacts in social and emotional situations. From the outset, he blushes, he reddens, he constantly pats his tie and adjusts his clothes, and he stumbles over his thoughts and words.

His class, national, cultural, and political identifications are variously and subtly assailed in his interactions with Lily and Miss Ivors, as are his familial and romantic senses of self in dealings with his aunts, remembrances of his mother, and scenes with his wife. He struggles to compose himself and to retain a sense of control in his dealings with each of these women. He strives to say what he believes is expected, and in turn he is surprised when the women do not conform to his expectations and social scripts. For example, he is caught off guard when Lily declares with great bitterness that men are 'all palaver and what they can get out of you' and feels as though her cry is somehow an accusation that encompasses him.[63] In similar fashion, he is flummoxed when Miss Ivors frankly voices her disapproval of his decision to write for the *Daily Express*: 'I'm ashamed of you . . . . To say you'd write for a rag like that. I didn't think you were a west Briton.'[64] After this charge, an attractive young woman of similar educational background is suddenly a 'girl . . . or whatever' with 'rabbit's eyes' who has 'tried to make him ridiculous before people.'[65] His over-personalized interpretations of any number of exchanges continue throughout the party and once he has arrived at the hotel after the party.

The story concludes with a quiet interlude between Gabriel and Gretta where Joyce again reveals his mastery with different registers of language. Gabriel's language is denotative, urban, educated, and ironic. Gretta is connotative, naïve, sincere, and idiomatic. Gabriel becomes aware of this difference, and this awareness fuels the awakened consciousness with which he is infused at the end of the story. The revelation about Michael Furey—Gretta's first love, who is long dead and consigned to memory—forces Gabriel to think about something other than real or imagined social representations. He is forced to think about something other than his conduct and instead he must glimpse the large cycle of life and death that ultimately governs our existence.

The awareness that suffuses Gabriel at the end of 'The Dead' suggests that there might be something different about this epiphany, a quality that sets it apart from the other stories. Gabriel has become aware of language's power and its limit. Gabriel comes to the realization that

> language, phrase-making, is not enough. Beneath and beyond
> the nervous restlessness of his own existence he glimpses the
> larger cycle of life and death, which throws his own febrile at-
> tempts at self-assertion into relief. At last truly 'generous' tears
> can fill his hitherto screened eyes.[66]

Gabriel is now aware of his limitations, and the limitations of a world-view in which the individual is both the beginning and the end. The story ends with an integration of the living and the dead, the present and the past, the west and the east, enveloped in the 'silver and dark' snow: '[h]is soul swooned slowly as he heard the snow falling faintly through the universe and faintly falling, like the descent of their last end, upon all the living and the dead.'[67] The limitations of a life governed by an over-concern with self-presentation become palpable as the story leaves aside the narrow concerns of a single individual for those of the sleeping and the dead.

D.H. LAWRENCE

In turning to D.H. Lawrence, we come to a writer for whom death, both metaphorically and literally, repeatedly prefigures spiritual re-birth and awakening. We also come to a writer whose stories arguably have the most complicated publication history of all the works discussed in this chapter. While Joyce's stories were much delayed, they were not subject to the same kind of ongoing revisions as were Lawrence's early stories. Lawrence consistently took advantage of the delay between the publication in a magazine and a story's final appearance in a book.[68] Lawrence's first collection of short stories, *The Prussian Officer and Other Stories*, was published in November 1914.[69] The collection included new work in addition to stories that had previously appeared in the *English Review*, *Smart Set*, *Nation*, *Metropolitan*, and *New Statesman*. Lawrence wrote his first three stories in response to a call for stories in the *Nottinghamshire Guardian*. The paper's 1907 story contest called for 'An Amusing Adventure,' 'A Legend,' and 'An Enjoyable Christmas.' Janice Harris has suggested that these categories illustrate the continuing dominance of assumptions that had been in play since the latter half of the eighteenth century with reference to the appropriate form and content of a short story. Into the nineteenth century, short stories tended towards three types: sketches, compressed novels, and cleverly plotted tales. Examples of all three types were readily found in a variety of nineteenth-century magazines, such as *Blackwood's*, *Household Words*, *Cornhill Magazine*, *The Ladies' Magazine,* and *The Queen*, with a preponderance of tales reliant on exotic settings and/or supernatural incidents for their surprise endings.

When Lawrence began writing, an interest in producing a different kind of short story was taking hold in England primarily by way of Continental writers such as Nikolai Gogol, Ivan Turgenev, Leo Tolstoy, Fyodor Dostoevsky, Anton Chekov, and Gustave Flaubert as well as the lingering influence of the *Yellow Book* and *The Savoy*. Writers like Chekov and Flaubert had abandoned drum-rolling climaxes; instead they offered sharp detailed observations of ordinary lives. Ford Madox Ford's editorial in the first issue of the *English Review* called for more stories that offered a picture of life as it is. He demanded a literature that advanced 'knowledge of the lives and aspirations of the poor man . . . . We are barred off from him by the invisible barriers: we have no records of his views in literature. It is astonishing how little literature has to show of the life of the poor.'[70]

Lawrence's working class origins positioned him within the very community that Ford's editorials encouraged writers take as their subject. With Lawrence, there was no need to write from the position of an observer or visitor, as had so many of the nineteenth-century novelists who had sought a wider social canvas for their work. Lawrence's father was a miner, and life in the mining village, which was dominated by the men's daily descent into the mining pit, was his childhood milieu. His early life amongst the miners was tainted by his mother's sometimes corrosive middle-class aspirations, thus providing him with an acute awareness of class boundaries. His early stories of family life and young love exposed a keen ability to depict the bitter disappointments and frustrations peculiar to family relations and love affairs. Lawrence's economic and intense short stories explore nothing less than human experience. As with the majority of the writers in this chapter, Lawrence's use of setting and imagery betrays a profound commitment to aesthetic unity. Setting and imagery work in close concert with one another to generate the desired mood and tone. Few details are superfluous in a Lawrence story, and meaning is implied through the cumulative weight of characters' responses to the situations in which they find themselves. The active raconteur disappears and—as in Joyce and Mansfield, in particular—the burden of drawing conclusions and discerning the significance of an ending falls to the reader. The story is told through the visual and auditory images. Reading a story by writers such as these is akin to reading poetry; there are a density and a precision in the use of language that demand great care on the part of the reader.

In that regard, the third story in Lawrence's first collection is an interesting anomaly; like 'The Dead' it is a long short story and, in spite of its length, it nevertheless has a suggestive power akin to the work of contemporaneous poets. The earliest version of 'Daughters of the Vicar'—then titled 'Two Marriages'—was completed in July 1911. The American magazine *Century* initially rejected the story. Lawrence rewrote it in July 1913 and changed the title to 'Daughters of the Vicar.' The second draft was rejected by the Northern Newspaper Syndicate and the American magazine *Smart Set*. The story was then revised extensively a third and final time in July 1914 in preparation for the autumn publication of *The Prussian Officer and Other Stories*. It is this version of the story with which the majority of contemporary readers are familiar and the one with which we will concern ourselves.

Here yet again a story affirms the impossibility of writing about individual struggles with intimacy without attending to the social networks within which a person is enmeshed. Lawrence's characters are
endowed with a biographical density against which they must rebel if
they seek to be reborn. Louisa Lindley and Alfred Durant learn to
shrug off their familial inheritances as they struggle to meet each other
unhampered by conventions and convictions not their own. In short,
they wish to be free of class prejudices. Through its depiction of the
fates of the other men and women by whom Louisa and Alfred are
surrounded, the story's structure emphasizes the heavy costs associated with false spirituality, the misdirection of will, and the denial of
the flesh. In particular, this is done so by opening and closing with
scenes exposing the deficiencies of the Lindley family.

The limitations of the parents and the consequences with respect to
the children's relationship to their community are made plain in the
opening vignette: 'Their father and mother educated them at home,
made them very proud and very genteel, put them definitely and cru-
elly in the upper classes, apart from the vulgar around them. So they
lived quite isolated.'[71] The parents are unable to conceive of social
relations except those defined by class. The father 'had no particular
character, having always depended on his position in society to give
him position among men.'[72] And when the mother cannot maintain
her sense of position within the community on account of their
intensely genteel poverty, she is eventually broken by 'her violent
anger and misery and disgust' and takes to her couch, adopting the
pose of the invalid.

In the second vignette, Lawrence contrasts the attitude of the
Lindley parents with the introduction of the Durants. The two families
are shown over their midday meals espousing contrasting positions
towards service in response to Alfred's decision to join the navy. In
spite of the differences, it is evident that the attitudes of Louisa and
Alfred contrast with those of their parents, foreshadowing their need
to break from the limiting constraints of the parental prejudices if they
wish to strive to fashion a life in which they are only indebted to their
own beliefs.

The first half of the story primarily depicts what Louisa will reject.
For the most part this is communicated through her reaction to her
sister's marriage. When Mary and Louisa reach twenty-three and
twenty-two, respectively, their father's bout with illness makes it necessary that a clergyman take up his church work for a few months.
This need brings Mr Massey to Aldecross and the family's home. The
perceived benefits of his arrival are not, however, exclusively spiritual
as is suggested by Mrs Lindley's willingness to incur new debts when
they learn that he came of 'an old Cambridgeshire family, had some
private means, was going to take a church in Northamptonshire with a

good stipend, and was not married.'[73] In time, however, the family's revulsion and disappointment in the inhuman little Mr Massey are sufficiently overcome by his money and social acceptability for them to approve of marriage between Mr Massey and Mary. Mary's acceptance of a marriage with Mr Massey contrasts with Louisa's revulsion.

Louisa recoils from Mr Massey; indeed '[h]is body was almost unthinkable, in intellect he was something definite.'[74] Mrs Lindley reacts by declaring him 'a little abortion.'[75] These reactions and words are set against Louisa's response to seeing Alfred recently returned from naval service when she and Mr Massey go to visit the ailing Mr Durant. When she thinks of Alfred that evening after she returns home and speaks with Mary,

> she remembered [his voice] again and again, [it] was like a
> flame through her; and she wanted to see his face more distinctly in her mind, ruddy with the sun, and his golden-brown
> eyes, kind and careless. . . . And it went through her with pride,
> to think of his figure, a straight, fine jet of life.[76]

Alfred is a man who demands a bodily response as opposed to an intellectual response in which the body must be denied. Mary, in marrying Mr Massey, must learn to become 'pure reason such as he was, without feeling and impulse.'[77] This exacts a price. She feels a certain shame in her private life, which she can keep hidden as she lives in a tiny village that is miles from the railway and she can offset her awareness that people feel uneasy before him. The uneasiness that other people feel restores her pride and affirms the sense of position that she so needs in this diminished life that she has forged for herself.

Louisa rejects her sister's choice and comes to distrust her sister's spirituality: 'It was no longer genuine for her. And if Mary were spiritual and misguided, why did not her father protect her? Because of money. He disliked the whole affair, but he backed away, because of the money.'[78] She also recoils yet further from her family whose willingness to disregard other values in favour of the consuming importance of material comfort and security disgusts her: 'They are wrong—they are all wrong. They have ground out their souls for what isn't worth anything, and there isn't a grain of love in them anywhere. And I will have love.'[79] Her convictions will separate Louisa from her family; her will to live by her own convictions rather than the will of family divide her from her blood:

> So Miss Louisa stood isolated from everybody. She and Mary
> had parted over Mr Massey. . . . She could not bear to think of
> her lofty, spiritual sister degraded in body like this. Mary was
> wrong, wrong, wrong: she was not superior, she was flawed, incomplete. The two sisters stood apart.[80]

Her distance from her family is emphasized in the eighth vignette—the story's mid-way point—when she flees her home and no one remarks on her exit. In fact, no one will remark until the final vignette of the story when she returns home with Alfred.

Louisa's exit takes her to the Durants and, specifically, Alfred. The second half of the story examines the awakening of the physical and spiritual awareness between Alfred and Louisa that leads her to reject her family. Beforehand, however, the reader learns further of what unites them. Where Louisa stands isolated from her family, Alfred is isolated from men with whom he feels no kinship. He is described as feeling spiritually impotent and less than a normal man. This grates hard on him, and '[h]e would have changed with any mere brute, just to be free of himself, to be free of this shame of self-consciousness.'[81]

A communion, which will be the antithesis of the union binding Mary and Mr Massey, is forged when Louisa and Alfred learn to acknowledge the independent other within each other, and when they learn to see each other instead of seeing what they have been taught to see: a miner; a clergyman's daughter. Louisa's desire to see is articulated in her pain when she sees him covered in pit dirt, stripped of a recognizable individuality. At his dying mother's request, she washes his back and in doing so witnesses the reemergence of his distinctiveness:

> His skin was beautifully white and unblemished, of an opaque, solid whiteness. Gradually Louisa saw it: this also was what he was. It fascinated her. Her feeling of separateness passed away: she ceased to draw back from contact with him and his mother. There was this living centre. Her heart ran hot. She had reached some goal in this beautiful, clear, male body. She loved him in a white, impersonal heat. But the sun-burnt, reddish neck and ears: they were more personal, more curious. . . . A person—an intimate being he was to her. She put down the towel and went upstairs again, troubled in her heart. She had only seen one human being in her life—and that was Mary. All the rest were strangers. Now her soul was going to open, she was going to see another. She felt strange and pregnant.[82]

She is alive to him and alive with a willingness to meet him in intimacy. Louisa's vision is matched by Alfred's own vision that concludes the tenth vignette. He is transformed by their contact and feels a new night 'gathering around him.'[83] He is awed by Louisa, but can conceive of her in the same thought as his mother with 'a sense of uplifting' just as she has recognized the possibility of an intimacy with him that previously has only been experienced with her sister.[84] The possibility of an allegiance between the two of them becomes palpable and desirable.

This antihierarchical intimacy is sharply contrasted with Mary's demeanour when Alfred presents himself at the vicarage to gather Louisa's things as she cares for his dying mother. She labels him an honest man and sees no more than that which she has expected to see, and so

> the patronage was applied as salve to her own sickness. She had station, so she could patronize. . . . she could not have lived without having a certain position. She could never have trusted herself outside of a definite place, nor respected herself except as a woman of a superior class. [85]

To admit the possibility of a different kind of relationship with Alfred would be to move into an indefinite place where social convention is not in effect—where there are no prescribed roles—and men and women come together freely in and of themselves.

Louisa and Alfred's silent communion, and the brevity of the final interview with the Lindley family in which their intention to marry is announced, is fitting. The couple are rejecting (social) expectation and roles and in doing so they move into unbroken ground in which they must work together. It is a choice that is not without struggle and not without its agonies:

> Then, gradually, as he held her gripped, and his brain reeled round, and he felt himself falling, falling from himself, and whilst she, yielded up, swooned to a kind of death of herself, a moment of utter darkness came over him, and they began to wake again as if from a long sleep. He was himself. [86]

In waking from death-in-life, the petty prejudices of the Lindley family—'You don't want to marry a collier, you little fool'—become irrelevant, though not painless, as does their insistence that Louisa is acting selfishly. Receiving no welcome from the Lindley family, the young couple will emigrate. Whether a new country will prove less hostile is ambiguous; it is clear, however, that the old country has little or no room for the unimagined in its stained and crowded landscape.

'Second-Best' is a considerably shorter story than 'Daughters of the Vicar,' and it was also written at the beginning of Lawrence's career. The earliest known manuscript dates to August 1911, when Lawrence was writing stories for the *English Review*. A slightly revised version of the story was published in the *English Review* in February 1912. Again, not unlike 'Daughters of the Vicar,' Lawrence extensively revised the manuscript in advance of publishing *The Prussian Officer and Other Stories*. This is the base-text on which the majority of the critics comment. The version has a neatness and ease that suggests increased assurance on Lawrence's part, as he becomes an ever more accomplished and highly regarded writer. Economy and depth combine in this short story where Lawrence chooses yet again to work with a pair of sisters. This time, however, there is an almost ten-year age difference between the two sisters. Nevertheless, the rapport between the sisters and their contrasting responses to the mole that Anne catches are effective tools with which to illustrate the elder sister's shifting attitudes towards isolation and sacrifice.

The title invites a blatantly straightforward reading: a young woman who has moved to the city returns to the country sacrificing herself to a simple local farmer when she cannot marry her first choice. In reality, however, there is a narrative ambivalence towards Frances and Jimmy Barrass that undermines so sure a reading. The conversations between Frances and her younger sister Anne imply that the absent Jimmy is a far from adequate first choice in this instance. Anne's self-confident and practical manner exposes her sister as unnatural, stand-off-ish, and self-conscious. Frances does not act instinctually as does her sister in her response to the struggling mole that nips her and so incurs her wrath and its death. Passion and practicality unite—They're vicious little nuisances, moles are'—in this gesture. Indeed, the gesture elicits a transformation in Frances' psychological state: '[she] suddenly, became calm; in that moment, grown-up.'[87]

Hers is by no means a perfect transformation characterized by an unwavering certitude as she still evinces 'a rather stubborn pride in her isolation and indifference,' but the scene which has played out on a hot summer's afternoon rouses her and she '[knows] what she [is] about.' She knows she will 'have something' just as Tom Smedley knows he wants a woman.[88] In becoming 'grown-up,' she has become masterful in the sense that she can master herself—control the aspect of herself that was earlier identified as whimsical by her sister. The readers become aware of the power and need to make choices as the conversation between Frances and Tom progresses on the subject of killing moles. In short, Frances declares that while she does not need to kill moles—she is not a farmer—she will venture to determine whether she can kill a mole and, in turn, learn whether she can align herself with the young farmer whose ways she likes. This declaration elicits mixed emotions in the pair: 'Their eyes met, and she sank before him, her pride troubled. He felt uneasy and triumphant and baffled, as if fate had gripped him. She smiled as she departed.'[89]

When they next meet, she comes to him with a dead mole in her hands. Frances and Tom are terrified and thrilled by the implications of her 'secret, persistent hunt.'[90] Man and woman both experience conflicting emotions, which they must master and to which they must submit. Furthermore, as with the majority of Lawrence's stories, there is no ending in the conventional sense. There is no joyful scene of perfect communion. In fact, the readers' experience of the story parallels that of the characters—Frances and Tom are not sure where their romance is headed, and neither are the readers. In short, as already suggested, the story's meaning cannot be inferred from the title, which ought not to be taken at face value.

'Odour of Chrysanthemums,' one of Lawrence's best-known stories, is similarly concerned with love and the difficulty of loving without the damaging interference of succumbing to culturally determined attitudes towards intimacy. This story, however, does not end with a marriage. Instead, it ends with the death of a marriage:

> 'Daughters of the Vicar' and 'Odour of Chrysanthemums' are
> like a great diptych, the wings of an altarpiece. They both por-
> tray the same central figure being ministered to, being washed,
> by a woman: the body of a miner in his physical beauty, mature,
> powerful and unblemished. The firm flesh and the white skin
> are revealed as the soiling mask of labour is washed away and
> he is uncovered as this other, strange and wonderful. In the first
> story the wonder is released and is potent; in the other it has
> been lost, negated.[91]

The earliest drafts of this story date from 1909. After significant revisions, the story was published in the *English Review* in June 1911. Three years later, Lawrence used the magazine text as his setting-copy for Duckworth but rewrote the ending. The earliest versions of the story are considerably more sentimental than the version published in the 1914 edition of *The Prussian Officer*. The completed story opens with the panoramic overview of the mining community in which the story is set. The 'dreary and forsaken' landscape gives way to a 'felt-covered fowl-house half-way down the garden' from which Elizabeth Bates emerges.[92] With this narrowing of scope, we move from a desecrated landscape to a scene of ruined love. There is perverse harmony between the setting and the events relayed in the story.

Elizabeth's dissatisfaction with her marriage is palpable from the outset. It is revealed in the set of her mouth 'closed with disillusionment.'[93] It is exposed in her response to her playing child; as she watches her son struggle with a piece of wood, 'she [sees] herself in his silence and pertinacity, she [sees] the father in her child's indifference to all but himself.'[94] The indifference and silence betoken the impossibility of connection between man and wife, which—paradoxically—they create together. He nevertheless consumes her. She is described as being 'occupied by her husband.'[95] Even in his absence, she is fretful and unable to drive him from her thoughts—that is, she is unable to drive her projected disappointments and resentments as to his perceived failings.

It is only when she is confronted by a body stripped of life that she comes to realize how they were divided irrevocably long before his death. With his death, however, there is no means by which the situation can be rectified. When the force of this realization hits her, Elizabeth feels 'countermanded':

> She saw him, how utterly inviolable he lay in himself. She had
> nothing to do with him. She could not accept it. Stooping she
> laid her hand on him, in claim. . . . Elizabeth embraced the body

building between England and Germany as mediated by a criticism of the culinary and personal habits of the English. The indelicacies of both nations stand revealed in this story, as does the belligerent posturing which mimics the activities of the nations' officials and envoys seemingly determined to lead Europe into war. The narrator's unwillingness to be baited, coupled with her decided lack of interest in food, distinguishes her from the other guests and their caricatures of British citizenry so obviously not realized in the woman sitting before them. This, however, goes unnoticed.

Her words and replies to their questions go unheeded until she vows that she does not know what her husband's favourite meal is. Indeed, her overtly political declaration that '[w]e certainly do not want Germany' is disregarded in favour of a disquisition on Herr Rat's spa treatments and meals. In contrast, her admissions that she has never really asked her husband about his favourite meal and that 'he is not at all particular about his food' elicit a head-shaking reaction from the group that pauses with 'their mouths full of cherry stones.'[102] The priorities and concerns of the guests appear distorted in view of the political backdrop against which the scene is played. This is an unusual story in the collection given that more frequently conversations in a Mansfield story explore the conflict between traditional roles and contemporary viewpoints, between women and men, between mothers and daughters leaving aside—for the most part—explicitly political commentary. However, Mansfield's ability here to offer an unusual or distorted angle from which to view a familiar scene is very much in keeping with the tone of the entire collection.

The narrative structure of the collection is also somewhat unsettling. As already mentioned, the majority of the stories are written in the first-person and narrated by an English-speaking woman; yet, her identity is not firmly established and there are inconsistencies from story to story. The narrator in the first story 'Germans at Meat' appears to have a husband; in the fourth story 'Frau Fischer,' there is a sense that the narrator may be fabricating a husband in response to the conversation she is having with Frau Fischer. More importantly, the inconsistencies, which inconclusively suggest the possibility that the narrator may have changed, draw attention to the shifting self-projections that men and women offer up depending upon on the people with whom they are interacting. 'Frau Fischer,' falls into this category. The widow Frau Fischer evinces such clearly stated views on everything from coffee to marriage that what she would like to see in her companions is rendered transparent by her actions and assertions.

The narrator strives to resist engaging with the effusive Frau Fischer, observing that the weather was 'too hot to be malicious, and who could be uncharitable, victimized by the flapping sensations which Frau Fischer was enduring until six-thirty.'[103] When Frau

Fischer bursts into the narrator's room, the juxtaposition between the narrator's view and those advanced by her visitor as well as the reading given to her by a Catholic priest becomes complete. The *Miracle of Lourdes* and the views of Frau Fischer are not in harmony with the attitudes held by the narrator, who likes empty beds and considers 'child-bearing the most ignominious of all professions.'[104] The widow strives to envelop the young woman before her in a vision of blessed maternal contentment and to rouse in her the indignities of a wife parted from her sea-faring husband.

Frau Fischer's remarks elicit the admission from the narrator to the readers that the husband created for the benefit of Frau Fischer has become so substantial a figure in the widow's hands that she can see herself 'pushing a perambulator up the gangway, and counting up the missing buttons on [her] husband's uniform jacket.'[105] In response, the narrator decides to 'wreck her virgin conception and send [her husband] down somewhere off Cape Horn.'[106] Frau Fischer, who assumes that after dinner there is much more to be discussed, does not, of course, witness the imagined drowning. The narrator is not reconciled to the same vision of feminine fulfilment and conduct as Frau Fischer. In spite of her near silence, that which she rejects has become readily apparent within a matter of pages. The story undercuts any still lingering myths that all women are cut of the same cloth and share the same desires.

In 'The Modern Soul,' the narrator continues quietly observing the guests at the pension, exposing how she has come to break with many of the day's conventions as regard to appropriate conduct and decorum for women. She exposes the 'modern soul' as in fact a troublingly conventional woman. The progressive attitudes adopted by the actress stand revealed as nothing more than poses below which the desire to enact womanhood in previously worn garments emerges. It is the quiet little English narrator who discloses a modern perspective by way of her suggestions and questions that shock those to whom her remarks are directed.

Her practical response to Fräulein Godowska's complaint that the tragedy of her life is her mother—'Living with her I live with the coffin of my unborn aspirations'—is met with physical revulsion. The 'modern soul' and declared admirer of Sappho collapses to the pavement in a fainting spell at the narrator's suggestion that she marry off her mother to the attentive Herr Professor. The narrator has very clearly misunderstood the degree to which the actress is interested in releasing her 'unborn aspirations' by whatever means possible. Before fainting Fräulein Godowska clutches her walking companion's arm and stammers, 'You, you . . . the cruelty. I am going to faint. Mamma to marry again before I marry—the indignity. I am going to faint here and now.'[107]

When the narrator fails to dissuade her from dramatically fainting on the Station Road, her response is anything but sympathetic: 'Very well ... faint away; but please hurry over it.'[108] Fräulein Godowska lingers motionlessly on the spot even when her companion walks away. The narrator breaks into a run when she finally realizes that the modern soul is not going to get up and that she is required to collect Herr Professor on behalf of the fallen soul. The professor who had earlier admiringly declared the lady 'modern' worries about the delicacy of reviving a fainting lady to the already unsympathetic narrator who dryly observes, 'Modern souls oughtn't to wear [stays].'[109] As the narrator's wry observations suggest, the distance between the romantic lead's declarations and actions is very far indeed. Her remarks also attest to the difference between adopting an up-to-date vocabulary and living by the principles that such words might be expected to imply. Fräulein Godowska's modernity is a pose—an attitude appropriate to her profession and the drama of her own self-construction—that is put aside when the matrimony plot comes to assume greater urgency in her life. Unlike the narrator, Fräulein Godowska by no means embodies a woman consciously breaking free from the nineteenth-century conventions in which she had been raised.

The overt artifice of the modern short story parallels modernism's commitment to formal experimentation as a means of transcribing social realties into literary form. Mansfield explored the distance between what is spoken and our actions, and in doing so drew attention to the transgression of social hierarchies and patterns. Lawrence interrogated the ways in which men and women annihilate each other through a denial of the physical and the failure to recognize the essential separateness of another soul. Joyce subverted the single-effect story to delineate his ambiguous internal dramas in his tales of life in working-class Dublin. Somerville and Ross used humour to draw attention to the inconsistencies and infelicities of unquestioningly assuming that power is the exclusive province of the upper-class English male. The writers deliberately utilize the genre's formal properties and, in doing so, dissonance—at the level of form—becomes a key element of the modern short story.

Stylistic experimentation is one of the means by which a writer can offer a critique of contemporary society and reveal its hypocrisies. The stories discussed here draw attention to the shifting relations between men and women in the opening decade of the twentieth century. While the stories examined in this chapter overwhelmingly privilege change and uncertainty in a domestic setting or the private sphere through repeated portraits of courtship and marriage, it is false to separate public and private. Sex relations are unquestionably conditioned and influenced by the attitudes and beliefs of the society in which women and men find themselves situated. In particular, the stories by Lawrence and Mansfield expose the difficulties of forging relationships in a changing society; men and women adopt new perspectives at varying rates complicating communication and the process of defining relationships. The short story as crafted by these writers and others is a snapshot capturing modern life in compressed, highly subjective episodes and fragments. The unexpected perspectives and revelations that characterize the short fiction of Somerville and Ross, Joyce, Lawrence, and Mansfield illuminate moments in which individuals are confronted with choices that present both personal and communal dilemmas. The public and the private intersect powerfully in the work of all four writers.

FOR FURTHER CONSIDERATION: SUGGESTED READING

Modernism

Bornstein, George. *Material Modernism: The Politics of the Page*. Cambridge: Cambridge University Press, 2001.

Bradbury, Malcolm, and James McFarlane (eds). *Modernism: 1890–1930*. 1976. London: Penguin, 1983.

DiBattista, Maria, and Lucy McDiarmid. *High and Low Moderns: Literature and Culture, 1889–1939*. Oxford: Oxford University Press, 1996.

Giddens, Anthony. *The Consequences of Modernity*. Stanford: Stanford University Press, 1990.

Kenner, Hugh. *The Pound Era*. Berkeley: University of California Press, 1973.

Levenson, Michael. *A Genealogy of Modernism: A Study of English Literary Doctrine, 1980–1922*. Cambridge: Cambridge University Press, 1984.

Nicholls, Peter. *Modernisms: A Literary Guide*. London: Macmillan, 1995.

Schwartz, Sanford. *The Matrix of Modernism: Pound, Eliot and Early Twentieth-Century Thought*. Princeton: Princeton University Press, 1985.

Williams, Raymond. *The Politics of Modernism: Against the New Conformists*. London: Verso, 1989.

The New Woman

Ledger, Sally. *The New Woman: Fiction and Feminism at the Fin de Siècle*. Manchester: Manchester University Press, 1997.

Marks, Patricia. *Bicycles, Bangs and Bloomers: The New Woman in the Popular Press*. Lexington: University of Kentucky Press, 1990.

Nelson, Carolyn Christensen. *A New Woman Reader: Fiction, Articles, and Drama of the 1890s*. Peterborough ON: Broadview Press, 2001.

Parsons, Deborah L. *Streetwalking the Metropolis: Women, The City and Modernity*. Oxford: Oxford University Press, 2000.

Richardson, Angelique, and Chris Willis (eds). *The New Woman in Fiction and in Fact: Fin de Siècle Feminisms*. London: Macmillan, 2001.

The Short Story

Bayley, John. *The Short Story: Henry James to Elizabeth Bowen*. Brighton: Harvester Press, 1988.

Dunn, Maggie, and Ann Morris. *The Composite Novel: The Short Story Cycle in Transition*. Toronto: Macmillan, 1995.

Flora, Joseph M. *The English Short Story, 1880–1945*. Boston: Twayne, 1985.

Hanson, Clare. *Short Stories and Short Fictions, 1880–1980*. London: Macmillan, 1985.

Head, Dominic. *The Modernist Short Story: A Study in Theory and Practice*. Cambridge: Cambridge University Press, 1992.

May, Charles. *The Short Story: The Reality of Artifice*. Toronto: Macmillan, 1995.

Shaw, Valerie. *The Short Story: A Critical Introduction*. London: Longman, 1983.

James Joyce

Attridge, Derek (ed.). *The Cambridge Companion to James Joyce*. Cambridge: Cambridge University Press, 1990.

Brannigan, John, Geoff Ward, and Julian Wolfreys (eds). *Re:Joyce: Text, Culture, Politics*. New York: St. Martin's, 1998.

Corcoran, Marlena, and Jolanta Wawrzycka (eds). *Gender in Joyce*. Gainesville: University Press of Florida, 1997.

Ellmann, Richard. *James Joyce*. Oxford: Oxford University Press, 1959.

Finney, Michael. 'Why Gretta Falls Asleep: A Postmodern Sugarplum,' *Studies in Short Fiction* 1995 Summer 32 (3): 475–81.

Howes, Marjorie. 'Tradition, Gender and Migration in "The Dead," or: How Many People Has Gretta Conroy Killed?' *Yale Journal of Criticism: Interpretation in the Humanities* 2002 Spring 15 (1): 149–71.

Kelly, Joseph. 'Joyce's Marriage Cycle,' *Studies in Short Fiction* 1995 Summer 32 (3): 367–78.

Leonard, Garry. *Reading 'Dubliners' Again: A Lacanian Perspective*. Syracuse: Syracuse University Press, 1993.

Osteen, Mark. '"A Splendid Bazaar": The Shopper's Guide to the New *Dubliners*,' *Studies in Short Fiction* 1995 Summer 32 (3): 483–96.

Porcel-Garcia, Maria Isabel. 'Gretta Conroy: The Dead Woman/The Dead One?' *Papers on Joyce* 1999 (5): 51–65.

Rice, Thomas Jackson. 'Paradigm Lost: "Grace" and the Arrangement of *Dubliners*,' *Studies in Short Fiction* 1995 Summer 32 (3): 405–21.

Wright, David. 'Interactive Stories in *Dubliners*,' *Studies in Short Fiction* 1995 Summer 32(3): 285–93.

D.H. Lawrence

Fernihough, Anne (ed.) *The Cambridge Companion to D.H. Lawrence.* Cambridge: Cambridge University Press, 2001.

Thorton, Weldon. *D.H. Lawrence: A Study of the Short Fiction.* New York: Twayne, 1993.

Volker, Schulz. 'D.H. Lawrence's Early Masterpiece of Short Fiction: "Odour of Chrysanthemums",' *Studies of Short Fiction* 1991 Summer 28 (3): 363–70.

Katherine Mansfield

Blake, Ann (ed.). *England Through Colonial Eyes in Twentieth-Century Fiction.* New York: Palgrave, 2001.

Fernihough, Ann. 'Introduction,' *In a German Pension.* London: Penguin, 1999.

Kaplan, Sydney. *Katherine Mansfield and the Origins of Modernist Fiction.* Ithaca: Cornell University Press, 1991.

Moran, Patricia. *Word of Mouth: Body Language in Katherine Mansfield and Virginia Woolf.* Charlottesville: University Press of Virginia, 1996.

Robinson, Roger (ed.). *Katherine Mansfield —In From the Margin.* Baton Rouge: Louisiana State University Press, 1994.

Somerville and Ross

Cahalan, James M. *Double Visions: Women and Men in Modern and Contemporary Irish Fiction.* Syracuse: Syracuse University Press, 1999.

Kelly, Aaron, and Alan Gillis (eds). *Critical Ireland: New Essays in Literature and Culture.* Dublin: Four Courts, 2001.

Kreilkamp, Vera. *The Anglo-Irish Novel and the Big House.* Syracuse: Syracuse University Press, 1998.

Laird, Holly. *Women Coauthors.* Urbana: University of Illinois Press, 2000.

NOTES

1 Oscar Wilde, for instance, was associated with Aestheticism and Decadence as are Walter Pater, Ernest Dowson, Richard Le Galliene, and Arthur Symons. Joseph Conrad's writing style is frequently called Impressionist, while W.B. Yeats' poetry of the 1890s ranks him among the Symbolists.

2 The Fabian Society was a socialist organization that espoused a belief in gradual rather than revolutionary change. It sought to persuade, through education and lectures, the British intellectual and political elite of the necessity of reforms that would assist those members of society least able to help themselves.

3 Triple-decker novel is the term used to refer to the three volume novels that were the norm in publishing from the 1840s until the mid-1890s. The novels were circulated by lending libraries, which charged their subscribers an annual fee that permitted them to borrow one volume at a time, and as many volumes as they wished annually. Charles Edward Mudie founded one of the best known of

these lending libraries—Mudie's—in 1842. To learn more about Mudie's and lending libraries see Guinevere L. Griest's *Mudie's Circulating Library and the Victorian Novel*, (Bloomington: Indiana University Press, 1970).

4 Sarah Grand's *The Heavenly Twins* was a controversial bestseller in England and the United States. The English edition of the novel was reprinted six times in its first year. The triple-decker novel (three volumes) deplored sexual ignorance and hypocrisy in marriage. It offered a disturbing portrait of a syphilitic wife and baby while also questioning gender roles through the depiction of twins Angelica and Diablo. The *North American Review* was a literary and cultural journal founded in Boston at the beginning of the nineteenth century; when Grand's article appeared in the Review, it was published out of New York and featured the work of such writers as Walt Whitman, Henry James, and Joseph Conrad.

5 Sarah Grand, 'The New Aspect of the Woman Question,' *A New Woman Reader: Fiction, Articles, Drama of the 1890s*, Carolyn Christensen Nelson (ed.), (Peterborough ON: Broadview, 2001) 142.

6 Carolyn Christensen Nelson, 'Introduction,' *A New Woman Reader: Fiction, Articles, Drama of the 1890s* ix. See also Patricia Marks, *Bicycles, Bangs, and Bloomers: The New Woman in the Popular Press* (Lexington: University Press of Kentucky, 1990). Girton was established in 1869 as the first residential college for women at Cambridge University.

7 Nelson ix–x.

8 Henry James, 'Preface' to 'The Lessons of the Master,' *The Art of the Novel: Critical Prefaces* (New York: C. Scribner's Sons, 1962) 219.

9 James 231.

10 Valerie Shaw, *The Short Story: A Critical Introduction* (London: Longman, 1983) 11.

11 James 231.

12 Dominic Head, *The Modernist Short Story* (Cambridge: Cambridge University Press, 1992) 1.

13 Nelson 3.

14 Head 1.

15 Shaw 43.

16 Anton Chekhov, *Letters on the Short Story, the Drama & other Literary Topics*, Louis S. Friedland (ed.) (New York: B. Blom, 1964) 17.

17 Edgar Allan Poe, Review of Nathaniel Hawthorne's *Twice-Told Tales*, in *The Complete Works of Edgar Allan Poe*, James A. Harrison (ed.), vol. 11 (17 vols, New York: T.Y. Crowell, 1902; repr. 1965) 107.

18 Poe 108.

19 Head 26.

20 Harris 11.

21 The *Irish R.M.* stories have never been out of print and the 1991 rebroadcast of the British Channel 4/UTV/RTE television series from the early 1980s based on the stories has continued to ensure healthy sales of the books in the UK.

22 James M. Cahalan, *Double Vision* (Syracuse: Syracuse University Press, 1999) 71.

23 Cahalan 80.

24 E.O. Somerville and Martin Ross, *Some Experiences of an Irish R.M.* (Nashville: J. Sanders & Co., 1998) 14.

25 Cahalan 85.

26 Somerville and Ross 72. See for example 'Oh Love, Oh Fire' and 'Lisheen Races, Second-Hand' in *Some Experiences of an Irish R.M.*

27 Somerville and Ross 38.

28 Somerville and Ross 46.

29 Somerville and Ross 48.

30 Somerville and Ross 48.

31 Somerville and Ross 51.

32 Somerville and Ross 51.

33 George Russell, an active Irish nationalist, edited *The Irish Homestead* from 1904 to 1923. *The Irish Homestead,* the weekly journal of the Irish Agricultural Organization Society (IAOS), featured editorials, national and rural news, poetry, and prose. According to George Bernard Shaw, the paper always contained 'one to three first-rate political and social articles, followed by instructions on how to keep bees . . . or what not' (Nicholas Allen, *George Russell and the New Ireland, 1905–1930.* Dublin: Four Courts Press, 10).

34 Stephen Daedalus was the hero of the lengthy naturalist novel on which Joyce was working when he began writing the *Dubliners* stories. *Stephen Hero* was an early version of Joyce's first novel, *A Portrait of the Artist as a Young Man,* which was published in 1916 after it appeared serially throughout 1914 in the London-based literary magazine *The Egoist.*

35 The letter was published in *Sinn Féin* (Dublin) and *Northern Whig* (Belfast).

36 A number of technical difficulties plagued the production of the first edition; not only were the printers perplexed by Joyce's unconventional punctuation, but Grant Richards failed to incorporate more than 200 corrections to the manuscript.

37 Head 77.

38 James Joyce, *Dubliners* (London: Vintage, 1993) 28.

39 Joyce 29.

40 Joyce 31.

41 Joyce 28.

42 Joyce 29.

43 Joyce 30.

44 Joyce 30–1.

45 Joyce 32.

46 Joyce 33.

47 Joyce 53.

48 Joyce 54.

49 Joyce 54.

50 Joyce 54.

51 Joyce 59.

52 Joyce 55.

53 Joyce 54.

54 Joyce 55.

55 Joyce 56.

56 Joyce 57.

57 Joyce 58.

58 Joyce 59.

59 Kelly 261.

60 Kelly 249.

61 Kelly 270.

62 Joyce 162.

63 Joyce 162.

64 Joyce 171.

65 Joyce 173.

66 Kelly 274.

67 Joyce 204.

68 The variations are frequently of sufficient significance to warrant the attention of critics; see, for example, Mara Kalnins, 'D.H. Lawrence's "Two Marriages" and "Daughters of the Vicar",' *Ariel 7* (January 1976) 32–49.

69 For ease of reference, this chapter discusses the versions of 'Odour of Chrysanthemums,' 'Second Best,' and 'Daughters of the Vicar' that appeared in *The Prussian Officer* (1914).

70 'The Month,' *English Review* (December 1908) 162-3.

71 D.H. Lawrence, *The Prussian Officer and Other Stories,* John Worthen (ed.) (Cambridge: Cambridge University Press, 1983) 41.

72 Lawrence 41.

73 Lawrence 48.

74 Lawrence 48.

75 Lawrence 48.

76 Lawrence 53.

77 Lawrence 56.

78 Lawrence 58.

79 Lawrence 58.

80 Lawrence 59.

81 Lawrence 68.

82 Lawrence 73.

83 Lawrence 75.

84 Lawrence 75.

85 Lawrence 76.

86 Lawrence 82.

87 Lawrence 117.

88 Lawrence 118.

89 Lawrence 120.

90 Lawrence 120.

91 Michael Black, *D.H. Lawrence—The Early Fiction* (London: Macmillan, 1986) 208-9.

92 Lawrence 181-2.

93 Lawrence 182.

94 Lawrence 184.

95 Lawrence 184.

96 Lawrence 196.

97 Lawrence 197, 198.

98 Lawrence 198.

99 *The Rainbow* (1915), *Women in Love* (1920), and *Kangaroo* (1923) are three ex-amples of Lawrence novels in which male and female characters skirmish—to varying degrees of success—in an attempt to forge viable romantic relationships.

100 In 1891, Florence Farr played Rebecca West in the first English production of Ibsen's *Rosmersholm*. At the turn of the century, this character—a compelling portrait of individualism—became an emblem of the New Woman. Farr was also well known for her performances in W.B. Yeats' play *Countess Cathleen* and G.B. Shaw's *Arms and the Man*. See Josephine Johnson, *Florence Farr: Bernard Shaw's 'New Woman'* (Totawa NJ: Rowman and Littlefield, 1975). 'Suffrage' means the right to vote; when Millicent Fawcett founded the National Union of Women's Suffrage in 1897, her supporters were known as suffragettes. The movement started peacefully, but when their demands were not met by the British government, large-scale marches and sometimes violent protests became increasingly commonplace. Women over thirty were eventually granted the right to vote in 1918, when the government passed the Representation of the People Act.

101 Circulation peaked at the end of November 1908, when circulation was estimated at 22,000; by 1913, circulation had settled at 4,500.

102 Katherine Mansfield, *In a German Pension* (London: Penguin, 1964) 13.

103 Mansfield 28.

104 Mansfield 31.

105 Mansfield 32.

106 Mansfield 32.

107 Mansfield 50.

108 Mansfield 50.

109 Mansfield 51.

CHAPTER 2

POETRY—TECHNOLOGY AND WAR

A Modernist Chronology—The 1910s

Arts & Literature	*Historical Events*
1910 E.M. Forster, *Howards End*	Japanese annexation of Korea
Post-Impressionist Exhibition in	Death of Edward VII
London	Accession of George V
Igor Stravinsky, *The Firebird*	Union of South Africa formed
1911 G.K. Chesterton, *The Innocence of*	National Insurance Act—provided medical
Father Brown	care and unemployment insurance for
Irving Berlin, *Alexanders Rag-time*	workers
Band	Roald Amundsen reaches South Pole
1912 Sarah Bernhardt, *Queen Elizabeth*	Sinking of the *Titanic*
Marcel Duchamp, *Nude Descending a*	Beginning of the Balkan Wars (1912–13)
Staircase	Nationalization of UK telephone service
George Bernard Shaw, *Pygmalion*	Royal Flying Corps (later RAF) founded
Arnold Schonberg, *Pierre Lunaire*	
1913 Willa Cather, *O Pioneers!*	Suffragette demonstrations in London
D.H. Lawrence, *Sons and Lovers*	
Marcel Proust, *Swann's Way*	
Igor Stravinsky, *Le Sacre du*	
Printemps	
1914 Founding of *Blast*	Home Rule Bill for Ireland passes in
Joseph Conrad, *Chance*	Parliament
James Joyce, *Dubliners*	Assassination of Archduke Franz Ferdinand,
	heir to the Austro-Hungarian Empire
	Outbreak of World War I on 28 June 1914
	4 August Britain declares war on Germany
	after the Germans invade France through
	neutral Belgium
1915 D.W. Griffith, *Birth of a Nation*	Sinking of the *Lusitania*
D.H. Lawrence, *The Rainbow*	First use of poison gas on Western Front
Somerset Maugham, *Of Human*	Gallipoli landings of British, Australian,
Bondage	New Zealand, and French troops
Dorothy Richardson, *Pointed Roofs*	
Virginia Woolf, *The Voyage Out*	
1916 H.D., Sea Garden	Battle of the Somme
D.W. Griffith, *Intolerance*	Easter Rising in Dublin
James Joyce, *A Portrait of the Artist*	Battle of Jutland
as a Young Man	Sinking of HMS *Hampshire*

1917	T.S. Eliot, *Prufrock and Other Observations* Carl Jung, *The Unconscious* Sergei Prokofiev, 'Classical' Symphony Leonard and Virginia Woolf found the Hogarth Press	Royal Family renames itself House of Windsor First major assault using tanks United States declares war on Germany Collapse of Czarist Russia
1918	James Joyces, *Exiles* Paul Klee, *Garten Plan* Lytton Strachey, *Eminent Victorians*	Royal Air Force established Central Powers surrender to the Allies Votes for women thirty years and over in Britain Sinn Féin win victory in Ireland
1919	Thomas Hardy, *Collected Poems* Pablo Picasso, *Pierrot and Harlequin* Ezra Pound, *Hugh Selwyn Mauberly* Robert Weine, *The Cabinet of Dr Caligari* Virginia Woolf, *Night and Day*	Treaty of Versailles signed in June 1919 officially ending World War I Sinn Féin establish own Parliament in Dublin British troops kill 370 people in Amritsar Massacre in the Punjab Nancy Astor first woman to take seat in British Parliament E.R. Rutherford splits atom

As the second decade of the twentieth century opened, Britons were faced yet again with the death of a monarch and with the spectre of a nation on the brink of turmoil· Edward VII's short rule came to a close on 6 May 1910. At the time of his death, the country was embroiled in a constitutional crisis. The Conservative-controlled House of Lords refused to pass a budget proposed by the Liberal Prime Minister Lloyd George, and a deadlock resulted. With the backing of the new King George V—who agreed to create enough new Peers if necessary to enable the passage of the budget in the Lords—the impasse ended. However, the budget standoff was symptomatic of greater social upheaval, as 1911 witnessed a nationwide strike of dock workers, miners, and railway men. Their strike brought the nation to a halt, forcing the Liberal government to pass the National Insurance Act which ensured that the worker, the employer, and the government all contributed to a fund that provided free medical treatment, sick pay, disability, and maternity benefits. Other measures were also passed over the next few years that improved the situation of the workers and their families: unemployment benefits, free meals for school children, and periodic medical exams. The costs of these programmes were largely borne through the taxation of wealthier Britons, thereby driving a wedge further between the classes. The Irish Question continued to simmer and it was to explode into violence at the Easter Rising of 1916 and then again at the end of the decade. In Europe, the first signs of trouble were on the horizon. Germany had supported the Afrikaners in their war against Britain, and the expansion of the German navy set off warning bells in London. German hostility against France, and events in the Balkans were soon to draw not only Britain but also all of Europe into a world war.

Literature was also undergoing a tremendous transformation as the 1910s opened. D.H. Lawrence's first novel *The White Peacock* was published in 1911 and was followed by *Sons and Lovers* in 1913 and *The Rainbow* in 1915. Lawrence's frank presentation of sexuality and of class and gender issues outraged many critics and readers, but his novels found favour with others in the reading public who hailed Lawrence's compelling psychological portraits, complemented by prose that was heavily imbued with symbolism, as modern work appropriate for the changing times. Other prose writers were also venturing into new territory. As we have seen, Katherine Mansfield transformed the short story genre and she continued to produce increasingly experimental stories throughout the 1910s. Although the stories had been written before 1910, the eventual publication of *Dubliners* in 1914 helped to establish Joyce as an important new fiction writer. Virginia Woolf, who had spent much of the first decade of the twentieth century writing literary journalism, was also branching out into fiction, writing a number of highly experimental short stories that were gathered together in volume entitled *Monday or Tuesday* that was published in 1919. The two novels that she published in this decade—*The Voyage Out* (1915) and *Night and Day* (1919)—are less experimental than her short stories, though they also showed signs of leaving behind conventional form and subject matter. Dorothy Richardson's *Pointed Roofs* (1915) and James Joyce's *A Portrait of the Artist as a Young Man* (1916) were the first English examples of a new mode of fiction: stream–of–consciousness. Late in the decade, Harriet Shaw Weaver began to publish Joyce's next novel *Ulysses* serially in *The Egoist* magazine, one of the leading publication venues for modernist work. The publication of this novel sealed Joyce's reputation as the leading experimental fiction writer of the period. In the meantime, Richardson would continue to work on her own experimental fiction, adding 12 more volumes over the next two decades to what was to become her monumental novel *Pilgrimage*. This multi-volume novel has garnered less critical attention than other key experimental prose works; nevertheless, Richardson's pioneering work alongside that of Mansfield, Lawrence, Woolf, and Joyce, in particular, would help to set the foundation for the explosion of experimental prose that occurred in the 1920s.

Prose fiction was not the only literary genre in the 1910s to be influenced by the aesthetics and formal experiments of literary modernism. Shaw continued to use his plays as forums in which to address social issues and he continued to employ experimental techniques to drive home his points. Heavily influenced by the Norwegian Henrik Ibsen's dramas, Shaw's plays made extensive use of symbolism and allusion, and he frequently resorted to satire in which to couch his social critiques. John Galsworthy, who is now better remembered for the novels that make up his *Forsyte Saga*, also wrote plays that dealt with social issues, with his 1910 play *Justice* presenting such a realistic portrait of the dismal conditions in prison that it stirred up popular support for prison reform. Apart from Shaw and Galsworthy, both of whom became Nobel laureates, few homegrown playwrights stand out. The 1910s were not British drama's finest decade. Such is not the case for another literary genre, poetry, which is the focus of this chapter.

KEY POETRY MOVEMENTS

The early twentieth century witnessed a renaissance, indeed a transformation, of poetry. Poets, like prose writers, wished to renew their art; and like prose writers, they sought to distance themselves from what they saw as the stagnant state of late Victorian literature. W.B. Yeats, whose association with the Irish Literary Revival had clearly marked him as someone interested in distancing himself from the conventions of the Victorian period, stands out as one of the early modernist poets. His poetry took on a new cast in the century's second decade as it moved away from the Celtic myths and legends that had infused his early work in order to address contemporary political issues more directly. Poems such as 'September 1913' or 'Easter 1916' record his sympathy with the Irish Nationalist cause and his dismay at the ways in which Irish issues were yet again being set aside because of England's other political concerns: in this case the Great War—World War I. The spare language of the poems marks a departure from his earlier, more ornate, efforts and signals a change in Yeats' poetic technique that moved him to the centre of the modernist movement. Long after having established himself as the pre-eminent late Victorian novelist, Thomas Hardy, like Yeats, also found new life as a poet in the second decade of the twentieth century. *Satires of Circumstance* (1914) contains some of the most memorable of his poems including 'The Convergence of the Twain' which is an ironic depiction of the fate of the *Titanic*, and 'Channel Firing,' Hardy's commentary on the beginning of the Great War. Yet despite, or perhaps because of, their stature as established men of letters, neither poet played as central a role in the poetic and aesthetic debates of this period as did a younger generation of men and women. Indeed, this younger generation was caught up in the enormous creative activity that took place prior to, and during, the Great War. The vibrancy of the poetry in this period is remarkable, with a wide range of poetic movements emerging; each contested the others' aesthetics through the various manifestos that they produced and published in little magazines, many of which were founded and run by the poets themselves.

Of all the poetic coteries that flourished in the 1910s, arguably the most important was Imagism. The poetics promulgated by its founders have influenced much of the poetry written in English throughout the twentieth century. This chapter opens with an examination of Imagism and its aesthetic underpinnings before looking at some poems written by key Imagist poets. However, Imagism was not alone in seeking directly to alter the form and function of poetry. Vorticism was also an important aesthetic and artistic force in the 1910s. While the Vorticist magazine *Blast* was limited to two issues, its influence was much more widespread and the poets whose works appeared in the two issues are amongst the most important of the period. We will look at Vorticist aesthetics as articulated by Ezra Pound and Wyndham Lewis, and also at 'Preludes,' one of T.S. Eliot's early poems that first appeared in *Blast*. This will afford us a sense of the movement's dynamic flavour and familiarize us with the aesthetic principles that influenced poets of this and subsequent generations.

The poetry associated with the Great War is the third important poetic movement that will be explored in this chapter. Unlike either Imagists or Vorticists, the war poets did not write with the primary intent of transforming their art. Rather, they sought to use poetry for one of its traditional purposes: singing the praises of heroes who head off to battle for the glory of their country. Though this may have been the initial intention of many, if not most of these poets, their encounters with a radically new form of warfare prompted them to alter just as radically the poems they wrote about war. It is this transformation that underscores even more forcefully the need for change that lies at the heart of the aesthetic terms articulated by the Imagists. Poetry comes alive again, ironically, on the battlefields of Europe; and in the process, poetry is forever changed.

IMAGISM

Imagism was a trans-Atlantic literary movement closely associated with a group of English and American poets working in London during the opening two decades of the twentieth century. The movement was rooted in the dissatisfaction with the moribund state of contemporary English poetry. As F.S. Flint's 1915 article 'History of Imagism' implies, the English philosopher and sometime poet T.E. Hulme is an important figure in the movement's history. Hulme vigorously advocated the advancement of poetic forms that did 'a more efficient job of communicating contemporary reality' than the tired conventions inherited from the previous century.[1] In 1908 Hulme joined the Poets' Club, an organization headed by Scottish banker Henry Simpson. Later that year, Hulme's influential 'Lecture on Modern Poetry' was delivered at the Poets' Club. This lecture was an early expression of his views on contemporary verse.[2] It promoted *vers libre* as a replacement for outworn forms of poetry. At the end of the year, examples of Hulme's own contributions to the revitalization of poetry appeared in a small booklet of verse entitled *For Christmas MDCCCVIII*. He contributed two poems: 'Autumn' and 'A City Sunset.'[3]

In 1909, Hulme broke away from the Poets' Club and began to meet with other poets on a much more informal basis at a Soho restaurant. Hulme, Flint, Joseph Campbell, Dermot Freyer, Florence Farr, and a few others met for the first time on 25 March 1909, at the Café Tour d'Eiffel just off Tottenham Court Road. In straightforward terms, the bond that united these writers was 'dissatisfaction with the poetry then being written.'[4] Introduced to the group by Florence Farr and T.D. Fitzgerald, Ezra Pound joined the regular Thursday evening meetings for the first time on 22 April 1909. Questions related to poetic technique were the primary topic of conversation among these young writers. Hulme, as befits a man who reputedly spent 'hours each day in search of the right phrase,' repeatedly insisted upon the importance of 'absolutely accurate presentation and no verbiage' when writing poetry.[5] These principles would become the cardinal rules of Imagism as later promoted by Flint and Pound.

The informal meetings trailed off during the winter of 1909, and little more was heard of these writers and their principles until November 1912. That autumn Pound published *Ripostes, whereto are appended the complete poetical works of T.E. Hulme, with prefatory note* (1912), a book of poems that included an appendix with five short poems by T.E. Hulme.[6] In his 'History of Imagism,' Flint described *Ripostes* as the sequel to the discussions that had been held in Soho a few years earlier. The appendix was accompanied by an explanatory note in which Pound made mention of 'the School of Images' and used the word 'Imagiste' for the first time. Pound did not name the poets with whom he associated the term but based on his later comments, it is likely that he was thinking of Hilda Dolittle (H.D.), Richard Aldington, and himself.[7]

In spite of Hulme's importance in articulating the aesthetic principles now associated with Imagism, literary history and Pound privilege H.D. as the inspiration for the articulation of a new school of poets. Legend has it that H.D. showed Pound and Aldington a group of poems over tea at the British Museum in October 1912. When Pound sent the poems to Chicago with the hope of having them published in Harriet Monroe's newly-founded *Poetry* magazine, he described the poems as being 'modern, for it is in the laconic speech of the Imagistes, even if the subject is classic' and so Imagism was born.[8] Monroe included three poems by H.D. in the January 1913 issue of *Poetry*: 'Hermes of the Ways,' 'Priapus,' and 'Epigram.' H.D.'s poems embodied much of what Hulme had been advocating since 1908, which in turn suggests why his critical writing is invaluable to an understanding of the principles informing Imagist poetry.

In the years leading up to World War I, Hulme argued for a new classicism in response to the romantic excesses of the nineteenth century. While many readers associate the terms *classical* and *romantic* with the literary periods, for Hulme the terms applied to ways of seeing the world. He maintained that the romantic sees 'man, the individual, [as] an infinite reservoir of possibilities'—the romantic believes that if 'you can so rearrange society by the destruction of oppressive order, then these possibilities will have a chance and you get Progress.'[9] In contrast, the classicist believes 'quite clearly the exact opposite to this. Man is an extra-ordinarily fixed and limited animal whose nature is absolutely constant. It is only by tradition and organization that anything decent can be gotten out of him.'[10] Hulme and poets influenced by him were of the conviction that modern poets needed to be students of the past and develop their own poetic forms appropriate to the moment in which they lived in order to best express their modernity.[11]

As was to be repeatedly the case with literary modernism, the critical work of the practitioners played an important role in giving the movement definite meaning. The second issue of *Poetry* magazine included two essays by Pound and Flint that were instrumental in publicizing Imagist aesthetic principles. Flint's essay 'Imagism,' in keeping with Hulme's influence and definition of classicism, insisted that the Imagists 'were not a revolutionary school; their only endeavour was to write in accordance with the best tradition, as they found it in the best writers of all time,—in Sappho, Catullus, Villon.'[12] However, in an effort to articulate how contemporary poets differed from those of the past, Flint declared that there were three cardinal principles associated with Imagism:

> 1. Direct treatment of the 'thing', whether subjective or objective.
> 2. To use absolutely no word that did not contribute to the presentation.
> 3. As regarding rhythm: to compose in the sequence of the musical phrase, not in sequence of a metronome.[13]

Pound's companion essay 'A Few Don'ts by an Imagiste' defined an image as 'that which presents an intellectual and emotional complex in an instant of time.'[14] An image works to generate a single effect. This definition was complemented by the further observation, '[i]t is the presentation of such a "complex" instantaneously which gives the sudden sense of liberation; that sense of freedom from time limits and space limits; that sense of sudden growth, which we experience in the presence of the greatest works of art.'[15] With characteristic bravado, Pound also declared, 'It is better to present one image in a lifetime than to produce voluminous works.'[16]

He did not, however, want his directives to be taken as dogma. He wanted poets to consider 'the three propositions (demanding direct treatment, economy of words, and the sequence of musical phrase) . . . as the result of long contemplation.'[17] In other words, the poet must find images—words—that best fit the object or subject under scrutiny as opposed to selecting phrases which he or she thought were appropriate or palatable. It was on these terms that he expressed admiration for H.D.'s poetry, which he described as '[o]bjective—no slither; direct—no excessive use of adjectives; no metaphors that won't permit examination. It's straight talk.'[18]

Flint's and Pound's essays helped articulate the shared objectives of Imagist poets to the reading public. Over the coming years *Poetry* and *The Egoist: An Individualist Review* published the work of an ever-increasing array of writers experimenting with poetic expression independent of the rules that had guided their predecessors. Flint, Aldington, Pound, H.D., Amy Lowell, John Gould Fletcher, William Carlos Williams, and D.H. Lawrence were among the many poets on

part of an Imagist poem: it is the poem. The plot or argument so integral to nineteenth-century poetry gives way to a single, dominant image in the poetry of Pound and the other Imagists. This leaves greater interpretative responsibility with the reader who, through reading and re-reading, must determine the full force and significance of the fresh and unfamiliar image offered by the poet.

It is, however, important to stress that the unfamiliar is not the same as the exotic. The objects on which the Imagists and others associated with the movement meditated were taken directly from the natural or urban landscape of the modern poet. The poems read like snapshots that arrest and re-awaken us to our immediate environment. An Imagist poem forces a reader to see beyond what he or she has been schooled to see by poets of an earlier age. For example, T.E. Hulme's poems take familiar images as their subject—the moon, a valley wood, the Embankment—and, in concrete terms, explore the significance that we, as readers, impart to the natural or urban objects. His poetry makes us see that we invest these objects with meaning, and in showing us this, his poems suggest that each reader and each reading reveals as much about ourselves as it does about the world it ostensibly describes. Hulme's most frequently anthologized poems, 'Autumn' and 'Above the Dock,' respond to natural images as experienced within the framework (or limitations) of human experience. In 'Above the Dock,' the moon is likened to 'a child's balloon':

> Above the quiet dock in midnight,
> Tangled in the tall mast's corded height,
> Hangs the moon. What seemed so far awayIs but a child's
> balloon, forgotten after play.[27]

That a moon 'tangled' in the mast of a ship can recall 'child's balloon' suggests a kind of reawakening on the part of the speaker to the perceptions lost as one hardens to convention and fact in adulthood. This is a vision 'forgotten after play,' and retrieved at 'midnight' long after a child's perspective has been put aside. Not only does the short poem offer a fresh metaphor describing the moon, but it also demonstrates what is lost when language and images harden into stock phrases and associations.

EZRA POUND

Pound's early Imagist poems are characterized by a striking resemblance to Japanese haikus. The haiku is a Japanese verse form consisting of seventeen syllables in three lines of five, seven, and five syllables respectively. Haikus express a single idea, image, or feeling. The form was established in the sixteenth century and originally it was the opening verse in a linked sequence. Imagists were attracted to the form because of its intense concentration of effect. In particular, Pound's short Imagist poems achieve their force through the juxtaposition of the natural world and that of man. Pound's 'In A Station of the Metro,' while its syllable count does not match that of a haiku, mimics the shape of a haiku. This short poem, first published in 1916, transforms a nameless crowd of city dwellers into an object of beauty:

> The apparition of these faces in the crowd;
> Petals on a wet, black bough.[28]

No one word is superfluous. Each word works in concert with another. The title becomes an integral part of the poem and gives it its haiku shape. It implies that the scene is taking place in but one station in a network of stations, which amplifies the sense of anonymity that pervades: this is but one crowd in a bustling cityscape. The faces in the crowd are transformed in the second and final line of the poem. The faces become petals, and the crowd becomes the wet, black bough. This crowd is but one black bough of a tree that becomes the natural analogue to the implied urban landscape to which this poem responds. To see beauty in the contrast between petals on a wet bough is an example of beauty which we see unprompted; in turn, the crowd is infused with an unexpected beauty through the comparison. The poem captures in miniature a moment during which we see how our immediate environment is transformed. A workaday scene of men and women boarding and disembarking from a metro station now has the beauty of a Post-Impressionist painting or a Japanese scroll.

'Fan-Piece, For Her Imperial Lord,' which appeared in the first Imagist anthology, relies on a similar juxtaposition between the natural world and hand-crafted objects. The effect, however, is somewhat different. In this three-line poem, the lines directly pertaining to the fan both begin at the left margin. The contrasting line, which contains the image to which the fan is compared, is indented, thus the blade of grass is visually and typographically distinguished from the fan thereby heightening the contrast on which the poem pivots. The white silk stretched against the frame of the fan is likened to frost on a grass blade. Just as the silvery white of the frost melts from view, the fan is no more permanent—no more lasting—than an instant of beauty in nature. The frost and the silk are both passing pleasures, one no more valuable than the other. The exquisite workmanship that goes into the creation of a fan-piece for an aristocratic woman is no guarantee of timeless appreciation:

> O fan of white silk,
>> clear as frost on the grass-blade,
> You are also laid aside.[29]

Although it is the silk fan that is addressed in this poem—'You are also laid aside'—the address to a hand-made object implies a direct address to man and to his vain belief that he lies outside the forces of time and nature. Each reader will respond to the images differently. Some will feel the undertone of longing that resonates in the final line and its implication that, in time, we will all be laid aside; our deaths parallel the laying aside of a once cherished object. Others will be drawn to the beauty of Pound's description of the fan and will marvel at the clarity and precision of his language. It is clear from these lines, however, that the effect of the poem on each reader is—to borrow once more from Hulme—to 'arrest [us], and to make [us] continuously see a physical thing, [and] to prevent [us] gliding through an abstract process.'[30]

H.D.

H.D.'s early poems incorporate an energy that is not evident in the poetry of Hulme or Pound. She is fascinated by the beauty inherent in the clash between natural forces. Where Pound and Hulme's poems suggest a crystalline formation—a static, brief moment of apprehension—H.D.'s poetry is dynamic. This difference aside, the poems found in her first volume of poetry, *Sea Garden* (1916), nevertheless conform to the principles set out by Pound and Flint in their various essays and lectures on Imagism. As Louis Martz observes in his introduction to *H.D.—Collected Poems, 1912–1944*

> she gives 'direct treatment of the "thing" whether subjective or objective'; she tries 'to use absolutely no word that does not contribute to the presentation'—though sometimes her exclamations overrun the mark; and as for rhythm, she certainly composes 'in the sequence of the musical phrase.'[31]

The doctrines of Imagism control H.D.'s responses to the natural world. Her early poems meet Pound's definition of the 'image' as that which

> 'presents an intellectual and emotional complex in an instant of time,' if we allow the 'complex' to hold the psychological overtones that Pound intends and if the complex is created by the interaction of many images within an 'instant' of time of considerable duration.[32]

H.D.'s poem 'Oread' simultaneously captures an instant of time and recalls the past with its invocation of the spirit of a Greek mountain-nymph who comprehends the waves of the ocean as the pines of her own shore:

> Whirl up, sea—
> whirl you pointed pines,
> splash your great pines
> on our rocks,
> hurl your green over us,
> cover us with your pools of fir.[33]

In a single unified image, the sea is described in terms of the land and the land in terms of the sea. The poem conveys an interdependence and correspondence between the two elements. In accordance with

Pound's definition of an image, the readers intellectually apprehend the posited connection between the land and water while simultaneously responding emotionally to the cry of the wood nymph. The standard structure of a metaphor no longer applies in 'Oread'; this poem is about land *and* sea—water becomes earth and earth becomes water. The sea is solidified in terms of its shape, movement, and colour. The pine forest is liquefied by the series of active verbs. Active verbs begin all but one line of the poem—*whirl, whirl, splash, hurl,* and *cover*—and contribute to its dynamic force. Motion, shape, colour, and form interact in a single dynamic vision—a dense image— that activates the readers' senses and transports them into a world of timeless physical sensations.

The second section of H.D.'s 'Garden' pivots on a series of commands.[34] This poem expresses the desire for a cool breeze to 'cut apart' and 'plough through' the summer heat. Hot thick air wraps around the second stanza—a stanza replete with images of ripe fruit— and prevents summer's bounty from dropping. The active verbs that fill the first and third stanzas call upon the wind to break the heat and wrest the fruit from the trees:

> *O wind, rend open the heat,*
> cut apart the heat,
> rend it to tatters.
>
> Cut the heat—
> plough through it,
> turning it on either side
> of your path.[35]

This is the perfect summer poem: it combines the heat of summer and the season's bounty without being unduly romantic or clichéd. 'Rend,' 'cut,' and 'plough' suggest a kind of violence that is not usually associated with summer. The verbs express the intense, almost desperate, desire for a cool wind. The poem activates our senses: we can feel the heat just as we can imagine the sensation of relief that a wind would bring. The breathy, plosive sounds of the middle stanza with its alliterative f's, th's, and p's combine with the imagery to create a sense of suffocation and breathlessness. In contrast, the first and third stanzas have a crisp force to them, the sharpness of a strong wind—with the repetition of strong one-syllable words and sharp t's. The rhythms of the opening and closing stanzas echo in sound the speaker's desire: the intense wish for a powerful wind to cut the oppressive heat.[36] The image of the wind cutting into heat—ploughing into the heat—evokes images of harvest and the cool air of autumn; in turn, the desirability of changing seasons is subtly implied in this short poem very much rooted in summer. The poem's strength lies in its ability to call to mind the desires evoked by summer heat in combination with images and language that do not rely on predetermined patterns and associations.

BLAST—
IMAGES FOR THE MACHINE AGE

In 1914 Pound's promotional activities turned to the endorsement of Vorticism—an interdisciplinary movement that shared many aesthetic concerns germane to Imagism. Pound and the English writer and painter Wyndham Lewis launched their new magazine, which they named *Blast,* mid-way through the year. Despite their many disagreements that strained their cooperation on this new venture, the two men agreed that Edwardian and Georgian writers had not been able to countermand the deadening influence of Victorian poetry. *Blast* was intended as a corrective to this state of affairs. Launched just weeks before the outbreak of World War I, the name was supposed to suggest 'an explosive charge that would blow away tired literary and social conventions'; furthermore, they intended it to be 'a calculated assault on good taste, both in its contents and, more immediately, in its form: an oversized, bright pink cover with the single word *BLAST* splashed diagonally across it.'[37]

The magazine promoted the literary and visual arts in its assault on the reading public. The content of *Blast* was heavily indebted to the polemical style of F.T. Marinetti, the founder of Italian Futurism.[38] Marinetti endorsed a modern aesthetic that venerated speed, technology, and power. With the intention of openly differentiating it from Futurism, Lewis defined Vorticism as follows:

> (a) ACTIVITY as opposed to the tasteful PASSIVITY of
> Picasso;
> (b) SIGNIFICANCE as opposed to the dull or anecdotal
> character to which the Naturalist is condemned;
> (c) ESSENTIAL MOVEMENT and ACTIVITY (such as the
> energy of the mind) as opposed to the imitative
> cinematography, the fuss and hysterics of the Futurists.[39]

In turn, Pound conceived of Vorticism as a whirlpool of human imagination and potentialities: 'the point of maximum energy.'[40] Pound saw art as a means by which to give structure and value to an otherwise formless modernity. According to Pound and Lewis, without art, the present had no particular value. Lewis hammered this point home when he declared that:

> A space must be cleared, all said and done, round the hurly
> burly of the present. No man can reflect or create, in the
> intellectual sense, while he is acting—fighting, playing tennis,
> or making love. *The present man in all of us is the machine.*
> The farther away from the present, though not too far, the more
> free.[41]

That said, as might be expected, the signatories to the Vorticist manifesto declared, 'We stand for the Reality of the Present—not for the sentimental Future, or the sacripant Past.'[42]

Lewis and his cohorts intended the magazine to send a 'death warrant' to the guardians of the past. The task of Vorticism and *Blast* was 'to make the rich of the community shed their education . . . to destroy politeness, standardization and academic, that is civilized, vision.'[43] As Peter Nicholls has put it, Lewis was lured by the thought of a modernism 'able to respond to the exciting challenge of modern dynamism and technology without capitulating to the sentimental lure of modernity's "eternal present".'[44] Lewis wanted to create an authentically modern art that would derive from the subordination of the technological to the aesthetic and from which 'the resulting force of design would differentiate his art from both the facile "automobilism" of Marinetti and the "safe" domestic materials of Picasso's recent still-lifes and assemblages.'[45] The content of *Blast* was chiefly editorial: both issues were bursting with a series of manifestos and statements of artistic intent.

Lewis set out to establish the legitimacy and importance of Vorticism through a series of rhetorical blasts and 'promotional' language. This process of legitimization was initiated well before the appearance of the first issue. On 1 April 1914, a full-page ad appeared in *The Egoist* announcing the launch of a new publication edited by Wyndham Lewis. The advertisement, with its oversize boldface type in capital letters, declared the new magazine's commitment to the 'Discussion of Cubism, Futurism, Imagisme and all Vital Forms of Modern Art.' In advance of publication, *Blast* had called attention to itself. It looked different and spoke differently from other periodicals. The bold typography of the *Blast* ad in the otherwise visually understated landscape of *The Egoist* drew explicit attention to these differences.

The 'Blast' and 'Bless' sections of the magazine endorsed an explicit aesthetic and ideological position. The magazine told readers what to like and what to dislike. 'Bless' the scaffolding around the Albert Memorial. 'Blast' the architect of the Regent Palace Hotel.[46] The 'blasts' simultaneously linked Vorticism with a rejection of the past and helped clarify the magazine's own aesthetic position. Through the strategic deployment of editorial material, Vorticism emerged as a well-marked brand of culture complete with its own sanctioned cultural and political affiliations. In addition to schooling them in what to read, *Blast* taught the subscribers how to read culture. Art and advertising are synonymous in *Blast*.

The second issue emphasized the importance of the symbiotic relationship between artists and the public. The editorials confirmed the magazine's desire to communicate with the public as opposed to the narrow coterie audiences often associated with modernist literary production. While neither issue sold more than a few hundred copies, it is important to stress that large sales were by no means the response explicitly sought by the contributors. The opening pages of the first issue declared:

> Blast will be popular, essentially. It will not appeal to any
> particular class, but to the fundamental and popular instincts in
> every class and description of people. TO THE INDIVIDUAL.
> The moment a man feels or realizes himself as an artist, he
> ceases to belong to any milieu or time. Blast is created for this
> timeless, fundamental Artist that exists in everybody. [47]

Lewis and Pound sought to inculcate readers of all classes in their vision of art, which held that art should be an independent and unconscious response to 'the crude energy flowing through us.' [48] The artist honours his instincts and is unconcerned with the beliefs of the herd. This would mean that the magazine would be appreciated by a small, select readership and its contributors would be writers and artists at the forefront of their crafts. By way of illustration, in addition to the op-ed pieces and manifestos, both issues of *Blast* included samples of new work by writers who would later be remembered as key figures in the history of Anglo-American modernism. The magazine published short stories by Rebecca West and Ford Madox Ford and poetry by T.S. Eliot and Ezra Pound. The issues included illustrations and reproductions of recent pieces by artists such as Edward Wadsworth, Frederick Etchells, Epstein, Henri Gaudier-Brzeska, Cuthbert Hamilton, Spencer Gore, and Wyndham Lewis.

T.S. ELIOT

T.S. Eliot is a dominant figure in twentieth-century literary history. His influence as a poet and a critic was felt on both sides of the Atlantic Ocean throughout his lifetime and long after his death in 1965. While this book is not specifically concerned with the work of the American-born Eliot, it is well worth taking the time to pause over one of his best-known early poems, 'Preludes,' which was first published in the 1915 issue of *Blast*. As with the other great poems— 'The Love Song of J. Alfred Prufrock,' 'Rhapsody on a Winter Night,' and 'Portrait of a Lady'—written in the early period of his career, 'Preludes' deals unflinchingly with loneliness, alienation, and isolation. The early poetry suggests that the loneliness and isolation frequently associated with the modern city derive from self-alienation and an inability to make sense of a chaotic, fast-paced world. He believed that contemporary writers who synthesized the seemingly unrelated sensations and experiences of modern men and women might show a way out of 'the immense panorama of futility and anarchy which is contemporary history.' [49]

In the words of the Vorticist manifesto, 'Preludes' is grounded in the 'Reality of the Present.' It is also a popular poem in the sense advocated by Pound and Lewis. The poem draws on 'the crude energy flowing through us'—it draws on the chaos of the city in which modern life in the industrialized world is embedded. The familiar images and rituals that dominate the poem are drawn from our collective urban experience. Eliot juxtaposes contrasting conceptions of time: clock-time is in tension with internal time. The passing of external time—or clock-time—is carefully measured and marked in each of the poem's four sections. The first 'Prelude' opens as 'The winter evening settles down'; in the second 'Prelude,' night gives way to the breaking dawn when 'morning comes to consciousness,' after which morning arrives in the third 'Prelude' when 'all the world came back/And the light crept up between the shutters.'[50] The fourth 'Prelude' returns the reader to the time of day at which the poem began—'At four and five and six o'clock' but it is now the following day. The temporal structure of the poem emphasizes both the sameness of days and the inevitable progress of time. This winter evening—as with other winter evenings—is characterized by the 'smell of steaks in passageways.' The phrasing suggests the speaker knows that it is 'six o'clock' because it smells like steaks—the scent of the 'burnt-out ends of smoky days.' The opening 'Preludes' depict a world characterized by mechanized actions determined by the passing of time. Anonymous feet and hands repeat the same actions over and over again; morning brings feet to the 'early coffee-stands' and one cannot help but think about 'all the hands/that are raising dingy shades/In a thousand furnished rooms.'

The poem's unvarying landscape, a city street upon which the scenes of each day are (re)played, reinforces the senses of stasis pervading the poem. This is also a timeless landscape: the landscape of the speaker's mind. In responding to the images—both encountered and recollected—that litter the poem, the speaker blends the past, present, and future. As Mary Ann Gillies has observed in her work on the representation of time in Eliot's poetry, '[t]he real sordid world of the poem, with its "burnt-out ends of smoky days" and its "faint stale smells of beer," exists simultaneously with the one alive in the mind of the poem's unnamed persona who is

> moved by fancies that are curled
> Around these images, and cling:
> The notion of some infinitely gentle
> Infinitely suffering thing.'[51]

The poem is anchored in the interiorized juxtaposition between the street scenes described in the present tense, which dominate the first two 'Preludes,' and the past recollections in the latter half of the poem. In the third 'Prelude,' the speaker remembers a woman 'Sitting along the bed's edge where/You curled the papers from your hair.'

Like the speaker, she too is constructed through a collage of images: 'You dozed, and watched the night revealing/The thousand sordid images/Of which your soul was constituted'; these images, however, as they are not those of the speaker, are not accessible. The reader encounters the woman as an image embedded in the soul of the speaker and nothing more; as such, she is part of both his past and his present meditation on the dark streets. Eliot is attempting to write that which cannot be measured; he is attempting to capture 'a continuous moment of undefinable time.'[52] The impossibility of the attempt as well as the inevitability that such attempts will reoccur is encapsulated in the final lines of the poem: 'The worlds revolve like ancient women/Gathering fuel in vacant lots.' The 'ancient women' are the present exhausted by past events but yet they still gather fuel so that there might be a future. When Eliot published the 'Preludes,' England was entrenched in the first year of a war that would irrevocably change the future of both Europe and literature.

WARRING WITH WORDS—
THE POETRY OF THE GREAT WAR

Imagism and Vorticism call for art that responds to the demands of the moment of composition. World War I is a profoundly public example of an event that demanded the rejection of outdated conventions and called for a poetic language suited to the events under scrutiny. The poetry of World War I exposes the strain of a violent collision between the present and the past. Critics estimate approximately seventy British poets wrote about World War I; nearly fifty of these poets were actively engaged in the war.[53] However these soldier-poets may have felt about war when they first enlisted, the full horror of the war came to affect their imaginations and their poetic technique. As the conflict dragged on soldiers and non-combatants alike began to express revulsion, anger, cynicism, disgust, and horror at the new forms of war that characterized this conflict. In turn, writers were compelled to find means of expressing the terrible truths they had experienced.

It is not an overstatement to suggest that, 'people were wholly unprepared for the horrors of modern trench warfare. World War I broke out on a largely innocent world that still associated warfare with glorious cavalry charges and the noble pursuit of ideals.'[54] As the war dragged on, patriotic celebrations of the glories of war gradually became a thing of the past. By the time Germany surrendered on 11 November 1918, more than eight million lives had been sacrificed to a war that had lasted four years and three months. This final section of Chapter 2 opens with the poetry of Rupert Brooke. It contrasts his highly patriotic poetry written at the beginning of the war, with poems by Siegfried Sassoon and Wilfred Owen, which were written later in the conflict. It will become clear through this contrasting of early and later war poetry, that as the war progressed, poetry began to adapt to the rhythms and technology of a machine war. This, however, is to get ahead of ourselves. We will begin with Rupert Brooke.

Rupert Brooke was educated at Rugby School and King's College, Cambridge. Between leaving school and the beginning of the war, he travelled extensively throughout Europe, North America, and the South Pacific. When the war broke out, he enlisted as an officer in the Royal Navy. In autumn 1914, Brooke took part in a brief but aborted naval expedition to Antwerp. While on leave in December 1914, he wrote the 'war sonnets' for which he is famous. Five months later, he was dead.[55] In June 1915, shortly after his death, his book of war poems, *1914 and Other Poems*, was published. Over the next ten years, *1914* and his *Collected Poems* sold hundreds of thousands of copies.

Brooke's poetry is an important touchstone against which to read the aesthetic implications of the horrors of a mechanized war. Now his poetry is frequently described as anachronistic. When these charges are levelled, it is important to remember that Brooke died before he could respond as a poet to the realities of modern warfare. Brooke did not experience the horrors of active combat. He did not experience the wholesale slaughter of men at Gallipoli and the Battle of the Somme. It is also worth remembering that 'these patriotic poems—and most especially *The Soldier*, in which Brooke seemed to have foreseen his own death—meshed perfectly with the temperament of the British people as the nation entered into war.'[56] In contrast, the early poems of Wilfred Owen struck a similarly patriotic and romantic note that he could not duplicate after repeated exposure to the atrocities that came with trench warfare. The later poems of Wilfred Owen depict nightmarish scenes that were unimaginable in advance of World War I.

When Brooke's 'The Soldier' was read aloud to great acclaim at St Paul's Cathedral in London on Easter Sunday in 1915, Brooke's words assured him immortality as a representative of a generation of patriotic Englishmen lost to a brutal war fought for reasons later difficult to identify. Brooke's poetry came to represent sacrifice and pride. It was on those terms that the public rallied around his posthumously published poetry. Not only was the content familiar but so too was the form. As with the other sonnets in *1914*, 'The Soldier' is a modified Petrarchan sonnet.[57] The poem's octave presents readers with an ennobling image of sacrifice. It is not simply that an English soldier has died, but his death will become the means by which foreign soil is enriched and made forever England; his sacrifice enriches and sanctifies the battlegrounds so far from home. 'A body of England's'—a body '[w]ashed by the rivers, blest by the suns of home'—leaves behind in death that which is presumed to make England great: in death, a soldier '[g]ives somewhere back the thoughts by England given,/Her sight and sounds.'[58]

At no point does Brooke make a direct reference to the war. He does not make direct references to battles or to the magnitude of the losses even in the opening months of the war. How the soldier might have died is not broached in this sonnet. In turn, his equation of death with dust is familiar and comfortable. Brooke does not confront his readers with scenes which men and women at home would have found unsettling and even beyond comprehension. Not only is Brooke's presentation of death conventional but so too is his portrait of England. The poem's sestet answers the octave with an England for which it is an honour to fight. England is no less than the country that bore this soldier, 'shaped, made aware,/Gave, once, her flowers to love, her ways to roam.' Furthermore, the sestet betrays the poet's sense that peace is imminent and shall be won on England's terms. Brooke's poems were written before there was an acute sense that this war might not be over within a matter of months. He was writing when it was still possible to imagine 'gentleness/In hearts at peace, under an English heaven.' Yet the reality of England during the war and the postwar England envisioned by other World War I poets is altogether something else. These poets provide a poignant and disturbing contrast to Brooke's vision of a noble race heroically sacrificing its sons for the common good.

SIEGFRIED SASSOON

Siegfried Sassoon's prewar poetry, and even the poetry that he wrote before experiencing combat firsthand, in no way suggests the corrosive force that characterizes the poems he wrote between 1916 and 1918. Sassoon's first major volume of verse, *The Old Huntsman and Other Poems* (1917), included prewar poems and his early war poems. Sassoon's early war poems are accomplished but conventional, the kind of work that he was soon to leave behind. Poems such as 'Absolution,' 'To My Brother,' 'France,' and 'The Dragon and the Undying'—all of which were collected in *The Old Huntsman*—resemble Brooke's war poems. The style is familiar and the sentiments expressed are those of a patriotic soldier fighting on behalf of his country. As with 'The Soldier,' there is a strong reliance on nature images and on abstract meditations on human experience. Both dominate the final stanza of 'The Dragon and the Undying':

> Yet, though the slain are homeless as the breeze,
> Vocal are they, like storm bewilder'd seas.
> Their faces are the fair, unshrouded night,
> And planets are their eyes, their ageless dreams.
> Tenderly stooping earthward from their height,
> They wander in the dusk with chanting streams,
> And they are dawn-lit trees, with arms up-flung,
> To hail the burning heavens they left unsung.[59]

81

The battlefield is not present, it is not a physical reality that assaults the readers, forcing them to encounter the horror of war from the comfort of the place in which they are reading the poem. Similarly, the nature images used—the slain are likened to the wind, seas, night, and planets—distance the reader from the fact that these are men—sons, brothers, husbands—who have died brutal deaths in muddy fields far from home.

By the time Sassoon wrote 'Counter-Attack,' also the title of his second volume of poems, his treatment of war and the dead was changing:

> The place was rotten with dead; green clumsy legs
> High-booted, sprawled and grovelled along the saps
> And trunks, face downward, in the sucking mud,
> Wallowed like trodden sand-bags loosely filled;
> And naked sodden buttocks, mats of hair,
> Bulged, clotted heads slept in the plastering slime.[60]

No longer are the dead compared to nature, but instead to inanimate objects—'sand-bags'—'wallowing' in the 'sucking mud,' exposing the indignity and inhumanity of a death in the trenches. The title—with its invocation of battle—indicates a poetic challenge as well as a poetic subject. First-hand experience of trench warfare transformed Sassoon as a poet. When the war began, he was a country gentleman who wrote poetry according to convention. During the war, however, this model began to fail him when observed reality no longer bore any relationship to the modes of pastoral prettiness that had previously characterized his verse.

Before the war, Siegfried Sassoon, the son of a wealthy Jewish family, was educated at Marlborough College and Clare College, Cambridge. After leaving university, he was able to divide his time between London and the country. When the war broke out, Sassoon served with the Royal Welch Fusiliers where he befriended fellow writer and soldier Robert Graves. He first saw action in late 1915, and shortly thereafter he received the Military Cross for his actions during the Somme Offensive of July 1916. After being injured in battle—he took a sniper's bullet in the chest—he was invalided back to England in April 1917. From this point onwards, his writing began to show signs of his changing attitude towards war. Sassoon refused to return to battle and wrote an open letter to the war department in which he suggested the conflict was being unnecessarily prolonged. Robert Graves' interventions on Sassoon's behalf prevented Sassoon from being court-martialled. Instead, Sassoon was committed to Craiglockhart War Hospital and treated for shellshock.[61] While Sassoon's protest was undercut by the military authorities' response to his open letter, his poems continued to attack the army, church, and government whom he held responsible for this murderous drawn-out war.

Nevertheless, he returned to the Western Front in 1918. Sassoon's later war poems are characterized by an unrelentingly realistic portrayal of modern warfare and the masterful use of direct speech and irony. Where Brooke's poems offered familiar refrains and were well-received by a public not ready to confront the reality of this war, Sassoon's poetry was frequently rejected as unpatriotic and grotesque. Two of Sassoon's books of war poetry were published during the latter half of the war. In contrast with *The Old Huntsman* (1917), the poems in *Counter-Attack* (1918) and then *Picture-Show* (1920) offer a much more direct expression of his views on the brutality and waste of war.

These poems reveal the unreality of participating in an interminable conflict. 'The Dug-Out,' for example, is a short and seemingly moderate poem that captures the horror of a world where men have been so overwhelmed by death that the speaker can no longer bear the sight of a sleeping soldier:

> Why do you lie with your legs ungainly huddled,
> And one arm bent across your sullen, cold,
> Exhausted face? It hurts my heart to watch you,
> Deep-shadow'd from the candle's guttering gold;
> And you wonder why I shake you by the shoulder;
> Drowsy, you mumble and sigh and turn your head . . .
> *You are too young to fall asleep for ever;*
> *And when you sleep you remind me of the dead.*[62]

Sassoon's poem illustrates the reality of the combatant's life: soldiers are ensnared in a world where death is more common than sleep and to see a man asleep is painfully akin to seeing yet another man dead. It is a simple and direct poem. It rejects metaphoric language. The images are nonfigurative.[63] The speaker describes a sleeping soldier in plain unadorned language. It is the speaker's response to the sleeping soldier that becomes a metaphor for the disorienting experience of life in the trenches—a reading that the two lines in italics reinforces. In *An Adequate Response*, Arthur Lane suggests that 'The Dug-Out' is

> a perfect example of the Coleridgean use of symbol 'not as a sign that stands for something other than itself but as a living part or instance in the larger reality it manifests.' The speaker in the poem demonstrates in the final two lines his own awareness of the symbolic significance of what at first seems to be little more than an everyday scene: a man asleep.[64]

By turning in on itself and explicitly indicating how to interpret its own dominant image, the poem enforces the requisite contrast between the theatre of war and the world of peacetime—a world where the dead are usually described as sleeping.

Sassoon's poems do not simply set out to depict in plain spare language the realities of a soldier's world. His poems also attack institutions. 'They,' which appeared in the earlier collection *The Old Huntsman* and foreshadows his shift in tone, is a critique of the church's abdication of humanitarian responsibility in wartime and the limitations of institutionalized religion. The two stanzas of equal length share the same rhyme scheme, thereby emphasizing the utter lack of sympathy between the words uttered by the Bishop and those of the returning soldiers. Not only does the Bishop have no conception of the physical reality of the soldiers' suffering, but he does not speak to them as a man of religion, only as a man more concerned with war and politics. This hypocrisy is Sassoon's subject. The order in which the two parties speak is also of importance to any reading of the poem:

> The Bishop tells us: 'When the boys come back
> They will be the same; for they'll have fought
> In a just cause: they lead the last attack
> On Anti-Christ; their comrades' blood has bought
> New right to breed an honourable race,
> They have challenged Death and dared him face to face.'
>
> 'We're none of us the same!' the boys reply.
> 'For George lost both his legs: and Bill's stone blind;
> Poor Jim's shot through the lungs and like to die;
> And Bert's gone syphilitic: you'll not find
> A chap who's served that hasn't found *some* change.'
> And the Bishop said: 'The ways of God are strange!'[65]

The cries of the soldiers expose the inadequacy of the patriotic platitudes spouted by the Bishop. His rhetoric is as irrelevant to the men on the front as it is to those who have returned home.[66]

Sassoon's poetry also plays with the expectations that can be generated by the decision to write a specific kind of poem. To choose to write a sonnet with the title 'Glory of Women' is to create the expectation that what follows will be a love poem. What follows, however, serves only to draw attention to the distance between a soldier's experience of the war and that of a woman on the home front. The repetition of 'you' and 'we' throughout the sonnet emphasizes the divide between the men and women; a nation at war is two nations: there are combatants and non-combatants. As the tone suggests, it is a division characterized by rancour and bitterness as expressed by the speaker's accusatory tone. 'Heroes,' 'decorations,' and 'chivalry' are what the women like, but these baubles and empty words do not express the horrors of war—the horrors which most women do not see because they are so far from the Western Front. The sonnet also links words like 'love,' 'worship,' and 'believe' with the women, while the soldiers are associated with 'wounded,' 'disgrace,' and 'killed.' Fittingly, the third sentence—'You make us shells'—implicates the women in a kind of double-murder: not only are the women making munitions which kill and maim the soldiers, but their naïve and false hopes in the soldiers make them 'shells' of their former selves and give the lie to the discrepancy between war as it was experienced and the war as it was conceived by women at home. The sonnet concludes with two images that would be hard for those at home to ignore: men retreating from 'hell's last horror . . ./Trampling the terrible corpses—blind with blood' and a German mother 'dreaming by the fire/While you are knitting socks to send your son/His face is trodden deeper in the mud.'[67] The avoidance of the truth becomes a sonnet of anger and despairing wonder.

'Survivors,' which focuses on men who have had combat experience, affirms the breadth of concerns evident in Sassoon's war poetry. The battlefield, the women and men on the home front, the institutions orchestrating the war effort and, as in this poem, the men who have survived the conflict all feature in his poetry and serve as the means by which he expressed his views regarding the war. His poems rarely incorporated references to the enemy with exception of poems like the 'Glory of Women' or the substitution of 'Gott' for 'God,' which only amplified the similarities between the warring camps. 'Survivors' is a strong example of a Sassoon poem illustrating his scepticism about the relevance of abstractions such as 'glory' and 'holy brightness' to the man who has been up at the front. His scepticism compels him to write what he has seen as opposed to what he is expected to write by those who have left England. Sassoon quickly came to realize that no amount of rest could alleviate the strain that the soldiers suffered in this war. The men in command were unaware of the side-effects of modern machine warfare upon the human body; as a result the soldiers were taxed beyond their ability to assimilate the experiences that they were enduring. Mental collapse was often inevitable in a situation where the attitude of the commanding officers and the doctors was 'war is war, and soldiers are to fight.'[68] Attitudes towards shell-shock—or neurasthenia as it was called then—were deplorable during World War I.

As the satirical tone of the first eight lines of 'Survivors' makes plain, unless a man was visibly wounded he was for the most part expected to continue fighting:

> No doubt they'll soon get well; the shock and strain
> Have caused their stammering, disconnected talk.
> Of course they're 'longing to go out again,'
> These boys with old, scared faces, learning to walk.
> They'll soon forget their haunted nights; their cowed
> Subjection to the ghosts of friends who died,—
> Their dreams that drip with murder; and they'll be proud
> Of glorious war that shatter'd all their pride. . .[69]

The poem makes bitterly plain the expectations of those who have not fought. The opening line conveys the misleading sense of hope with the assured 'no doubt' symptomatic of the public's sense of the war back in England. This is the disassociated, unfeeling voice of a public that believes all soldiers are willing and indeed desire a return to the front. And so we read of boys 'with old, scared faces,' which belie their age, enjoined to forget the ghosts of the dead and instead to be proud of their part in the 'glorious war that shatter'd all their pride.' The satirical tone is dropped in the final couplet. The rhymed couplet, which pairs 'glad' with 'mad,' makes a direct and unambiguous statement. Men have been destroyed— 'broken'—by this conflict:

> Men who went out to battle, grim and glad;
> Children, with eyes that hate you, broken and mad. [70]

The simplicity with which the final assertion is made affirms the message that the anger cloaked in satire that predominates in the first eight lines is anything but misplaced. Sassoon's grim war poems are a testimony to his own experiences during World War I and those of the men by his side left 'broken and mad.'

WILFRED OWEN

Wilfred Owen was one of the masses of men who did not survive the war. His poetry, however, remains a powerful account of one man's aesthetic response to the conflict. Owen's poetry merges the frank depiction of war's horrors found in the poetry of Sassoon with the formal and technical skill we associate with the writing of Keats and Shelley. Or, as Sassoon himself put it, 'My trench-sketches were like rockets, sent up to illuminate the darkness. . . . It was Owen who revealed how, out of realistic horror and scorn, poetry might be made.' [71]

The son of a railway superintendent, Owen's education began at the Birkenhead Institute and then continued at the technical school in Shewsbury after his father's appointment as Assistant Superintendent for the Western Railway. After failing to attain entrance to the University of London, Owen served as a lay assistant to a country vicar. As his preparation to become a clergyman progressed, he became increasingly dissatisfied with the church's response to poverty and suffering. In 1913, he severed ties with the church and moved to Bordeaux to teach English. When the war broke out the following year, Owen initially hesitated before enlisting. In 1916, he received his commission to the Manchester Regiment (5th Battalion) and spent the rest of the year training in England. After the bloody Battle of the Somme, in May 1917, Owen was invalided out of the front line with shellshock and sent to Craiglockhart War Hospital in Edinburgh. Sassoon arrived at the same hospital in July.

Owen benefited from the older poet's experience and encouragement. He wrote the bulk of his war poems between his first meeting with Sassoon in August 1917 and his return to active service in June 1918. Owen's earliest poems were published in the hospital magazine *Hydra*, over which he assumed editorship shortly after he arrived at the hospital. Owen returned to France in September 1918, three months after being graded fit for general action. He was killed in action on 4 November 1918—one week before Germany's surrender.[72] His poems were published two years later by Chatto and Windus in 1920, under the supervision of Sassoon.

Before his death, Owen wrote a draft preface for a collection of his poems that famously outlined his intentions as a war poet:

> This book is not about heroes. . . .
> Above all I am not concerned with Poetry....
> My subject is War, and the pity of War.
> The Poetry is in the Pity.[73]

He does not claim to have distanced himself from his subject: his subject is that in which he finds himself entrenched. This is not, however, to suggest that his poetry is not artful. Owen's poetry is simultaneously disciplined and passionate. Broadly speaking, the war poems are characterized by his masterful use of alliteration, onomatopoeia, assonance, half-rhyme, and pararhyme.[74] His elegiac sonnets are but one example of his attempts to work against the reader's expectations through the subversive use of conventional forms and symbolism.

That said, 'Anthem for Doomed Youth' attempts to capture the pathos of an untimely death. Adhering to the formal conventions of a sonnet, Owen—like Sassoon—manipulates the form to offer an understated and haunting indictment of the rhetoric so frequently spouted in response to reports of casualties. The sonnet refuses to employ the ritualized abstractions used to palliate the living. Owen opens with a question, 'What passing-bells for these who die as cattle?' and responds with the brutal truth, 'Only the monstrous anger of the guns.' The means and sounds of death are not buried in abstract metaphors. Owen refuses to use figurative language throughout the octave by focusing relentlessly on the instruments of death: rifles and shells. By framing his refusal in religious language, Owen further draws attention to the inadequacies of the tools available with which to mourn the dead. There is no anthem, only 'the stuttering rifles' rapid rattle' and the 'shrill, demented choirs of wailing shells.'[75]

The sestet does not offer any respite, metaphoric or otherwise, from the sonnet's subject. The sestet argues that the only appropriate response to death is simple acknowledgement of the dead. Neither 'candles' nor 'flowers'—the standard props of the mourner—can supplant the necessity of acknowledging the consequences of war:

> What candles may be held to speed them all?
>   Not in the hands of boys but in their eyes
> Shall shine the holy glimmers of goodbyes.

> The pallor of girls' brows shall be their pall;
> Their flowers the tenderness of patient minds,
> And each slow dusk a drawing-down of blinds.[76]

The sonnet anchors grief in the actual experience of death instead of in empty language and hollow rituals; '[b]y refusing to take flight into the fantasy world of metaphor-manipulation, Owen create[s] a poem out of images which represent reality. . . . The result is immediacy, which [is] his intention.'[77]

As with 'Anthem for Doomed Youth,' '*Dulce Et Decorum Est*' takes a familiar framework but refuses to work within the conventions that have come to be associated with the form. In '*Dulce Et Decorum Est,*' Owen jams together a series of heroic quatrains; this has the effect of obscuring the poem's regularity and creating the appearance of a realistic, apparently unshaped, report from the front as befits the poem's battlefield setting. The effect is an intense immediacy that mimics documentary reportage and hides the craft much as the chaos of the battlefield masks the orders and counter-orders governing the activities of the foot soldiers. Any hints of lyric cadence evident in the opening lines of the poem fade rapidly as the men struggle to battle exhaustion while removing themselves from imminent danger.

The exhaustion that pervades the opening stanza is pierced by the panic that accompanies the gas attack:

> GAS! GAS! Quick, boys!—An ecstasy of fumbling,
> Fitting the clumsy helmets just in time.[78]

Through the distorting and disorienting lens of the gas mask—'as under a green sea'—the speaker witnesses the death of a fellow soldier. The report of a scene filled with horrors that put the lie to inherited notions of heroism becomes the stuff of nightmares for the survivor in the broken quatrain that simply repeats the second word 'drowning' instead of completing the rhyme:

> Dim, through the misty panes and thick green light,
> As under a green sea, I saw him drowning.
>
> In all my dreams, before my helpless sight,
> He plunges at me, guttering, choking, drowning.[79]

The stern final stanza gives its attention to those not directly involved in the sequence of events described in the opening three stanzas. Here the readers at home— 'you'—are the subject of address. The speaker attempts to convey the horror of the battlefields to uncomprehending readers in England through an evermore urgent piling up images.[80] In the rudimentary table of contents accompanying the draft preface, Owen listed 'Indifference at Home' as the 'Motive' for this poem.[81] The despair and shades of guilt that haunt the opening three stanzas give way to Owen's primary concern—moral infection and corruption:

> If you could hear, at every jolt, the blood
> Come gargling from froth-corrupting lungs,
> Obscene as cancer, bitter as the cud
> Of vile, incurable sores on innocent tongues,—
> My friend, you would not tell with such high zest
> To children ardent for some desperate glory,
> The old Lie: Dulce et decorum est
> Pro patria mori. [82]

The narrator attempts to change places with the reader—'If in some smothering dreams you too could pace/Behind the wagon that we flung him in'—in an effort to demand that readers serve as a kind of witness to the horror of the described events. In doing so, he strives to negate the civilian's impulse to render the exploits of soldiers in terms intended to glorify and romanticize warfare.

'Disabled,' which has much in common with Sassoon's poem 'Survivors,' leaves behind the battlefields of Europe and turns to the subject of the men who returned home maimed and derelict. Owen writes as an observer. The poem alternates between direct observation and the presentation of the soldier's thoughts, thereby creating the impression that the soldier is too damaged to speak for himself. The story of the soldier's sacrifice—'he threw away his knees'—emphasizes his double loss. The loss of his limbs and the loss of a virile masculinity are conflated in the third stanza:

> He's lost his colour very far from here,
> Poured it down shell-holes till the veins ran dry,
> And half his lifetime lapsed in the hot race
> And leap of purple spurted from his thigh. [83]

His youth is spilled on fields far from home in a parody of sexual ejaculation. The use of erotic language to describe the loss of blood reinforces the poem's subject: destruction—*not* creation. The blood spilling from his thigh does not bring him the same glory as the 'blood-smear down his leg/After the [football] matches' where he was 'carried shoulder high' in celebration (not in helplessness).

The lines which follow offer an account of the series of clichés that led him to join the army in spite of being underage: because 'he'd look like a god in kilts'; 'to please his Meg'; 'For daggers in plaid socks; of smart salutes;/And care of arms: and leave: and pay arrears:/Esprit de corps.' [84] Never were there thoughts of the enemy or dreams of battles or fear. At no point, when he came to join, were his illusions disabused or countered: 'He didn't have to beg,/Smiling they wrote his lie: aged nineteen years.' The culpability—the guilt—of those smiling is the observer's knowledge; he knows full well the power of the lies and elisions upon which the war effort depends.

The man's voice emerges at the end of the poem when the full extremity of his fate becomes evident. A projection of his future follows the description of his homecoming—where '[s]ome cheered him home, but not as crowds cheer Goal'—and solicitude came only in the form of man who 'enquired about his soul.' The narrator describes a life of passive dependency doing 'what things the rules consider wise.' A stark sense of isolation and abandonment overwhelms the shivering man:

> How cold and late it is! Why don't they come
> And put him into bed? Why don't they come?[85]

Fighting on behalf of his country, he has been left utterly dependent on the care of institutions; this state of dependency, in turn, exposes the limits of institutionalized concern. Cold and isolated, the disabled soldier is cut off from the games of his youth and the warm glances of lovely young girls. All that he valued has been taken from him, and the nation to which he sacrificed himself has as good as abandoned his shell of a body. Owen unflinchingly recognizes and acknowledges the systemic indifference and avoidance upon which the war is predicated.

The most powerful war poems respond directly to the war and the reality of life at home after combat. The writer's choice to work within the limitation of his experience strengthens the poetry, which gains its force from the fierce commitment to imagery and rhythms entrenched in observed reality. The Imagist principles advanced by T.E. Hulme reverberate in the work of Sassoon and Owen.[86] The realistic, grim work of Sassoon and Owen and others such as Robert Graves, David Jones, and Issac Rosenberg in combination with the daily casualty lists that were published on the front pages of British newspapers provided a sobering counterpoint to the heroic images and patriotic rhetoric manufactured at home. By the end of the war, more than a million British troops—an average of fifteen hundred per day—had been killed in action. As suggested by the poems examined here, the war's primary legacies were disillusionment and cynicism. Nationalism, institutions, technology, and progress were treated with intense suspicion after the war. As poets discovered in the trenches and those at home were to learn later, this war was unlike any other war in the annals of history. The fruits of modernity and progress had arrived with a vengeance. A sense of physical and moral exhaustion came with the end of the war. It will come as no surprise to discover that the literature of the 1920s is burdened by a desire to wake up from the nightmare of history and haunted by the violence of the war that separates it from the wilful innocence of the years leading up to the conflict.

FOR FURTHER CONSIDERATION: SUGGESTED READING

Imagism

Des Imagistes: An Anthology. London: Poetry Workshop, 1914.

Some Imagist Poets: An Anthology. Boston: Houghton Mifflin, 1915–17.

Gross, Harvey Seymour. *Sound and Form in Modern Poetry*. Ann Arbor: University of Michigan Press, 1996.

Hughes, Glenn. *Imagism & the Imagists: A Study in Modern Poetry*. New York: Humanities Press, 1960.

Pratt, William, and Robert Richardson (eds). *Homage to Imagism*. New York: AMS Press, 1992.

Pratt, William. *The Imagist Poem: Modern Poetry in Miniature*. Ashland: Story Line Press, 2001.

Poetry of World War I

Booth, Allison. *Postcards from the Trenches: Negotiating the Space Between Modernism and the First World War*. Oxford: Oxford University Press, 1996.

Fussell, Paul. *The Great War and Modern Memory*. Oxford: Oxford University Press, 2000.

Graham, Desmond. *The Truth of War: Owen, Blunden, Rosenberg*. Manchester: Carcanet, 1984.

Quinn, Patrick, and Steven Trout (eds). *The Literature of the Great War Reconsidered: Beyond Modern Memory*. New York: Palgrave, 2001.

Stephen, Martin. *The Price of Pity: Poetry, History, and Myth in the Great War*. London: L. Cooper, 1996.

F.S. Flint

Pondrom, Cyrena N. (ed.) 'Selected Letters from H.D. to F.S. Flint: A Commentary on the Imagist Period.' *Contemporary Literature* 10.4 (1969): 557–86.

H.D.

Collecott, Diana. *H.D. and Sapphic Modernism 1910–1950*. Cambridge: Cambridge University Press, 1999.

Taylor, Georgina. *H.D. and the Public Sphere of Modernist Women Writers 1913–1946*. Oxford: Oxford University Press, 2001.

T.E. Hulme

Ferguson, Robert. *The Short Sharp Life of T.E. Hulme*. London: Allen Lane, 2002.

Rae, Patricia. *The Practical Muse: Pragmatist Poetics in Hulme, Pound and Stevens*. Lewisburg: Bucknell University Press, 1997.

Wilfred Owen

Sillars, Stuart. *Structure and Dissolution in English Writing, 1910–1920*. London: Macmillan, 1999.

Siegfried Sassoon

Campbell, Patrick. *Siegfried Sassoon: A Study of the War Poetry*. London: McFarland, 1999.

Moeyes, Paul. *Siegfried Sassoon, Scorched Glory: A Critical Study*. New York: St. Martin's, 1997.

Sillars, Stuart. *Structure and Dissolution in English Writing, 1910–1920.* London: Macmillan, 1999.

NOTES

1 Robert Ferguson, *The Short Sharp Life of T.E. Hulme* (London: Allen Lane, 2002) 48.

2 'Lecture on Modern Poetry' was not published until 1938.

3 'Autumn,' which will be discussed later in this chapter, is a more compelling demonstration of his poetic theories than 'A City Sunset.'

4 Ferguson 55.

5 F.S. Flint, 'History of Imagism,' *Egoist* (1 May 1915) 70. This article appeared in the *Special Imagist Number,* which included articles on the poetry of F.S. Flint, Richard Aldington, H.D., John Gould Fletcher, and D.H. Lawrence. It also included new poems by Aldington, H.D., Fletcher, Flint, Lawrence, Amy Lowell, Marianne Moore, and May Sinclair.

6 In advance of Pound's book *Ripostes,* these five short poems by T.E. Hulme appeared in *The New Age* (25 January 1912: 307) under the heading 'The Complete Poetical Works of T.E. Hulme.' Typical of what is now known as Imagism, the poems conveyed clear visual images and were examples of what Hulme thought young poets ought to be doing.

7 Hilda Doolittle adopted the pen name H.D. at Pound's suggestion in 1912.

8 Ezra Pound, *The Letters of Ezra Pound*, D.D. Paige (ed.), (London: Faber, 1951) 45.

9 T.E. Hulme, *Speculations* (London: Routledge & Kegan Paul, 1924) 116.

10 Hulme 116.

11 T.S. Eliot famously made a similar case in his essay 'Tradition and the Individual Talent' which appeared in his first volume of critical essays, *The Sacred Wood* (1920).

12 F.S. Flint, 'Imagisme,' *Poetry* (March 1913) 199.

13 F.S. Flint, 'Imagisme,' *Poetry* (March 1913) 199.

14 Ezra Pound, 'A Retrospect,' in *Literary Essays of Ezra Pound*, T.S. Eliot (ed.) (London: Faber, 1968) 4.

15 'A Retrospect' 4.

16 'A Retrospect' 4.

17 'A Retrospect' 4.

18 The Letters of Ezra Pound 45.

19 William Pratt, 'Introduction,' *The Imagist Poem: Modern Poetry In Miniature* (Ashland OR: Story Line, 2001) 27.

20 Walt Whitman, 'Section 21,' 'Song of My Myself,' *Leaves of Grass* (New York: Aventine Press, 1931) 49.

21 T.E. Hulme, 'Lecture on Modern Poetry,' *Further Speculations* (Minneapolis: University of Minnesota Press, 1955) 74.

22 'A Retrospect,' 9.

23 Hulme, 'Notes on Language and Style,' in *Further Speculations* 84.

24 Further Speculations 79.

25 Speculations 134–5.

26 Pound, 'Vorticism,' *Fortnightly Review, XCVI, n.s.* (1 September 1914) 469.

27 T.E. Hulme, 'Above the Dock,' *The New Age* (25 January 1912) 307.

28 Ezra Pound, 'In A Station of the Metro,' *Personae: The Shorter Poems of Ezra Pound* (New York: New Directions, 1990) 111.

29 Ezra Pound, 'Fan-Piece, For Her Imperial Lord,' *Des Imagistes, An Anthology* (London: The Poetry Bookshop) 45.

30 Speculations 96.

31 Louis Martz, 'Introduction,' Louis Martz (ed.), *H.D. Collected Poems, 1912–1944* (Manchester: Carcanet, 1984) xiii.

32 Martz xiii.

33 H.D. 'Oread.' *Egoist 1* (February 1914) 55. Nymphs are Greek female divinities associated with nature. The Oread is a mountain nymph associated with Aphrodite, the goddess of love.

34 This poem was frequently anthologized in the collections of modern poetry during the late 1910s and 1920s under the title 'Heat.'

35 H.D., 'Garden,' *Collected Poems* (Manchester: Carcanet, 1984) 25.

36 For the most part, H.D.'s early poems explore the natural world and/or man's relationship with that world; the final poem in *Sea Garden*, 'Cities,' foreshadows H.D.'s later interest in the worlds people make for themselves, physical or imagined.

37 Kevin Dettmar and Jennifer Wicke (eds), *The Longman Anthology of British Literature*, 2nd ed., vol. 2c (New York: Longman, 2003) 2,167.

38 Futurism was a literary movement that began in Italy at the beginning of the twentieth century. Futurism's primary proponent, the Italian artist F.T. Marinetti (1876–1944), founded the magazine *Poesia* in 1905. He wrote the first and second futurist manifestos, which he published in the Paris paper *Le Figaro* in 1909. The manifestos advocated a complete break with tradition and called for adoption of new forms, new subjects, and new styles appropriate to the advent of a mechanical age. After World War I, the movement came to have political associations with Italian Fascism and an indirect effect on Dadaism, expressionism, and surrealism.

39 Dettmar and Wicke 2,167.

40 Ezra Pound, 'Vortex,' *Blast* (20 June 1914) 153.

41 Wyndham Lewis, 'Essay on the Objective of Plastic Art in Our Time,' *Wyndham Lewis on Art: Collected Writings 1913–1956*, Walter Michael and C. J. Fox (eds), (London: Thames and Hudson, 1969) 213.

42 The signatories to the Vorticist manifesto were Richard Aldington, poet, critic, and novelist; Malcolm Arbuthnot, photographer; Lawrence Atkinson, artist; Henri Gaudier-Brzeska, sculptor; Jessie Dismoor, artist; Cuthbert Hamilton, artist; Ezra Pound; William Roberts, painter; Helen Sanders, designer; Edward Wadsworth, painter; and Wyndham Lewis. See *Blast* (20 June 1914) 43. According to the *OED*, sacripant refers to 'a boastful pretender to valour.'

43 *Blast* (20 June 1914) 7.

44 Peter Nicholls, *Modernisms: A Literary Guide* (London: Macmillan, 1995) 173.

45 Nicholls 174.

46 Queen Victoria commissioned the ornate Albert Memorial to commemorate Prince Albert. The gilded bronze and granite structure was completed in 1876

after four years of building. The Gothic shrine incorporates a sculpture of Albert and carved representations of the Continents, the industrial arts, the sciences, and angels. The Regent Street Hotel (Piccadilly) was the second hotel commissioned by the Lyon food empire. Upon completion, it was the largest hotel in Europe, with 1,280 rooms.

47 *Blast* (20 June 1914) 7

48 *Blast* (20 June 1914) 7

49 T.S. Eliot, '*Ulysses*, Order and Myth,' *Dial* (November 1923) 483.

50 T.S. Eliot, 'Preludes,' *Blast* (July 1915) 48–9.

51 Mary Ann Gillies, *Henri Bergson and British Modernism* (Montreal and Kingston: McGill-Queen's University Press, 1996) 81.

52 Gillies, 81.

53 See also Catherine Reilly's *Scars Upon My Heart* (London: Virago, 1981) for background on the work of female writers during World War I. Thousands of young women participated in the war effort as nurses and ambulance drivers and were exposed first-hand to the horrors of modern warfare.

54 John Stallworthy and David Daiches (eds), *The Norton Anthology of English Literature*, 7th ed., vol. 2c (New York: Norton, 2000) 2,049.

55 Brooke had died of dysentery and blood poisoning on a troop ship sailing for Gallipoli.

56 Dettmar and Wicke 2,184.

57 A traditional Petrarchan sonnet has an octave (eight lines) rhyming *abbaabba* and a sestet rhyming *cdecde* or *cdcdcd* or any other combination except a rhyming couplet. The octave develops a thought or argument, which the sestet then completes.

58 Rupert Brooke, 'The Soldier,' *The Collected Poems of Rupert Brooke* (New York: Dodd, Mead & Company, 1931) 115.

59 Siegfried Sassoon, 'The Dragon and the Undying,' *Collected Poems 1908–1956* (London: Faber, 1961) 12

60 Sassoon, 'Counter-Attack,' *Collected Poems* 68.

61 Pat Barker's 1991 novel *Regeneration*, later adapted into a film of the same title (1997), is a fictional account of the goings-on at Craiglockhart War Hospital during World War I. The third novel of her trilogy, *Ghost Road*, which won the 1995 Booker Prize, focuses on Sarah (a young woman working in a munitions factory) and the poet Wilfred Owen. Sassoon's 'Declaration Against the War' read as follows: 'I am making this statement as an act of wilful defiance of military authority, because I believe that the war is being deliberately prolonged by those who have the power to end it. I am a soldier, convinced that I am acting on behalf of soldiers. I believe that this War, on which I entered as a war of defence and liberation, has now become a war of aggression and conquest. I believe that the purpose for which I and my fellow soldiers entered upon this war should have been clearly stated as to have made it impossible to change them, and that, had this been done, the objects which actuated us would now be attainable by negotiation. I have seen and endured the sufferings of the troops, and I can no longer be a party to prolong these sufferings for ends which I believe to be evil and unjust. I am not protesting against the conduct of war, but against the political errors and insincerities for which the fighting men are being sacrificed. On behalf of those who are suffering now I make this protest against the deception which is being practised on them; also I believe that I may help to destroy the callous deception with which the majority of those at home regard

the contrivance of agonies which they do not, and which they have not sufficient imagination, to realize.' Sassoon, *Memoirs of an Infantry Officer* (London: Faber, 1930) 308.

62 Sassoon, 'The Dug-Out,' *Collected Poems* 102.

63 In literary studies, figurative language refers to different figures of speech—such as metaphors, similes, images, and symbols—that deviate from literal language to achieve a particular effect. Nonfigurative language, in turn, refers to the use of standard or literal language in writing or speech.

64 Arthur Lane, *An Adequate Response: The War Poetry of Wilfred Owen and Siegfried Sassoon* (Detroit: Wayne State University Press, 1972) 98.

65 Sassoon, 'They,' *Collected Poems* 23.

66 See Robert Graves' *Good-bye to All That* (1929) for further commentary on the Anglican chaplains' failure to attend to their men's spiritual welfare, and their conspicuous absence from the fighting areas. This, however, did not tend to apply to the Roman Catholic chaplains.

67 Sassoon, 'Glory of Women,' *Collected Poems* 79. By no means should it be imagined that no women responded with empathy and horror to the war; these poems represent generalized impressionisms. Female writers like Vera Brittain, whose brother, her fiancé, and several friends were killed in the war, also tackled the subject of the 'trivialization' of war in their work: 'Four years, some say consolingly. Oh well,/What's that? You're young. And then it must have been/A very fine experience for you' ('The Lament of the Demobilized').

68 Lane 150.

69 Sassoon, 'Survivors,' *Collected Poems* 90. 'Stammering, disconnected talk' was a symptom of shellshock.

70 Sassoon, 'Survivors,' 90.

71 As quoted in Dettmar and Wicke 2, 188.

72 The term 'armistice' refers to the cessation of hostilities between warring countries as a prelude to peace. With reference to World War I, the Armistice refers to the agreement between Germany and the Allies signed on 11 November 1918. German troops and resources were exhausted; it was no longer practical to continue prosecuting the war. The terms of the surrender were punitive and demanded the surrender and destruction of German arms.

73 Wilfred Owen, 'Preface,' *The War Poems of Wilfred Owen*, Jon Silkin (ed.) (London: Sinclair-Stevenson, 1994) xxxix.

74 Pararhyme is the rhyming of two words with identical or similar consonants but different stressed vowels, such as *hall* and *hell,* of which the second is usually lower in pitch. It was common in Icelandic, Irish, and Welsh verse. There are early signs of it in English in the poetry of Henry Vaughn; however, English poets did not use it regularly until Gerard Manley Hopkins and W.B. Yeats began their experiments with it. Wilfred Owen, T.S. Eliot, and W.H. Auden are among other well-known twentieth-century poets who regularly used pararhyme. The technique often produces a feeling of dissonance, failure, and unfulfilment, which in the case of Owen's war poetry reinforces the works' basic themes.

75 Wilfred Owen, 'Anthem for Doomed Youth,' *The Poems of Wilfred Owen* (London: Hogarth Press, 1985) 76. Owen's use of alliteration in line three— 'rifles' rapid rattle,' which mimics the unchanging, unceasing sounds of a rifle—emphasizes the distance between the sounds of the battlefield and those of a church service, with its 'bells,' 'prayers,' and 'choirs.'

76 Owen, 'Anthem for Doomed Youth' 76.

77 Lane 131.

78 Owen, '*Dulce Et Decorum Est,*' *The Poems of Wilfred Owen* 117.

79 Owen, '*Dulce Et Decorum Est,*' 117. Heroic quatrains are four-line iambic pentameter stanzas rhyming *abab*.

80 There are four existing drafts of this poem; one draft has the dedication 'To Jessie Pope etc.' and two others read 'To a certain Poetess.' Jesse Pope published patriotic war verse throughout World War I: *Jesse Pope's War Poems* (1915), *More War Poems* (1915), and *Simple Rhymes for Stirring Times* (1916).

81 Owen, 'Preface' xl.

82 'Ardent' here means 'hot with desire for,' but it also stands for 'burned,' 'charred.' The Latin translates as: 'it is sweet and fitting (proper) to die for one's country.'

83 Owen, 'Disabled,' *The Poems of Wilfred Owen* 152.

84 Owen, 'Disabled' 152, 153.

85 Owen, 'Disabled' 153. The refrain 'Why don't they come?' echoes a 1914 recruiting poster that read, 'Will they never come?' It is also worth noting that many posters likened sport to the army and that recruiting drives frequently took place at football matches.

86 T.E. Hulme was killed by a direct hit from a large shell on 28 September 1917. He is buried in the Military Cemetery at Koksijde, West-Vlaanderen in Belgium, where he is described as 'One of the war poets' (Ferguson 270).

CHAPTER 3

THE NOVEL AND MODERN FASHIONS

A Modernist Chronology—The 1920s

Arts & Literature	*Historical Events*
1920 D.H. Lawrence, *Women in Love*	Votes for American women
Katherine Mansfield, *Bliss and Other Stories*	Communist Party of Great Britain (CPGB) founded
Henri Matisse, *L'Odalisque*	Eleven British officers shot by IRA in
George Bernard Shaw, *Heartbeat House*	Dublin
Edith Wharton, *The Age of Innocence*	Royal Irish Constabulary open fire at football fans killing twelve people
	Government of Ireland Act—
	Parliaments for Belfast and Dublin
	First meeting of the League of Nations
	Oxford admits women for degrees
1921 Charlie Chaplin, *The Kid*	New Economic Policy in the USSR
Edvard Munch, *The Kiss*	Formation of the Irish Free State and
John Dos Passos, *Three Soldiers*	Northern Ireland
Luigi Pirandello, *Six Characters in Search of an Author*	
1922 Bertolt Brecht, *Drums in the Night*	Founding of the British Broadcasting
T.S. Eliot, *The Waste Land*	Corporation (BBC)
James Joyce, *Ulysses*	Benito Mussolini becomes dictator of
Fritz Lang, *Dr Mabuse*	Italy
Sinclair Lewis, *Babbit*	
Virginia Woolf, *Jacob's Room*	
1923 Aldous Huxley, *Antic Hay*	IRA Irregulars suspend hostilities
Dorothy L. Sayers, *Whose Body?*	Wembley Stadium officially opened
W.B. Yeats awarded the Nobel Prize for Literature	First American radio broadcast heard in England
1924 H.D., *Heliodora*	Election of Britain's first Labour
E.M. Forster, *A Passage to India*	government under the leadership of
Thomas Mann, *The Magic Mountain*	Ramsay MacDonald
Cecil B. de Mille, *The Ten Commandments*	Lenin dies; succeeded by Josef Stalin
Sean O'Casey, *Juno and the Paycock*	
1925 Charlie Chaplin, *Gold Rush*	National Party of Wales founded
Theodore Dreiser, *An American Tragedy*	British Empire Exhibition in London
F. Scott Fitzgerald, *The Great Gatsby*	
Adolf Hitler, *Mein Kampf*	
Franz Kakfa, *The Trial*	
George Bernard Shaw awarded the Nobel Prize for Literature	
Gertrude Stein, *The Making of Americans*	
Virginia Woolf, *Mrs Dalloway*	
1926 H.D., *Palimpsest*	Samuel Report calls for the
William Faulkner, *Soldier's Pay*	reorganization of the coal industry in
Ernest Hemingway, *The Sun Also Rises*	Britain
T.E. Lawrence, *The Seven Pillars of Wisdom*	General Strike in support of the miners throughout Britain
Henry Moore, *Draped Reclining Figure*	Television demonstrated by John Logie Baird

1927	Jacob Epstein, *Madonna and Child*	Trades Disputes Act in Britain restricting the ability of workers to strike
	Sigmund Freud, *The Future of an Illusion*	
	Martin Heidegger, *Being and Time*	German Economy collapses on 'Black Friday'
	Virginia Woolf, *To the Lighthouse*	
		Charles Lindbergh makes first solo cross-Atlantic flight
1928	Sergei Eisenstein, *Oktober*	National Party of Scotland founded
	Aldous Huxley, *Point Counter Point*	Alexander Fleming discovers penicillin
	D.H. Lawrence, *Lady Chatterley's Lover*	Right to vote extended to British women over the age of twenty-one
	W.B. Yeats, *The Tower*	
	Virginia Woolf, *Orlando*	
1929	Robert Graves, *Goodbye to All That*	Second Labour minority government under the leadership of Ramsay MacDonald
	Alfred Hitchcock, *Blackmail*	
	Virginia Woolf, *A Room of One's Own*	
	Opening of the Museum of Modern Art (MOMA) in New York	Collapse of Wall Street markets in New York heralds the Great Depression

The Great War ended in 1918, but battle weary Britain faced a number of significant economic, social, and political challenges as the 1920s began. The economies of Europe were devastated by the war, and re-covery was slow to come. The sales of manufactured goods declined as former British colonies and other nations, such as the United States, were producing their own goods and no longer relied on British im-ports to the same extent. Returning veterans found it difficult to find employment, since the major industries that had fed the war effort—steel, shipbuilding, munitions, and aeroplane production, in particu-lar—no longer had ready markets. To make matters worse, it would take additional capital to help the industries retool to deliver goods to postwar markets and there was a shortage of investment money. Com-petition from industries in other countries further complicated the situation. Other industries that had geared up production for the war effort—coal, cotton, and other textiles, for instance—now found themselves with a surplus that could not be sold; as a result, workers in those sectors were laid off. The resulting high rates of unemploy-ment compounded the sense of alienation and unrest felt by many in the working classes. The General Strike of 1926, which started in the coal fields and spread to other heavy industries, saw more than two million workers strike in order to protect current pay rates and in pro-test over working conditions and high unemployment. Although the rhetoric and tactics on both sides were to leave relations in the coal industry strained for decades to come, the strike was essentially peace-ful. Nevertheless, miners came out of the strike worse off, and a fur-ther crisis loomed large at the close of the decade and the beginning of the Great Depression. Women also felt betrayed by the new peace, since their places in the workforce were jeopardized by the waves of returning veterans who believed that women should give up their jobs in factories and other industries to the men who had fought for British freedom. In addition, the battle for universal suffrage for women was not yet complete, as the Electoral Reform Bill of 1918 had only ex-tended the vote to women over thirty. It was not until 1928 that uni-versal suffrage was extended to women.

Despite having emerged from the Great War victorious, British prestige overseas was entering into a period of decline. The Irish situation became critical and skirmishes between British Army forces and Irish paramilitary groups intensified at the end of the war. As we will see later in the chapter, the Irish question was to loom large throughout the 1920s. The various colonies that had come to Britain's assistance during the war were also expressing desire for greater autonomy. Imperial conferences in 1926 and 1931, which involved Britain and its predominantly white colonies of Australia, New Zealand, South Africa, Ireland, Canada, and Newfoundland, resulted in the 1931 Statute of Westminster which acknowledged that these colonies were to be autonomous communities in the British Empire—thus giving them equal status with Great Britain. Such privileges were only granted later to other British colonies, and in the case of Britain's most populous colony India, independence came only after significant violence and bloodshed, as will be discussed later in the chapter. As the 1920s drew to a close, Britain was thus much diminished, economically, socially, and politically.

Yet for some in Britain, especially for the privileged classes, the 1920s were a vibrant age in which fashion, music, art, and literature flourished. The 1920s were the era of the flapper, jazz, cocktails, country parties, and motoring trips. It was also the age in which modernism established itself as the primary cultural movement. Short fiction and poetry continued to be important modernist literary genres. Katherine Mansfield published two significant collections of short stories before her death in 1923. The posthumous publication of a number of other stories and her journals and letters later in the decade solidified her presence at the forefront of experimental fiction. Poetry, too, continued to flourish in the 1920s, with both Yeats and Hardy publishing verse collections. Yeats' *The Tower* (1928) contains some of his finest late lyrical poems, including 'Sailing to Byzantium.' The poem most closely associated with the '20s is perhaps T. S. Eliot's *The Waste Land* (1922), which in many ways was regarded as the anthem of the postwar generation. Eliot himself came to assume a central importance in literary culture, since his literary criticism, his editing of the *Criterion*, and his poetry all helped to shape the reception of literary modernism.

However, it was the novel that dominated the literary landscape of the 1920s as the writers who had spent much of the previous decade or two experimenting with prose reached the peak of their powers. *Women in Love* (1920), *Ulysses* (1922), *Mrs Dalloway* (1925), and *Point Counter Point* (1928) are but a few of the many books that are read and studied in the twenty-first century. These novels have come to epitomize a body of literature that expresses sympathy with a broad range of characters and that adopts an increasingly multi-perspectival narrative structure. The early twentieth-century writers' commitment to subjectivity and interiority had transformed the literary landscape by the 1920s. *A Passage to India* (1924) and *The Last September* (1929), the novels with which this chapter is concerned, offer readers intense psychological portraits of women and men experiencing geographic, national, and spiritual dislocation.

HOW TO READ A MODERN NOVEL

The publication of James Joyce's *Ulysses* (1922) so significantly changed the contours of the modern novel that the relationship between the 'plain' reader and the modern novel became a topic of serious critical interest. Books on the subject flourished. Elizabeth Drew's *The Modern Novel: Some Aspects of Contemporary Fiction* (1926) is an engaging example of a book written for the purpose of introducing the non-specialist reader to the art of the modern novel.[1] Drew's *The Modern Novel* assessed recent work by James Joyce, Arnold Bennett, Aldous Huxley, H.G. Wells, Virginia Woolf, Willa Cather, Joseph Conrad, Samuel Butler, and Dorothy Richardson. As this list suggests, Drew privileged no one school of writing over another. In her estimation, the good novel was that which

> succeeds in communicating vividly the writer's experience, and there can be no rules for what form succeeds in doing that—except the rules of success! . . . Provided that the reader feels he simply must finish the book, the novelist has succeed in his aim and his form has justified itself.[2]

According to Drew, the means by which the novelist achieves success is less important than the achievement itself. The best in literature sustains a reader's attention: it awakens the reader's senses to the experience we call life.

Drew identifies three basic characteristics of the modern novel: its emphasis on interiority, its use of a highly speculative tone, and its active appeal to the reader. With reference to interiority, she argues that '[t]he history of the serious novel during the last fifty years is the history of more and more subtle means of presenting the intricacies of human relationships, of accenting the elements of the unseen and unexpressed in the affairs of life.'[3] The modern novelist is not simply concerned with the world of action but also with the story taking place 'inside the human being himself': 'the [characters] become the impulses and movements of the mind and imagination, and we have scene after scene illustrating the dynamics of the spirit.'[4] Drew names Woolf as the best example of this school of writing, not in the least because her writing has 'no obscure and enigmatical goal which the average reader cannot understand.'[5] Woolf's goals are enumerated in her essay 'Mr Bennett and Mrs Brown,' which Drew recommends unhesitatingly to her readers.

In no uncertain terms, this well-known and oft-cited essay declares that, 'Edwardian tools are the wrong ones . . . to use.'[6] According to Woolf, the Edwardians—Arnold Bennett, H.G. Wells, and John Galsworthy—placed 'enormous stress upon the fabric of things. They have given us a house in the hope that we may be able to deduce the human beings who live there.'[7] She argues that this convention has become an obstacle, an impediment, to capturing 'Mrs Brown' in a 'way which makes her more living and more real' and captures the nuances of her internal experiences.[8] In contrast, she praises the efforts of the Georgians—D.H. Lawrence, E.M. Forster, Lytton Strachey, T.S. Eliot, and James Joyce—who are actively striving to destroy 'the very foundations and rules of literary society' in an attempt to rejuvenate fiction and poetry alike.[9] Happily, '[s]igns of this are everywhere. Grammar is violated; syntax disintegrated' in an effort to offer fresh perspective and insight into the lives and thoughts of ordinary men and women.[10]

After reviewing the essay itself, Drew turns to Woolf's own fiction as an example of original, supple, and dramatic writing that seeks to capture inner lives of ordinary people. In particular, *Jacob's Room* (1922) is singled out for this purpose. According to Drew, Woolf builds Jacob up 'wholly out of suggestion and implication and fleeting glimpses mirrored in the eyes and remembrance of all who came in contact with him.'[11] He does not live simply because the narrator has described him and given him an address: '[h]e lives because he is present in the consciousness of the people who see him in the street, or sit near him in the British Museum, or on the top of a bus . . . . On just such a fine-spun thread of connection and significance is his reality sustained.'[12] While Drew has some reservations about this technique when it utterly disregards the material aspects of life—because 'Life is not only inner life'—she nevertheless emphasizes that:

> This new technique of presenting characters from oblique angles with nothing but the play of glancing lights and shadows upon its half tones, does convey, however, a particular flavour of life on the emotional palate, which is most significant of the present day. . . . The aim of such writers is, presumably, to give an impression of the ceaseless activity of life, while at the same time suggesting the sense of its inconclusive character—its inexorable habit of merely adding day to day instead of building itself into the convenient symmetry of a plot.[13]

This inconclusiveness of character relates to the second characteristic of the modern novel that is of considerable interest to Drew.

Drew defines the work of the modern novelist as speculative and agnostic. The modern novelist refuses to 'make any absolute statements' because, for her, life is 'infinitely formidable and perverse, an implacable and impenetrable force without any apparent symmetry or design.' According to Drew, this is the terrain that Forster explores in *A Passage to India*—'the most interesting novel of 1924.'[14] *A Passage to India* and novels like it reject 'the confident and somewhat glib assurances of the old standard truth.'[15] Nevertheless, Drew carefully stresses the modern novelist is not a 'disillusioned pessimist' who believes in 'evil triumphant,' but rather an individual who 'as far as the universe is concerned . . . feels that, with every discovery in knowledge, we find that we know less and less about it':

> [t]his uncertainty which meets his mind on every side has revolutionized his moral outlook. His moral values have shifted: the outlines of the vices and the virtues have lost their firmness: he no longer pretends to find existence emotionally intelligible.

> Life refuses to make any absolute statements; it remains infi-
> nitely formidable and perverse, an implacable and impenetrable
> force without any apparent symmetry or design.[16]

Not only is uncertainty everywhere, but so too—and this is Drew's
third point—is a fundamental reconfiguration of the relationship between writers and readers. She emphasizes that an '[a]ppreciation' of
the new fiction 'depends on [a] partnership, on the establishment of
understanding between writer and reader.'[17] Drew deftly argues that
readers must be willing to adapt to the objectives of the day's serious
novelists and accept that modern novelists are characterized by 'an
almost brutal candour in unmasking individual counterfeit human beings, so do they expose mercilessly the shallow thinking and feeling
behind the conventional attitudes towards collective human problems.'[18] Woolf makes similar claims in 'Mr Bennett and Mrs Brown'
in which she ventures to 'remind [readers] of [their] duties and responsibilities':

> Your part is to insist that writers shall come down off their
> plinths and pedestals, and describe beautifully if possible, truth-
> fully at any rate, our Mrs Brown. You should insist that she is
> an old lady of unlimited capacity and infinite variety; capable of
> appearing in any place; wearing any dress; saying anything and
> doing heaven knows what.[19]

Woolf warns readers that their insistence may not initially be re-
warded as writers strive to develop new tools best suited to their purposes, but asks that they '[t]olerate the spasmodic, the obscure, the
fragmentary, the failure. Your help is invoked in a good cause.'[20] This
good cause, as far as Woolf is concerned, will result in 'one of the
great ages of English literature'—an age persuasively celebrated in
Drew's book.[21]

As *The Modern Novel* affirms, Woolf's injunction in 'Modern
Fiction' to capture the 'incessant shower of innumerable atoms . . . as
they fall, [and] as they shape themselves into the life of Monday or
Tuesday' had become a commonplace in English literary culture.[22]
Writers were rapidly refining the means by which to record and explore the 'myriad impressions' that an ordinary mind receives in the
course of an ordinary day, whether 'trivial, fantastic, evanescent, or
engraved with the sharpness of steel.'[23] To do so required writers to
'record the atoms as they fall upon the mind in the order in which they
fall, [and] trace the pattern, however disconnected and incoherent in
appearance, which each sight or incident scores upon the consciousness.'[24] In electing to trace 'the atoms' as they fell, the modern novelist demonstrated that writers (and readers) must 'not take it for granted
that life exists more fully in what is commonly thought big than in
what is commonly thought small.'[25]

Ulysses, which Woolf praises in 'Modern Fiction,' deftly combines the 'big' and 'small' with its mythic template recalling Homer's *Odyssey* and the detailed scrutiny of contemporary Dublin, as Leopold Bloom navigates altogether modern and domestic dangers over the course of a single day. The effect is two-fold: first, Everyman—as opposed to a Greek hero—is the subject of the novel and, second, by way of the double story, in spite of all its revolutionary pyrotechnics, Joyce exposes a continuous parallel between contemporaneity and antiquity, between the past and the present. In turn, with the publication of *Ulysses* two further primary characteristics of modernist novels as conceived by Woolf are affirmed. First, it showcases a profound interest in the inner workings of the ordinary mind. Second, it betrays an intense interest in the individual's response to the contemporary moment as filtered through the weight of history, whether that history be personal, sexual, religious, or national.

The intense scrutiny of the individual subject that we associate with modernism had implications not only for the representation of British metropolitan subjects, but also for the examination of people and experiences beyond England's borders. Writers who are now included in the modernist canon frequently came from anywhere but from within the confines of the educated English middle-class. Somerville and Ross, W.B. Yeats, and James Joyce were Irish. D.H. Lawrence was a provincial working-class writer. Katherine Mansfield was from New Zealand. Ezra Pound, H.D., and T.S. Eliot were American. E.M. Forster was a closeted homosexual. Elizabeth Bowen was Anglo-Irish. Given this diversity, it is unsurprising to discover that among the more powerful works of literature written in the 1920s, a number of them do not take place in middle-class England.

Modernism and the work of these writers in particular inclines towards doubt of things presented steadily and whole in favour of things as they are unsteadily and partially represented. The range of values under scrutiny and viewed with scepticism in the opening decades of the twentieth century is as varied as the citizenship of the aforementioned writers. As writers at the beginning of the twentieth century witnessed increased fragmentation, they became increasingly suspicious about narratives of progress, social unity, and national or racial superiority. In this climate, it was difficult for British writers to ignore that the age of empire was coming to an end.

THE GEOGRAPHY OF THE MODERN NOVEL

The Boer War had marked both the high point of British imperialism and the beginnings of a reaction against the Empire abroad and at home. The British fought, and lost, the bloody and costly war in South Africa between 1899 and 1902 in order to establish political and economic control over the independent Boer republic. This was the first colonial conflict to elicit widespread protest in England and generate debate about Britain's role and responsibilities in relation to her overseas possessions—in particular, with reference to the colonies clamouring for independence, such as India and Ireland. Debate on this subject intensified during and after World War I given that the war was in part reputedly being fought to affirm the rights of small independent nations. Imperialists and anti-imperialists would continue to be in direct conflict with one another in parliament, in the press, and in literature long after the end of World War I.

The literary concerns of this chapter lie in India and Ireland by way of Forster's and Bowen's respective explorations of relationships, both personal and political, in what were, or were soon to be, former colonies of Britain. Gender, politics, and the complexities of uncertain allegiances loom large in *A Passage to India* and *The Last September*. Before embarking on an examination of each novel, however, it is necessary to take a detour into a discussion of the political climates in India and Ireland in advance of the 1920s. These discussions will allow us to see more clearly the complex political situations that inform both novels.

We will begin in India. The British had long been in India before Forster's first visit to the subcontinent in 1912. English trading centres in Madras, Bombay, and Calcutta had been established during the reign of Elizabeth I.[26] For more than two hundred years, the British East India Company had controlled trade in the region. No significant changes were made to the administration of India until the Mutiny of 1857–8.[27] The immediate cause of the mutiny was the cartridge for the new Enfield rifle, which had to be bitten before it was loaded. Rumours circulated that the cartridge was greased with cow fat and pig lard. As the cow is sacred to Hindus and the pig is considered unclean by Muslims, both religious groups were offended. After soldiers at Meerut mutinied and killed their officers in May 1857, it took British troops over a year to quell the rebellion. There were other, more political reasons for the Mutiny, including an intensifying resentment on the part of Indians, Hindu, and Muslim alike, over the Westernization of India and the fear that native customs, religions, and social structures were being irrevocably eroded by the ongoing control of India by a foreign power. After the Mutiny was put down, the 1858 India Act abolished the East India Company and transferred the company's powers to the Crown, which was represented in India by the Viceroy. This change, however, did little to alleviate the original concerns, and an organized independence movement soon took hold in India.

Within fifteen years of the Mutiny, the British approved the foundation of the Indian National Congress. Members of the Congress came from all over the country and represented the many religious groups and castes found in India. However, the Congress quickly lost favour with the British when it began to advocate self-government. The efforts of the Congress—and later the Muslim League—aside, in the eyes of many, meaningful change in the governance of India was slow to come and violence against the British began to escalate in the early 1900s.[28] For example, in response to the division of the Bengal state, there were a number of bombings and shootings. In an attempt to improve the situation, the British government passed the Morley-Minto Reforms in 1909, which expanded the provincial legislative councils to include elected Indian officials and enlarged the Viceroy's advisory council to include an Indian. Improved relations and the seeming acceptance of the inevitability of reform on the part of the British government secured India's support in World War I—in return for which support the British promised India a major role in its own government. After the war, the Montagu-Chelmsford Reforms increased both the powers of the provincial legislatures and the number of Indians elected to the central legislature; that said, however, the Viceroy and his governors retained veto power.

These changes aside, Indians continued to believe that the reforms did not provide them with sufficient control of their own country and the protests continued. The postwar years proved difficult for India both politically and economically. After the war, British officials who had fought in the war returned to their posts in the Indian Civil Service and ousted their Indian subordinates who had served in their stead, acting as though nothing had changed in India during their absence. In turn, Indian soldiers returned from the trenches only to find that they were no longer invaluable allies but had instead reverted to the status of 'natives.' Tension and further conflict were inevitable. A new level of disaffection with British rule was reached with the passage of the Rowlatt Acts early in 1919. The 'black acts,' as they came to be called, were peacetime extensions of the wartime emergency measures which limited Indians' civil liberties, including the right to trial by jury.

The Rowlatt Acts were pushed through the Supreme Legislative Council in spite of the unanimous opposition of its Indian members. Indian leaders viewed the autocratic enactment of such legislation, following the conclusion of a war in which India had loyally supported Britain, as an unwelcome example of treachery and an abandonment of promised reform in favour of repression. Mahatma Gandhi, who had returned to India from South Africa during the war and was recognized throughout India as one of its most promising leaders, called upon Indians to disobey the Rowlatt Acts. His calls launched a nationwide movement demanding a repeal of the repressive measures. Gandhi's appeal was strongly supported in the Punjab where nationalist leaders addressed mass protest rallies from the provincial capital of Lahore to Amritsar, the sacred capital of the Sikhs.[29] Gandhi attempted to attend these rallies but he was arrested at a border station and taken back to Bombay under the orders of Sir Michael O'Dwyer, the lieutenant governor of the Punjab.

On 10 April 1919, the nationalist leaders, Dr Kichloo and Dr Satyapal, were arrested and deported by the Punjab's deputy commissioner Miles Irving. When their followers attempted to march to Irving's bungalow to demand the release of their leaders, they were fired upon by British troops. The enraged protesters rioted in the old city of Amritsar, burning British banks, killing several Englishmen, and attacking two Englishwomen. In response, General Dyer was summoned from Jullundur with troops to restore order. Although there were no further disturbances, on the afternoon of 13 April 1919, Dyer marched fifty armed soldiers into the Jullianwallah Bagh (Gardens) and ordered them to open fire without warning on a meeting attended by some 10,000 unarmed men, women, and children. Dyer's troops fired 1,650 rounds of ammunition into a crowd that had no way of escaping the Bagh since the soldiers were positioned at the only exit. Four hundred civilians were killed and approximately 1,200 people were wounded. When Dyer withdrew, the dying and the wounded were left without medical attention. Lieutenant Governor O'Dwyer fully approved of the Jullianwallah Bagh massacre, and two days later issued a martial law decree for the entire Punjab. The Jullianwallah Bagh Massacre in Amritsar transformed millions of patient and moderate Indians from loyal supporters of the British Raj into men and women who would never again trust, let alone cooperate with, a government capable of defending such actions. The following year Mahatma Gandhi launched his first Indian *satyagraha*—'clinging to the truth'—campaign. After the Amritsar Massacre, Indian history became an almost constant struggle for self-rule.

E.M. Forster arrived in India two years later. The politics of mobs and the use of language to control a colonized people factor powerfully into Forster's final novel. A novel about race, colonialism, and gender, *A Passage to India* draws heavily upon the incidents and political climate of the day.[30] In part, it tells the story of a man who hardens on account of persecution and can no longer take his rulers as a joke:

> [Aziz] was without natural affection for the land of his birth,
> but the Marabar Hills drove him to it. Half closing his eyes, he
> attempted to love India. She must imitate Japan. Not until she is
> a nation will her sons be treated with respect. He grew harder
> and less approachable.[31]

He withdraws from British India and retreats to an independent Indian state a few hundred miles west of the Marabar Hills. Through the lens of the individual—individuals like Aziz—Forster explores race relations, history, and politics in a vast country, which the web of colonialism and greed, masked by the pretence of duty, tried so long to contain and control.

IMITATING GOD—LANGUAGE AND SYMBOLISM IN *A PASSAGE TO INDIA*

Forster first began working on *A Passage to India* in 1912, but he did not complete the novel until 1924. The book was published in June 1924 to favourable reviews and brisk sales: 'in the United States alone, 30,000 copies were bought before the end of July, and by the end of the year, most of the first printing of 17,000 British copies and 54,000 American copies had been sold.'[32] For the most part, English and Indian reviewers approved of the novel; in contrast, however, Anglo-Indians expressed a distinct dislike for the book. As St Nihal Singh observed in the Calcutta-based *Modern Review*, Anglo-Indians were not 'used to being talked about in this manner' and so likely hated 'Mr Forster for giving them away.'[33] It is difficult to disregard the importance of talk in *A Passage to India* as indeed, arguably, very little actually takes place beyond a subtle analysis of the power of words—the power of accusations—to unsettle the never easy relations between Indian and Englishman, between woman and man. Making sense of the misunderstandings, or muddles, that litter the landscape of this novel is a difficult proposition; that said, a discussion of language in relation to questions of dominance and control is better considered after an examination of the kind of novel that Forster was writing when he published *A Passage to India*.

Forster is not nearly so experimental a novelist as Joyce or Woolf; nevertheless, he is considered a representative Georgian by none other than Woolf in 'Mr Bennett and Mrs Brown.' Why? Because *A Passage to India* fuses realist and symbolist elements. Forster does not exclusively anchor his story in clock-time. He counterbalances the clock—the traditional reliance on story, time, and place—with other aspects of the novel: in particular, plot, pattern, rhythm, and time as discussed in his book *Aspects of the Novel* (1927). Plot organizes the materials of the story not sequentially but causally when unanticipated connections are exposed as the story unfolds. Pattern gives a sense of timeless completion and wholeness. Rhythm conveys an underlying pulse and movement. Time suggests musical patterns as opposed to adherence to the conventional dictates of chronology.[34] This is to suggest that Forster's own commentary on the novel hints at how his work might be seen to outstrip the deployment of character and incident typical of realist narratives. The emphasis on plot, pattern, rhythm, and time as defined by Forster draws attention to the non-realist elements of *A Passage to India* and to the novel's reliance on repetition and patterning to create a sense of completion and aesthetic integrity.

The novel, which is divided into three sections, is laden with recurrences, analogies, and repeated figures. Repetition is an important 'aesthetic device whereby this novel is stitched internally and woven into an aesthetic unity.'[35] The wasp is one such figure. Its association with three different characters modifies both the symbol and our sense of the characters' spiritual outlook as expressed through his or her attitude towards the winged insect. As the analysis that follows will suggest, the primary difference between the viewpoints can be caricatured as inclusive, as opposed to exclusive. The ecumenical cast of Mrs Moore's spirituality is evident immediately. She is first introduced in the mosque near the Club, from which the first section of the book takes its name, where she conducts herself with grace and sincerity for no reason other than her sense that 'God is here.'[36] That this is not god as worshipped or expressed in the churches of her own country 'makes no difference' to her, as what is importance is the presence of God. Mrs Moore's willingness to affirm differences in fundamentally similar thoughts or objects is emphasized at the end of Chapter 3. For example, when Mrs Moore and her son discuss Aziz, she is all too aware that Ronny's description is a false summary of the man and that 'the essential life of him had been slain.'[37] Mrs Moore rejects such reductions throughout the novel. After her encounter with Aziz and then her son, her resistance is further reinforced when dressing for bed she finds a wasp on a peg. She murmurs 'Pretty dear' while observing that '[s]he had known this wasp or his relatives by day' and 'they were not as English wasps.'[38] Little interested in judgment, she strives to accept and acknowledge.[39]

The second wasp is associated with Mr Sorley, the young missionary who lives 'out beyond the slaughterhouses.' He fears that 'perhaps it is futile for men to initiate their own unity' as they may 'but widen the gulfs between them by the attempt.'[40] He is of the view that in 'our Father's house are many mansions . . . and there alone will the incompatible multitudes of mankind be welcomed and soothed.'[41] There are, however, limits in Sorley's mind as to the extent to which all are included in God's mercy: 'he admitted that the mercy of God, being infinite may well embrace all mammals. And the wasps? He became uneasy during the descent to wasps, and was apt to change the conversation . . . We must exclude someone from our gathering, or we shall be left with nothing.'[42] He cannot conceive of a world view in which everything exists and nothing has value, or one in which everything has value. He cannot conceive of a philosophy in which there is no need for a hierarchy of values in order for there to be value. What value has heaven if all are present? What value has the club if Indians are admitted? His hesitation to envelop the wasp in the mercy of God draws attention to the rather more serious consequences of the hesitations to accept and embrace evidenced by the action of men and women, Englishmen and Indians, throughout the novel.

The final appearance of the wasp is not linked with hesitations as to whether God would have us include or exclude the wasp from mercy. The third appearance of the wasp coincides with the celebration of the birth of God—the birth of Shri Krishna. Professor Godbole's choir is playing a new rhythm in celebration, and it evokes seemingly unrelated images:

> Godbole, though she was not important to him, remembered an old woman he had met in Chandrapore days . . . he did not select her, she happened to occur among the throngs of soliciting images, a tiny splinter, and he impelled her by his spiritual force to that place where completeness can be found. Completeness, not reconstruction. His senses grew thinner, he remembered a wasp seen he forgot where, perhaps on a stone. He loved the wasp equally, he impelled it likewise, he was imitating God.[43]

In celebrating God, Godbole welcomes the divinity of the universe—a universe that includes a wasp, Mrs Moore, and himself. He does not resist but rather, as did Mrs Moore, he accepts and strives to imitate God. Why do so? Because all share in God's bounty, and 'owing to the nature of the gift . . . blessed is the man who confers it on another, he imitates God.'[44] For Godbole, it matters little that he is Brahmin and Mrs Moore is Christian; it makes no difference because it is his duty,

> as it was his desire, to place himself in position of the God and to love her, and to place himself in her position and to say to the God, 'Come, come, come, come.' This was all he could do. How inadequate! But each according to his own capacities, and he knew that his own were small. 'One old Englishwoman and one little, little wasp,' he thought, as he stepped out of the temple into the grey of a pouring wet morning. 'It does not seem much, still it is more than I am myself.'[45]

Godbole's vision suggests a spiritual philosophy that has little in common with the views of Mr Sorley and his brethren. By the end of the book, the wasp asleep on the peg where Mrs Moore was about to hang her cloak has become implicated in the interpretative strategy privileged by the novel. *A Passage to India* insists upon a complex weaving of associations and congruencies as opposed to the overly simplistic impulse to generate a series of binary oppositions—the impulse to include and exclude.

While parallel structures and repetition generate 'meaning which goes beyond story, people, even setting,' how characters speak and what they say to one another also play important roles in a novel exploring what can and cannot be said when people are locked into power relations determined by race and sex.[46] The novel pivots on an unspoken charge of rape in which an Indian man is accused of having assaulted an English girl. This incident draws attention to the habitual elisions and stereotyping that form a part of daily life in British India. English and Indian men share the same subject position in relation to their women. Men express their subjectivity by objectifying and silencing women. Language in the novel reduces the other to a physicality that denies the irreducibility and multiplicity of the individual subject. People are reduced to 'types.' Through language, the Indian man is subject to the white man's power, and as such he is feminized and emasculated. As the Anglo-Indian community's response to the Marabar Caves incident suggests, Aziz and Adela are both reduced to stock characters appropriate to the unfolding drama. They are not permitted to speak for themselves; instead, legal officials and their respective communities speak on their behalf.

The novel also explores the (im)possibility of bridging gaps. Early in the book, Aziz, Hamidullah Begum, and Mahmoud Ali discuss whether friendship with an Englishman is possible. The men trade stories about 'types' in which the only differences allowed between the English are physical, otherwise they are all 'exactly the same, not worse, not better.'[47] They dismiss exceptions with the cliché 'The exception does not prove the rule.'[48] It is accepted that the differences between the Turtons and the Burtons are no more profound than the recognition that 'Red-nose mumbles, Turton talks distinctly, Mrs Turton takes bribes, Mrs Red-nose does not and cannot, because so far there is no Mrs Red-nose.'[49]

The English are similarly constrained. However, the consequences of their actions are much more sinister; it is less complicated to rule a nation of objectified stereotypes than to govern a nation of individuals with legitimate needs and desires. Everyone is ensnared in the rhetoric of the system in which they find themselves participating. They are unwilling to break free of historically inscribed types. Within this conceptual framework, the English even type themselves. They ascribe to themselves a fixed set of judgements, gestures, and sayings all of which are taken to affirm their social positions and the necessity of their presence in India. Aziz is reduced to 'some native subordinate or other' who let down Major Callendar, while Ronny is elevated to 'the type we want, he's one of us.'[50] The mode on both sides is one of reduction:

> both groups represent their synecdochal reductions as capturing
> 'the truth', including the truth of the other's moral state. For the
> English . . . the mania for reductive categorising goes hand and
> hand with a dramatisation of difference and superiority inherent
> in their position of power: power not only to define the catego-
> ries but to enforce the 'truths' they supposedly convey; for the
> English, knowledge, representation, and power are one.[51]

Cecil Fielding, the principal of the local college, exposes language for what it is: a system of enforced truths that a person can inadvertently or deliberately violate; in turn, the Anglo-Indian community mistrusts him. This mistrust is intensified when he makes an infelicitous observation that 'the so-called white races are really pinko-grey. He only says this to be cheery, he does not realize that "white" has no more to do with a colour than "God save the King" with a god, and that it is the height of impropriety to consider what it does connote.'[52]

In *A Passage to India*, inequality and oppression are more likely to be expressed verbally than physically. This is well illustrated by Ronny's ready adoption of the vocabulary and attitudes of the entrenched Anglo-Indian who has little interest in the possibility of reform. Furthermore, Ronny's profession reinforces his association with the power of language. As the local magistrate, any sentences he metes out to Indians are done so through the formal apparatus of the judicial system and legal code, which is of course a powerful expression of the potential physical force of language. Ronny's willingness to learn the lingo and the jargon suitable to a 'pukka sahib' satisfies the English desire for conformity, but the consequences of his unquestioning adoption of the Anglo-Indian code are not lost upon his mother who remarks:

> 'You never used to judge people like this at home.'
> 'India isn't home,' he retorted, rather rudely, but in order to silence her he had been using phrases and arguments that he had picked up from older officials, and he did not feel quite sure of himself. When he said, 'of course there are exceptions' he was quoting Mr Turton, while 'increasing the izzat' was Major Callendar's own.[53]

He aspires to the 'higher realms of knowledge, inhabited by Callendars and Turtons, who had not been one year in the country but twenty and whose instincts were superhuman.'[54] Ronny, for example, mimics the reductive instincts of his superiors when he takes Aziz's 'missing' collar stud as symptomatic of the 'fundamental slackness' of all Indians.[55]

Aziz is most humiliatingly consigned to the status of 'type' or object after his arrest. Once accused of committing an insult against an English girl, Aziz does not speak again until after the trial. His letters, his photographs, and his race are used against him. British officials strip away his individuality and, in turn, there is no possibility for him to respond to the charges against him. He becomes a victim of the misuse of power:

> In contrast to the white man's position, which is conterminous with the (phallic) power of 'the law', the Indian man is to be symbolically 'raped' by the accusation of rape, a position crucial for maintaining the white man's power and one that carries

as much centrality in the intertwined discourse of sex and race as rape itself.[56]

For this discourse to work effectively, the alleged 'insult' of one Englishwoman becomes an occasion to fear for and protect all Englishwomen, 'simultaneously reducing them to objects of protection and using them as an excuse to reassert white male power over both their women and their potential attackers.'[57] Adela—like Aziz— is stripped of her individuality and reduced to a symbol of affronted English womanhood. The description of the gathering at the Club after Aziz's arrest demonstrates the swiftness with which the particulars of the case are set aside for a generalized view of the incident:

> They had started speaking of 'women and children'—that phrase that exempts the male from sanity when it has been repeated a few times. Each felt that all he loved best in the world was at stake, demanded revenge, and was filled with a not unpleasing glow, in which the chilly and half-known features of Miss Quested vanished, and were replaced by all that is sweetest and warmest in the private life.[58]

Adela can be accommodated in this setting so long as she provides the answers that everyone in the Anglo-Indian community wishes to hear.

Adela, however, has been suspect long before the trip to the Marabar Caves. Her desire to see the real India and Indians is never regarded favourably by the other Anglo-Indian women. Mrs Turton—the Collector's wife—deems her 'ungracious' and 'cranky.'[59] After the incident, 'pukka' or not, in spite of her unpopularity, she nevertheless 'brought out all that was fine in their character'; her position, not her character moved them: 'she was the English girl who had had the terrible experience.'[60] However, once back at Ronny's bungalow, after a single conversation with the wearied Mrs Moore now quite determined to leave India, Adela utters the name that everyone has been avoiding—'Aziz, Aziz': his name had 'become synonymous with the power of evil. He was "the prisoner," "the person in question," "the defence," and the sound of it now rang out like the first note of a new sympathy.'[61] Once Adela speaks his name, it is not difficult to go a step further and 'withdraw everything.'[62] Miss Quested is no longer the insulted English girl in need of protection. She is now the English woman who 'renounced her own people.'[63] In turn, Adela does not marry Ronny. She does not stay in India. Aziz is not judged guilty. He does not go to jail. The outcome expected and desired by the Anglo-Indian community is not fulfilled.

As Gillian Beer observes, negative structures predominate in this novel—'no,' 'not,' 'never,' and 'nothing' permeate the text: '[n]egation and negativity in this novel are related in complex ways to place and space (interiority and exteriority) and to the diverse shapes of inclusion and exclusion' evident throughout the book.[64] The novel opens with a phrase of exclusion, drawing the reader's attention to the Marabar Caves in advance of meeting the characters who will go to the caves: 'Except for the Marabar Caves—and they are twenty miles off—the city of Chandrapore presents nothing extraordinary.'[65] The landscape in which the city is situated dominates the opening pages of the book. People are important only in so much as they live and die while 'the town persists, swelling here, shrinking there, like some low but indestructible form of life.'[66] The city does not determine the appearance of the land: 'The sky settles everything—not only climate and seasons but when the earth shall be beautiful.'[67] The desires of individual men and women do not matter. *A Passage to India* ends as it begins, with humanity silenced by the landscape. In the final scene, Fielding asks Aziz for friendship and communion:

> But the horses didn't want it—they swerved apart; the earth didn't want it, sending up rocks which riders must pass single file; the temples, the tank, the jail, the palace, the birds, the carrion, the Guest House, that came into view as they issued from the gap and Mau beneath: they didn't want it, they said in their hundred voices, 'No, not yet,' and the sky said, 'No, not there.'[68]

In so beginning and ending, the novel emphasizes indeterminacy; it privileges the unsaid and that which cannot be said yet.

The description of the Marabar Caves offered at the tea party emphasizes the novel's reliance upon creating meaning or definitions through exclusion and absence. Instead of reading a description of the caves, the reader learns the caves are *not* large, *not* like the caves at Elephanta, *not* holy, *not* ornamented, and yet *not* an 'empty brag.'[69] Contrary to Aziz's assumption, 'Godbole was not concealing *something*, but *nothing*.'[70] The value of nothing simply has yet to become apparent. Beer reminds us that the word has two natures. The first nature is the one with which we are most familiar: our sense that it expresses stasis, or vacancy. However, when 'nothing' is embedded within a sentence, 'it makes the whole organization of that sentence restless and unstable, expressive of contrary impulses.'[71] The value of hierarchies and exclusionary social tactics is undercut when 'nothing has value.'[72] Mrs Moore murmurs, 'Everything exists, nothing has value' after her experience in the first cave where she emerges panicked and catches herself looking 'for a villain, but none was there.'[73] She sits 'motionless with horror' and begins to lose 'all interest' in the mundane details of everyday life. She realizes that there was nothing evil in the cave, only the villagers who wished to honour her. As she sits beneath the hot Indian sun, Mrs Moore is gradually overcome by a shocked awe at the vastness of the universe expressed by the echo in the cave.

Mrs Moore strives to accept all that exists, even that which is more than the 'feeble mind can grasp'—acceptance as expressed in Godbole's song of the milkmaiden who calls to Shri Kishna:

> 'I say to Shri Kishna, 'Come! come to me only.' The god
> refuses to come. I grow humble and say: 'Do not come to me
> only. Multiply yourself into a hundred Krishnas, and let one go
> to each of my hundred companions, but one, O Lord of the
> Universe, come to me.' He refuses to come. This is repeated
> several times. The song is composed in a raga appropriate to the
> present hour, which is the evening.'
> 'But he comes in some other song, I hope?' said Mrs Moore
> gently.
> 'Oh no, he refuses to come,' repeated Godbole, perhaps not un-
> derstanding her question. 'I say to Him, Come, come, come,
> come, come, come. He neglects to come.'[74]

Here absence—like nothingness—is a condition of God as it is of nothingness—a state that we do well to remember also implies presence. Or as Godbole explains, 'absence implies presence, absence is not non-existence.'[75]

'For this reason desire and absence are interlocked: absolutes capable of expression only in negative form'; these are absolutes through which it is possible to recognize new truths.[76] Adela, for example, climbs towards the second cave thinking about the absent Ronny—thinking about their temperaments and the marriage:

> What about love? . . . She and Ronny—no, they did not love
> each other. . . . The discovery had come so suddenly that she
> felt like a mountaineer whose rope had broken. Not to love the
> man one's going to marry! Not to find it out till this moment!
> Not even to have asked oneself the question until now! Some-
> thing else to think out. Vexed rather than appalled, she stood
> still, her eyes on the sparkling rock.[77]

For Adela, truth comes when she is apart from Ronny and, more importantly, when she is separated from the social structures that would have permitted her to decide to marry a man whom she does not love. Mrs Moore's absence is apparent on two significant occasions: in the second Marabar cave and in the courtroom at Aziz's trial. On the second occasion, however, her absence is more complete than in the first instance on account of her death while en route to England. Nevertheless, as Godbole would say, 'absence is not non-existence.' The invocation and Indianization of Mrs Moore at the trial has a kind of power that her physical presence could not equal: 'In vain the Magistrate threatened and expelled. Until the magic exhausted itself, he was powerless.'[78] After this Adela is able to speak 'more naturally and healthily than usual.'[79] Prior to that Adela was reciting words scripted by Mr McBryde. Now, however, she realizes that she cannot recall the event that must accompany these words if they are to be more than hollow platitudes demanded by the roused Anglo-India community:

> Her vision was of several caves. She saw herself in one, and she
> was also outside it, watching its entrance for Aziz to pass in.
> She failed to locate him. It was the doubt that had often visited
> her, but solid and attractive, like the hills, 'I am not –' Speech
> was more difficult than vision. 'I am not sure. . . . I cannot be
> sure . . .'[80]

It is in 'hard prosaic tones' that she 'withdraw[s] everything': 'though the vision was over, and she had returned to the insipidity of the world, she remembered what she had learnt.'[81] She must renounce her own people.

In the final section of the novel, 'Temple,' the absent continues to be present:

> God is not born yet—that will occur at midnight—but He has
> also been born centuries ago, nor can He ever be born, because
> He is the Lord of the universe, who transcends human proc-
> esses. He is, was not, is not was . . . .
> 'Thou art my father and mother and everybody.'[82]

Children, servants, rulers, professors, priests, and musicians—everyone is present at the festival for the God without attributes. The birth of the transcendent God is celebrated in ceremony, song, and games because this birth is the annihilation of all sorrow 'not only for Indians, but for foreigners, birds, caves, railways, and the stars; all became joy, all laughter; there had never been disease nor doubt, misunderstanding, cruelty, fear.'[83] In turn, '[t]he corridors, the courtyard, were filled with benign confusion. Also the flies awoke and claimed their share of God's bounty.'[84] It is a joy in which all share and of which 'No definite image survived: at the Birth it was questionable whether a silver doll or a mud village, or a silk napkin, or an intangible spirit, or a pious resolution had been born. Perhaps all these things! Perhaps none! Perhaps all birth is an allegory.'[85]

Whichever one or all of these things that the festival might signify, Godbole's 'strange thoughts' and the novel itself challenge 'through the habitual negativity of its language the beleaguered humanism of its characters . . . [Forster] sees what lies beyond the human need not be null or void.'[86] What lies beyond the human is the desire and the duty to place oneself in the position of God and to say to God, 'Come, come, come, come.'[87] Godbole's sentiments regarding the unity of all living beings notwithstanding, *A Passage to India* inherits and interrogates 'the discourses of the Raj' as opposed to offering a solution to the problems of interpreting and negotiating British India.[88] The novel examines the language of conquest and domination. However, agencies of power and knowledge all have their limitations, and the novel incorporates—as far as is possible—the unexpressed: '*A Passage to*

India is . . . a book *about* gaps, fissures, and exclusions.'[89] It questions British rule in India and the possibility of a single objective truth.

THE IRISH QUESTION

As in *A Passage to India*, the geography of Elizabeth Bowen's *The Last September* plays an integral part in the story. The feeling of dislocation surrounding Lois is in keeping with the ambivalent position of the Anglo-Irish after World War I. The story of inequity and Anglo-Irish landowners, however, begins centuries earlier. The Irish Question is a long-standing example of the conflict between imperialist and anti-imperialist forces. Bowen's story has its roots in the early sixteenth century when Henry VIII set out to reassert England's influence in Ireland. His son, Edward VI, and his daughter, Elizabeth I, continued their father's policies, which meant that for over a century land was seized and granted to English and Scottish Protestants, creating the Protestant majority that still exists in Northern Ireland. By 1704 the Protestant Ascendancy held most of the land in Ireland. Catholics were forbidden to purchase, inherit, or rent land. They were unable to participate in the Irish Parliament, banned from the army and restricted in their rights to practise Catholicism. During the eighteenth and nineteenth centuries the legal position of Catholics improved, though their living conditions were much affected by famines, mass emigration, and limited economic growth. One consequence to the impoverished conditions in which many Irish Catholics lived was an intensification of nationalist feelings. Throughout the late 1800s, the demand for home rule intensified. Home rule meant that Ireland would remain a part of Great Britain but it would control her own domestic affairs in an Irish parliament. The Protestants in Ulster—North Ireland—were opposed to home rule because they feared being a minority in an otherwise overwhelmingly Catholic country. The British Parliament defeated the First and Second Home Rule Bills in 1886 and 1892. Undeterred, Irish journalist Arthur Griffith founded Sinn Féin in 1905, determined to press for home rule. Around the same time, the Irish Republican Brotherhood (IRB) became active. The IRB was a secret organization that advocated the formation of an independent Irish republic. Home rule appeared inevitable in 1914 when the British Parliament passed the Third Home Rule Act; unfortunately, the outbreak of World War I prevented the act from taking effect immediately.

The 'Troubles' immediately informing *The Last September* are rooted in the 1916 Easter Rising. The aftermath of the Rising marked a coming together of the republican movement and mainstream Irish nationalism, which had previously accepted the promise of postwar autonomy under British rule enshrined in the Third Home Rule Act. Early in the war, the majority of Irish supported Britain as advised by the leader of the Irish Parliamentary Party, John Redmond, but republicans led by Patrick Pearse—a prominent member of the IRB—thought that the war gave Ireland a chance to gain independence and they enlisted the assistance of Germany.[90] In April 1916, the British intercepted an arms delivery from Germany and arrested the nationalists' emissary Sir Roger Casement. The Irish Volunteers, a force set up in November 1913 in support of the aims of the moderate nationalists, were ordered not to take any action.[91] Nevertheless, an estimated 1,000 insurgent Volunteers rose against some 4,500 British troops and 1,000 police and in protest occupied government buildings in Dublin.

The rebels were defeated quickly by the British use of artillery fire. Hundreds of people, including civilians, were killed and wounded. After the Easter Rising, the British arrested over 3,000 people and the fifteen rebel leaders were executed in early May 1916. Widespread public revulsion at the executions marked the beginning of a change in Irish opinion and fuelled an increased alienation from the British administration in Ireland. Before the Rising, the rebels were seen as a detriment to the nationalist cause. However, as freed detainees began to reorganize the Republican forces, nationalist sentiment swung towards the then small Sinn Féin party. The surviving Republican leaders infiltrated Sinn Féin and deposed its monarchist leadership. After the takeover, Sinn Féin and the Irish Parliamentary Party (IPP) fought a series of inconclusive electoral battles until the December 1918 General Election that was fought on the basis of Sinn Féin's commitment to the formation of a republic.

Sinn Féin swept the polls and seventy-three members were elected to represent Ireland in parliament. The newly elected members of parliament, however, chose not to go to London. Instead they formed the first independent parliament in Dublin. They called themselves the Dáil Éireann (House of Deputies). On 21 January 1919, the Dáil declared Ireland an independent republic. The British ignored the declaration. In retaliation, the newly formed Irish Republican Army (IRA)—formerly the Irish Volunteers—took guerrilla action against the British forces and loyalists through the formation of arson gangs, attacks on British barracks, and ambushes of military convoys. In kind, the British government responded by creating the Black and Tans, a paramilitary force. The British government advertised for men willing to face a rough and dangerous task with the intention of forming a special auxiliary force to assist the Royal Irish Constabulary (RIC) in policing the increasingly hostile Irish population. The first recruits arrived in Ireland on 25 March 1920. The men were paid ten shillings a day—a salary attractive to unemployed war veterans. While officially in Ireland as a police force, the Black and Tans were viewed by republicans as an army of occupation.

The most notorious atrocity with which the Black and Tans are associated is Bloody Sunday.[92] On 21 November 1920, in response to the assassination of fourteen British secret service officers, the Black and Tans surrounded a football match and shooting broke out. Twelve people were killed and over sixty people were injured. Without diminishing the intensity of the fighting and the atrocities on both sides, many commentators, then and now, have described the tactics of the Black and Tans as state-supported terrorism. Shortly thereafter, in December 1920, the Government of Ireland Act established two parliaments—one in Dublin and a second in Belfast—but both subordinate to London. Unionist Ulster, which had a Protestant majority, accepted the act and formed the state of Northern Ireland. The Belfast parliament was opened by George V on 22 June 1921. In sharp contrast, the Dáil Éireann rejected the act and southern Ireland began fighting for complete independence. After more fighting of considerable violence, the IRA and the British army declared an uneasy truce in July 1921. The Irish Free State was created in December 1921.

Bowen has set *The Last September* amid this period of intense turmoil. Passion and terror lie beneath the surface of Bowen's novel. Bowen herself is closely associated with the waning ascendancy culture that shaped her childhood and aesthetic sensibility. Born in Dublin to a land-owning Anglo-Irish family, she had a childhood characterized by loss and geographic dislocation. Her novels frequently take as their primary subject the plight of young women in complex emotional situations, which are not expressly of their own making. In particular, Bowen's explorations of her characters' struggles for selfhood are inseparable from the domestic spaces in which they are situated:

> Her heroines both flee from and seek houses that function as
> symbols of a psychic shelter that defines and threatens them. . ..
> Bowen's protagonists inhabit and reject a variety of domestic
> settings that present themselves as possible solutions to a sense
> of homelessness.[93]

Lois is one such heroine. As an orphan, she is dependent upon her aunt and uncle for her position both within Anglo-Irish society and Danielstown, the home she shares with them.[94] While *The Last September* is very much about Lois, it also examines the personal cost of a life devoted to the ideals of aristocratic society and a strategy of denial during one of the major political crises of modern Irish history.

INHERITED LOYALTY

The book 'takes its pitch from that lovely, too mortal month which gives the novel its name' and 'the Troubles'—'the guerrilla conflict between the Irish, in arms for freedom, and the British troops still garrisoning the land.'[95] The Naylors—Lois' aunt and uncle—are torn between their traditional hospitality towards the occupying British garrison and their loyalty to their tenants. Bowen described the position of Anglo-Irish families such as the Naylors as ambiguous and heartbreaking: 'Inherited loyalty to England—where their sons went to school, in whose wars their sons were killed, and to whom they owed in the first place their lands and powers—pulled them one way; their own latent blood-and-bone "Irishness," the other.'[96] The circumstance of Hugo Montmorency mirrors the fragility of the family's situation. Hugo, who has failed to find a home or role for himself since selling his land, responds to the questions 'How far do you think this war is going to go? Will there ever be anything we can all do except not notice?' with a devastatingly honest assessment of the situation. Hugo suggests that the Anglo-Irish can do little as they are lacking in legitimacy and do not belong to either side: 'Don't ask *me*. . . . A few more hundred deaths, I suppose, on our side—which is no side—rather scared, rather isolated, not expressing anything except tenacity to something that isn't there—that never was there.'[97]

All of the characters are trapped by their history, but Lois is doubly trapped. She is trapped by the past and the conventions associated with her gender and class. Living in a home that is not her own, Lois ambivalently fulfills the roles assigned to her because she dare not rebel and disassociate herself from the privileges and reassurance that Danielstown affords her. Nevertheless, in spite of her dependence on her position as obedient niece, she is restless and craves experience. It is this restlessness that takes Lois out into the shrubbery after a dull dinner where she is startled by a man walking purposefully through the dark foliage: 'there passed within reach of her hand, with the rise and fall of a stride, a resolute profile, powerful as thought. In gratitude for its fleshliness, she felt prompted to make some contact: not to be known seemed like a doom: extinction.'[98] Lois does not feel fear. Instead, she is reminded of the inadequacies and limitations of her own life and ambivalent feelings towards Ireland: 'She could not conceive of her country emotionally: it was a way of living, an abstract of several landscapes, or an oblique frayed island, moored at the north but with an air of being detached and washed out west from the British coast.'[99] Lois does not tell anyone about the encounter; she prefers to harbour the secret and personalize the significance of the event. She feels as though, '[c]onceivably, she had just surprised life at a significant angle in the shrubbery.'[100]

As the novel progress, Lois' desire to experience life at a more 'significant angle' intensifies. The first encounter with her soldier Gerald Lesworth after the shrubbery incident is revealing in this regard. When he mentions the attack on the RIC barracks in Ballydrum five nights earlier, Lois responds provocatively,

'Do you know that while that was going on, eight miles off, I
was cutting a dress out, a voile that I didn't even need, and
playing the gramophone? . . . How is it that in this country that
ought to be full of such violent realness, there seems nothing for
me but clothes and what people say? I might just as well be in
some kind of cocoon.'[101]

Gerald cannot—or rather will not—listen to what she is saying in spite
of his claim, 'I could listen all day to you talking.'[102] She has just announced that she did not feeling anything in response to the attack,
which garners Gerald's nonsensical response: 'you've got the most
wonderful power of feeling.'[103] Lois' exasperated claim that 'you
[Gerald] never take in a word I say. You're not interested in what I tell
you about myself' seems entirely justified.[104] Gerald responds to Lois
as a 'woman', and as such 'it wasn't to be expected or desired she
should understand.'[105] His response is all the more inappropriate given
Lois' desire to shed the cocoon and fall into realness, however violent
that step might prove.

Critics such as Heather Bryant Jordan have suggested that, 'Lois and
Gerald's love affair epitomizes the misunderstandings and bitterness
that separated the Anglo-Irish and the British.'[106] Lois is a member of
a community in an equivocal position; 'interest and tradition should
make [Lois and her family] support the British [but] affection ties
them to the now resistant people of their surrounding community.'[107]
As such, the possibility of union between Lois and Gerald seems
unlikely even in these early exchanges, especially when Lois likens
the situation in which Ireland finds itself to that of a woman—specifically, a woman irritated by England.[108] Men and England expect Lois
and Ireland to assume roles they would rather leave aside for a new set
of opportunities and responsibilities.

Tennis parties and conversations at cross purposes recede a second
time when Lois and Marda Norris come across a sleeping gunman in a
decaying mill on the estate. Ten years apart in age, Marda and Lois
share a loose connection to Ireland. Lois has been raised and educated
in England. Marda is about to marry a rich Englishman. The scene at
the mill is the novel's dramatic centre:

> [it] represents a powerful initiation of both women into the life
> of their own country. In fusing sexual and political imagery,
> Bowen integrates two narratives: the story of a young woman's
> attempted passage into adulthood and an account of Ireland's
> historical transformation into the twentieth century.[109]

The incident frightens Lois into thinking 'I must marry Gerald' while
simultaneously drawing attention to her willingness to keep secret her
meeting with a rebel who strives to destroy the system that keeps her
in check.[110]

In spite of their willingness to be agreeable, the rebel treats Lois and
Marda as Ireland has been treated; he dismisses them as female ser-

vants to the male political process. There is no difference between the gunman, Gerald, Hugo, or Lawrence. All of the men consign Lois to a domestic space and assume that marriage is the only appropriate activity for a young woman. The gunman commands, 'It is time . . . that yourselves gave up walking. If you have nothing better to do, you had better keep in the house while y'have it.'[111] As her thoughts of Gerald suggest, Lois' immediate impulse is to obey this traditional and constricted identification of the female with the domestic, which does not question or challenge the assumption that women have no role beyond the steps of a home. Nevertheless, in spite of their fear, the women are willing to protect the gunman and do not breach the promise made to remain silent; a promise to which Lois alludes when she repeatedly asserts to Hugo, 'We swore— . . . We swore. . . . There never was anybody, we never saw anybody, you never heard.'[112] The landless and childless Hugo can do little but protest against what he perceives to be the women's foolhardy conduct, little aware that the women, and Lois, in particular, conceive of him as irrelevantly anchored in 'old conceptions' and the past.[113] When the two women discuss Hugo's conduct, the injured Marda with her bloodied hand remarks, 'I hope I shall have some children; I should hate to be barren.'[114] Her declaration binds her to the future, and with an explicit desire for fecundity and change. While the scene contains no explicit acknowledgement of the possibility of women's political agency, Bowen 'figures, in narrative form, that both women imaginatively harbour a terrorist within themselves.'[115] This secret is buried deep within them and left unacknowledged even before the mill.

After Marda departs for England, Lois' contradictory impulses continue to haunt her as she wavers between marrying Gerald and seeking an unidentified alternative means by which to begin her life. She is without will—without direction. Lois does not act but instead reacts to the situations in which she finds herself. Her attitude towards her eventual engagement to Gerald is ambivalent. Mere moments after asking Lawrence 'what do you think I am for' and realizing that she cannot recollect her 'last sense of Gerald,' Lois concludes, 'All the same it . . . *is* something definite.'[116] The 'definite' quality of being engaged has appeal in the absence of other compelling options. Lawrence's suggestion that she go on with her German is received with hesitating sincerity when he hands her two grammars, a dictionary, and a Thomas Mann novel. Lois is malleable and changeable.

Lady Naylor takes advantage of her niece's malleability in her efforts to thwart any lasting attachment between Lois and Gerald. Her own meandering conversations recall Lois' mental peregrinations. Lady Naylor, however, punctuates her seemingly idle observations with pointed comments and suggestions deliberately intended to influence any decisions that Lois may make:

'I am surprised at them all having time. . . . However, if they danced more and interfered less, I dare say there would be less trouble in the country. It appears that in Kerry . . .' [Lady Naylor's] voice became colder with inattention and dwindled away. Lois was certain she eyed the pink blotter. This zigzag approach to Gerald, this ultimate vagueness, were sinister. Lady Naylor, after some moments of odd and oppressive silence observed that the sweet-peas were dying. 'The water must be unhealthy, it's going green. In fact, all the flowers need doing. Perhaps after tea—How would you like to go to a school of art?'

'Marvellous,' said Lois after reflection.[117]

With references to sweet-peas and soldiers, Lady Naylor's speech yokes together the domestic and the political. In doing so, her subversive views surface with blame for the recent trouble apportioned to the dancing soldiers. The impossibility of such a marriage hardly needs affirming with the further inquiry as to whether Lois would like to attend a school of art. Nevertheless, Lois' response is important but it exposes her as accepting and compliant.

In similar fashion, Lady Naylor's oblique but effective conversation with Gerald, shortly before his death, neatly curtails the possibility of the novel ending with a wedding. Bowen rejects the marriage plot to which so many readers had grown accustomed in the stories of young girls. In fact, when the marriage plot is derailed by Lady Naylor and Lois expresses a subdued appreciation of her aunt at a dinner with the Trents, the reader is more aware than ever that the ending does not constitute a failure to marry, but rather it represents a choice redolent with implicit political implications. As Robert Caserio observes, 'when Lady Naylor, of all people, decided that Lois must not be engaged to the English soldier, the unity-in-political-unconsciousness of women consolidates itself. It enacts a version of the nationalists' violence against empire: the fire in the house comes from within, from Lady Naylor, not just from without.'[118] Lady Naylor is refusing an English marriage for her niece. Gerald assumes that the objections are on account of class. He is unaware of Lady Naylor's ambivalent feelings towards the soldiers and the English quite unrelated to specific details of his personal circumstances. Throughout the novel, she is repeatedly critical of England and, in particular, English wives who 'tell one the most extraordinary things, about their husbands, their money affairs, their insides. They don't seem discouraged by not being asked.'[119] Of greater relevance, however, are Lady Naylor's views on Marda's upcoming marriage to an Englishman. Lady Naylor views this marriage as a loss: Marda will be lost to her Irish family once 'the veil of an international marriage descended,' making criticism or discussion of the English impossible. Marda will be doubly subdued as a married Anglo-Irish woman.

After his meeting with Lady Naylor, Gerald begins to doubt Lois' feelings for him. In turn, as soon as he doubts her, she cannot reassure him. If she is to react to him convincingly, she needs his love and faith. Without him believing in her, she cannot attempt to believe in him; nothing is left of what brought them together, and they are both 'entirely lost.'[120] They are lost in large part because Gerald would not have understood Lois' reaction to his death. When word of Gerald's death reaches her at Danielstown, Lawrence suggests:

> 'I expect—I don't know—one probably gets past things.'
> 'But look here, there are things that one can't—' (She meant:
> 'He loved me, he believed in the British Empire.') 'At least, I
> don't want to.'
> 'Perhaps you are right,' he said, studying, with an effort of sight
> and of comprehension, some unfamiliar landscape.[121]

Lois cannot reconcile Gerald's love for her and his belief in the Empire. His firm faith in Empire is unfathomable to a girl who harbours secrets of rebel activities and is little moved by news of ambushes on British soldiers. She can little fathom that she considered marrying a man with whom she was so out of sympathy on account of simply desiring 'something definite'—her seeming need for definite purpose regardless of the emotional and intellectual practicality cannot be readily forgotten. It can, however, be laid aside and left to smoulder while touring in Europe. Lois is absent when rebels burn Danielstown to the ground early the following year. History and circumstance have determined that Lois shall not idle in the Big House. She must adopt new affiliations now that violence has entered into what was her home and forced change. The dangerous consequences of an ambivalent passivity are violently revealed in the torching of the Big House.

Like Forster before her, Bowen has written a quietly incendiary novel. While *The Last September* is not as formally innovative as some of the novels discussed in Elizabeth Drew's *The Modern Novel*, it does unquestionably encompass what Drew identified as the primary characteristics of the modern novel: an interest in the inner workings of the ordinary mind and a commitment to registering an individual's response to the contemporary moment as filtered through the weight of history whether personal, sexual, religious, or national. Lois is just a girl—or so she seemed to Gerald. Bowen exposes the limitations of such a view, and artfully examines the conflict between Ireland and England without privileging the story of guerrilla warfare and public declarations. Human relations become the template against which the past must be understood as inflecting the present. Lois' parentage, gender, religion, and nationality powerfully shape the story and the reader's response. Lois' indecision and inability to act decisively are not simply the limitations of a girl on the brink of womanhood; rather, by reading them against the backdrop of the 'Troubles' and the palpable tension between Lois and the other female characters, we can see that Bowen's novel challenges the readers' conception of art at the same time as it challenges their views about women and politics. Lois doubts and rejects a conventional, unquestioning allegiance with the local garrison and the English. She does not believe in Empire. She does not believe in England. She inclines towards doubt of things presented steadily and whole in favour of things as they are unsteadily and partially represented. If not pressed to make a choice and choose sides, Lois could come to have much in common with the wandering emasculated Hugo. The fire at Danielstown may, however, preclude such a fate once the Big House's 'door [stands] open hospitably upon a furnace.'[122] The necessity of making a choice—of choosing sides—and striking an allegiance is intensifying.

Adela and Lois are a new kind of heroine: heroines who do not marry and cannot conform to societal expectations as formulated by the old guard. Adela, unlike Lois, however, does make choices. Adela chooses to speak Aziz's name and in speaking it she refutes the unspoken charge of rape. In doing so, Adela knowingly forecloses any prospect of marrying Ronny. She does so because she is willing to scrutinize the values and attitudes evinced by her country in its occupations of another. She is willing to view with scepticism the choices and allegiances fostered by the Anglo-Indian community. She is willing to accept an uncertain future without a prefabricated happy ending. In contrast, Lois is willing to keep secrets and as such she cannot break free in the way that Adela does. For Lois, the possibility of speaking out can simply be inferred, delayed to some future moment when her self knowledge mirrors the new reality in which the Irish find themselves after achieving independence from Britain.

Despite the different fates of their heroines, both novels present the intricacies of human relationships, accenting the elements of the unseen and unexpressed in the affairs of life. The modern novelist is revealed as not simply concerned with the world of action but also with the story taking place 'inside the human being himself' and 'the dynamics of the spirit.'[123] Bowen and Forster ably adhere to Woolf's injunction that writers 'record the atoms as they fall upon the mind in the order in which they fall, [and] trace the pattern, however disconnected and incoherent in appearance, which each sight or incident scores upon the consciousness.'[124]

FOR FURTHER CONSIDERATION: SUGGESTED READING

The Modern Novel

Adorno, Theodor. 'Perennial Fashion—Jazz,' *Prisms*, Samuel and Shirley Weber (trans.). Cambridge MA: MIT Press, 1981.

Ayers, David. *English Literature of the 1920s*. Edinburgh: Edinburgh University Press, 1999.

Caserio, Robert. *The Novel in England, 1900–1950: History and Theory*. London: Prentice Hall, 1999.

Dettmar, Kevin, and Stephen Watt (eds). *Marketing Modernisms: Self-Promotion, Canonization, Rereading*. Ann Arbor: University of Michigan Press, 1996.

Hapgood, Lynne, and Nancy Paxton. *Outside Modernism: In Pursuit of the English Novel, 1900–30*. New York: St. Martin's, 2000.

Miller, Tyrus. *Late Modernism: Politics, Fiction, and the Arts Between the World Wars*. Berkeley: University of California Press, 1999.

North, Michael. *Reading 1922: A Return to the Scene of the Modern*. Oxford: Oxford University Press, 1999.

Elizabeth Bowen

Bennett, Andrew, and Nicholas Royle. *Elizabeth Bowen and the Dissolution of the Novel: Still Lives*. New York: St. Martin's, 1995.

Corcoran, Neil. 'Discovery of a Lack: History and Ellipsis in Elizabeth Bowen's *The Last September*,' *Irish University Review: A Journal of Irish Studies* 2001 Autumn–Winter 31 (2): 315–33.

Williams, Julia McElhattan. '"Fiction with the Texture of History": Elizabeth Bowen's *The Last September*,' *MFS: Modern Fiction Studies* 1995 Summer 41 (2).

E. M. Forster

Armstrong, Paul B. 'Reading India: E. M. Forster and the Politics of Interpretation,' *Twentieth-Century Literature* 38 (1992): 365–85.

Beer, John, (ed.). *A Passage to India: Essays in Interpretation*. London: Macmillan, 1985.

NOTES

1 See also Charles Duff, *James Joyce and the Plain Reader—An Essay* (London: Desmond Harmsworth, 1932).

2 Elizabeth Drew, *The Modern Novel* (London: Jonathan Cape, 1926) 22–3.

3 Drew 246.

4 Drew 246.

5 Drew 255.

6 Virginia Woolf, 'Mr Bennett and Mrs Brown,' *A Woman's Essays*, Rachel Bowlby (ed.) (London: Penguin, 1992) 82.

7 Woolf, 'Mr Bennett and Mrs Brown' 84.

8 Drew 256.

9 Woolf, 'Mr Bennett and Mrs Brown' 84.

10 Woolf, 'Mr Bennett and Mrs Brown' 84.

11 Drew 256.

12 Drew 256–7.

13 Drew 260–1.

14 Drew 35.

15 Drew 34.

16 Drew 34, 35.

17 Drew 15.

18 Drew 39.

19 Woolf, 'Mr Bennett and Mrs Brown' 86, 87.

20 Woolf 87.

21 Woolf 87.

22 Virginia Woolf, 'Modern Fiction,' *The Crowded Dance of Modern Life*, Rachel Bowlby (ed.) (London: Penguin, 1993) 8.

23 Woolf, 'Modern Fiction' 8.

24 Woolf, 'Modern Fiction' 9.

25 Woolf, 'Modern Fiction' 9.

26 Queen Elizabeth I, the daughter of King Henry VIII and Anne Boleyn, ruled between 1558 and 1603.

27 A 'mutiny' is an open rebellion on the part of a body of people normally subject to strict discipline, such as soldiers or sailors, and shows an open disregard for discipline and order imposed by a constituted authority, such as the military or the government. The use of the word 'mutiny' suggests an inherent imperialistic bias in standard English accounts of the event. In contrast, Indian histories frequently refer to the same event as the Sepoy Rebellion.

28 India's many Muslims were reluctant supporters of the Indian National Congress because the majority of its members were Hindus. The Muslims feared it would be to their disadvantage if the Congress became too powerful. In response, they formed the Muslim League in 1906 to improve the position of Muslims in India.

29 The majority of the Indians who fought for Britain in World War I were from the Punjab, which in turn helped account for the intensity of the postwar frustration and anger in the Punjab.

30 For further information on correspondences between the novel and historical events, see G.K. Das, '*A Passage to India*: A Socio-Historical Study,' John Beer (ed.), *A Passage to India: Essays in Interpretation* (London: Macmillan, 1985) 1–15.

31 E.M. Forster, *A Passage to India* (New York: Harcourt Brace: 1984) 298.

32 Tony Davies (ed.), 'Introduction,' *A Passage to India* (Buckingham: Open University Press, 1994) 1.

33 Philip Gardener (ed.), *E.M. Forster: The Critical Heritage* (London: Routledge & Kegan Paul, 1973) 269.

34 See E.M. Forster's *Aspects of the Novel* (New York: Harcourt, Brace & World, 1927) for further discussion of his views on the novel.

35 Wilfred Stone, 'The Caves of *A Passage to India*,' *A Passage to India: Essays in Interpretation* 23.

36 Forster 18.

37 Forster 34.

38 Forster 34.

39 This is in direct contrast with her son; as her comments in Chapter 3 suggest, Ronny Heaslop has become quite willing to judge since arriving in India. When his mother remarks, 'You never used to judge people like this at home,' he retorts, 'India isn't home' (Forster 33).

40 Forster 37.

41 Forster 37.

42 Forster 38.

43 Forster 321.

44 Forster 325.

45 Forster 326.

46 E.K. Brown, *Rhythm in the Novel* (Toronto: University of Toronto Press, 1950) 57–8.

47 Forster 7.

48 Forster 9.

49 Forster 8.

50 Forster 23–4.

51 Brenda R. Silver, 'Periphrasis and Rape in *A Passage to India*,' Jeremy Tambling (ed.), *E.M. Forster: New Case Books* (London: Macmillan, 1995) 176–7.

52 Forster 65.

53 Forster 33.

54 Forster 86.

55 Forster 87.

56 Silver 182.

57 Silver 180.

58 Forster 203.

59 Forster 27.

60 Forster 199, 235.

61 Forster 224–5.

62 Forster 256.

63 Forster 257.

64 Gillian Beer, 'Negation in *A Passage to India*,' *A Passage to India: Essays in Interpretation* 46.

65 Forster 3.

66 Forster 4.

67 Forster 5.

68 Forster 362.

69 Forster 79–80.

70 Beer, 'Negation' 49.

71 Beer, 'Negation' 50.

72 Forster 165.

73 Forster 165, 163.

74 Forster 198, 85.

75 Forster 198.

76 Beer, 'Negation' 52.

77 Forster 168.

78 Forster 250.

79 Forster 251.

80 Forster 254.

81 Forster 257.

82 Forster 317.

83 Forster 322–3.

84 Forster 325.

85 Forster 325–6.

86 Beer, 'Negation' 58. The *Bhagavad Gita* – 'the Song of God' – is one of three principal texts that define the essence of Hinduism, the other two being the Upanishads and the Brahma Sutras. The *Gita* was written between 500 and 200 BC.

87 Forster 326.

88 Benita Parry, 'The Politics of Representation in *A Passage to India*,' *A Passage to India: Essays in Interpretation* 27.

89 Beer, 'Negation' 45.

90 The Irish Republican Brotherhood acted on the old republican principle that 'England's difficulty was Ireland's opportunity.'

91 As above, the IVF (Irish Volunteer Force) had been formed in 1913 by moderate nationalists frustrated by the delay in Britain's granting self-government to Ireland. The IVF had recruited nearly 200,000 men by mid-1914, but the organization formally split over whether its volunteers should enlist in the British Forces and fight in the European war. More than 10,000 men strongly opposed fighting on behalf of the British. These men retained the original IVF name. The Military Council of the Irish Republican Brotherhood hoped to convince these men to participate in the Uprising. IVF leaders, however, notably Eoin MacNeill, rejected a wartime uprising on grounds of principle.

92 'Bloody Sunday' also refers to a more recent event in the history of Northern Ireland. On 30 January 1972, fourteen people were killed by British soldiers during an anti-internment rally in Londonderry.

93 Vera Kreilkamp, *The Anglo-Irish Novel and the Big House* (Syracuse: Syracuse University Press, 1998) 142.

94 The term 'Anglo-Irish ascendancy' refers to the Protestant oligarchy that all but controlled Ireland from the eighteenth century through to the early twentieth century. The dominant landowners were the descendants of the original recipients of English land grants, beginning in the sixteenth century.

95 Elizabeth Bowen, 'Preface,' *The Last September* (New York: Knopf, 1964) vi, ix.

96 Bowen, 'Preface' x.

97 Bowen, *The Last September* (London: Penguin, 1987) 82.

98 Bowen 34.

99 Bowen 34.

100 Bowen 34.

101 Bowen 49.

102 Bowen 49.

103 Bowen 49.

104 Bowen 49.

105 Bowen 49. Gerald's attitude recalls that of Hugo Montmorency when he first observes Lois over dinner and he can do nothing other than suppose 'that unformed, anxious to make an effort, she would marry early' (28). Hugo cannot imagine any other possibility for Lois. It is, however, Lois's inability 'to begin' (191), rather than a true love of Gerald, that bids her consider marriage.

106 Heather Bryant Jordan, *How Will the Heart Endure: Elizabeth Bowen and the Landscape of War* (Ann Arbor: University of Michigan Press, 1992) 51.

107 Jordan 51.

108 Bowen 49.

109 Kreilkamp 156.

110 Bowen 125. The deserted mill on to which Lois and Marda stumble when out for a walk with Hugo in Chapter 15 is a ghostly reminder of England's prohibitions against Irish industry during the nineteenth century.

111 Bowen 125.

112 Bowen 126–7.

113 Bowen 127.

114 Bowen 128.

115 Robert Caserio, *The Novel in England, 1900–1950* (New York: Twayne, 1999) 255.

116 Bowen 162, 161.

117 Bowen 164.

118 Caserio 254.

119 Bowen 134.

120 Bowen 192.

121 Bowen 203.

122 Bowen 206.

123 Drew 249.

124 Woolf, 'Modern Fiction' 9.

CHAPTER 4

DOCUMENTING THE POLITICS OF ENGAGEMENT

A Modernist Chronology—The 1930s

Arts & Literature	Historical Events
1930 W.H. Auden, *Poems* William Faulkner, *As I Lay Dying* Sigmund Freud, *Civilisation and its Discontents* F.R. Leavis, *Mass Civilisation and Minority Culture* Evelyn Waugh, *Vile Bodies*	Gandhi begins campaign of civil disobedience in India First Nazis elected to the German Reichstag
1931 W.H. Auden, *Paid on Both Sides: A Charade* Charlie Chaplin, *City Lights* Fritz Lang, *M* Henri Matisse, *The Dance* Virginia Woolf, *The Waves*	Britain abandons the gold standard; National Government formed to deal with economic crisis Collapse of German banking system Royal Navy mutiny at Invergordon over pay cuts Statute of Westminster establishing formal legislative independence from Britain for the Dominions and the Irish Free State
1932 Bertolt Brecht, *The Mother* John Galsworthy awarded the Nobel Prize for Literature Aldous Huxley, *Brave New World*	Depression unemployment peaks in Britain at nearly 3,000,000 Great Hunger March of unemployed to London Gandhi arrested and later released George V makes the first Christmas Day broadcast Sir Oswald Mosley founds the British Union of Fascists
1933 W.H. Auden, *The Dance of Death* T.S. Eliot, *The Use of Poetry and the Use of Criticism* Gertrude Stein, *The Autobiography of Alice B. Toklas* Virginia Woolf, *Flush*	Adolf Hitler becomes Chancellor of Germany Franklin Roosevelt launches the 'New Deal' to combat the economic Depression in America Oxford Union debates 'This House will in no circumstances fight for King and Country'
1934 Robert Graves, *I, Claudius*	*Queen Mary* launched on the River Clyde British Union of Fascists holds rallies in Birmingham and London Hitler begins as Führer of Germany Mao Tse-tung's 'Long March' begins in China
1935 W.H. Auden and Christopher Isherwood, *The Dog Beneath the Skin* Salvador Dali, *Giraffe on Fire* T.S. Eliot, *Murder in the Cathedral* George Gershwin, *Porgy and Bess* Clifford Odets, *Waiting for Lefty* George Orwell, *Burmese Days* Dmitri Shostakovich, *Symphony No. 1*	Sectarian rioting in Belfast Invention of radar Penguin Books founded by Allen Lane Italy invades Abyssinia

1936	W.H. Auden and Christopher Isherwood, *The Ascent of F6* Charlie Chaplin, *Modern Times* John Grierson, *Night Mail* Piet Mondrian, *Composition in Red and Blue* Stevie Smith, *Novel on Yellow Paper* Dylan Thomas, *Twenty-five Poems*	Spanish Civil War breaks out BBC launches first continuous television services in London Death of George V Abdication of Edward VIII Accession of George VI Left Book Club publishes its first book
1937	George Orwell, *The Road to Wigan Pier* Pablo Picasso, *Guernica* J.R.R. Tolkien, *The Hobbit*	Jet engine first demonstrated Irish Free State abolished and replaced by the sovereign state of Eire Chamberlain becomes Prime Minister Zeppelin *Hindenburg* destroyed by fire in USA Golden Gate Bridge opens in San Francisco
1938	W.H. Auden and Christopher Isherwood, *On the Frontier* Belá Bartók, *Violin Concerto* Elizabeth Bowen, *The Death of the Heart* George Orwell, *Homage to Catalonia* Virginia Woolf, *Three Guineas*	Germany invades and annexes Austria Munich Agreement between Hitler and Chamberlain British Empire Exhibition in Glasgow
1939	W.H. Auden and Christopher Isherwood, *Journey to a War* Henry Green, *Party Going* T.S. Eliot, *The Family Reunion* James Joyce, *Finnegans Wake* Pablo Picasso, *Night Fishing at Antibes*	Britain promises to support Poland in event of German aggression Britain gives Germany an ultimatum over the invasion of Poland Evacuation of children from London begins Britain declares war on Germany and first troops of the British Expeditionary Force leave for France

As the 1920s drew to a close, most European nations were still constrained by crippling debts accrued during World War I; there was a climate of widespread economic depression with further inflation triggered by the Wall Street stock market crash in 1929. As global markets contracted throughout the world, the collapse of the New York markets heralded the beginning of the Great Depression. Demand for British products rapidly diminished and the effects were devastating and immediate. By the end of 1930, British unemployment had more than doubled and exports had fallen in value by 50%. The desperate state of the unemployed was underscored by the Great Hunger March of 1932, which saw violent clashes in Hyde Park between the police and thousands of marchers and their supporters. Throughout the decade, workers would take their cause to the streets, protesting persistent unemployment and government failure to deal with rising poverty amongst the working class. The '30s also witnessed the rise of fascism, particularly in Europe. Fascist Benito Mussolini had come to power in Italy early in the 1920s, becoming *de facto* dictator after he formed the government in 1922. Adolf Hitler became Chancellor of Germany in 1933, marking the rise to power of his National Socialist Party—the Nazis. In Spain, Generalissimo Francisco Franco led fascist Nationalist forces during the Spanish Civil War, and assumed power as dictator of Spain in 1939. In Britain, Oswald Mosley left the Labour party to form the British Union of Fascists in 1932, marking the entry of fascism into British politics.[1] There was also some concern that the new King—Edward VIII—had fascist leanings. Though the constitutional crisis of 1936—which saw Edward abdicate his throne in favour of his younger brother who became George VI—was blamed on Edward's decision to marry the twice-divorced American Wallis Simpson, Edward's subsequent visit to Hitler in Germany in 1937 lent credibility to fears about both the influence of fascism in elite circles of British society and the degree to which the establishment was out of touch with rank and file society. Indeed, one of the most famous scenes from the 1930s—Prime Minister Neville Chamberlain's return from his 1938 visit to Hitler in which Chamberlain proclaims that they have reached a deal that will bring 'Peace in our Time'—epitomizes the failure of the British establishment to take full measure of the political, economic, and social turmoil of the 1930s. Many Britons, consumed by economic woes at home and fears of another war in Europe, would have agreed with W.H. Auden's description of the '30s as 'A low, dishonest decade.'

Yet the 1930s were also a decade in which art and literature continued to flourish. Many of the modernists who had established themselves as writers of note earlier in the century produced important work throughout the 1930s. T.S. Eliot maintained his position as a leading poet, publishing *Ash Wednesday* in 1930 and the first of the

Four Quartets—'Burnt Norton'—in 1936. He also composed a number of verse plays for radio and stage production, with *Murder in the Cathedral* (1935) the most successful of them. Eliot continued his work as a leading critic and spokesman of modernist literature, which in turn helped to advance the critical consolidation of modernist aesthetics in British literary culture. As a director of Faber & Faber—a post he had assumed in 1925—he helped to foster the writing careers of the next generation of poets, including W.H. Auden, Louis MacNeice, and Stephen Spender. W.B. Yeats was active in the 1930s: several volumes of new poems were published including *Stories of Michael Robartes and his Friends* (1932), *The Winding Stair* (1933), and *Dramatis Personae* (1935). The publication of Yeats' *Collected Poems* (1933) and *Collected Plays* (1934) established him as one of the most important poets, if not the most important, of his era. Virginia Woolf was to write and publish some of her finest prose during the '30s, with *The Waves* (1931), *The Years* (1937), and her polemical essay *Three Guineas* (1938) all in print by the end of the decade. James Joyce's *Finnegans Wake* appeared serially throughout the decade and in 1939 it was finally published in volume form. Yet it is also the case that alongside these established modernists, the 1930s saw the emergence of new writers who developed their own unique voices and styles. These writers have often been called second-generation modernists, and it is these younger men and women with whom this chapter will be primarily concerned.

When the London-based Group Theatre was founded in 1932, W.H. Auden, often considered a leading second-generation modernist, was asked to serve as their literary advisor and in-house writer.[2] This invitation was extended on the strength of his first play, *Paid on Both Sides*, published in a 1930 issue of T.S. Eliot's *Criterion*.[3] Originally conceived as a charade to be performed by a group of houseguests, *Paid on Both Sides* explored the destructive consequences of a feud between two families. It rejected an explicitly realist framework in order to draw attention to the hidden emotions and convictions shrouded by the characters' public facades. With its mixture of prose and verse, *Paid on Both Sides* requires the audience to contemplate their own disguises and the subterranean motives informing personal actions in the public and private spheres. The following year, Auden helped write the Group Theatre manifesto. This communally-generated document articulated the company's position on collaboration and creativity:

> The GROUP THEATRE is a co-operative. It is a community, not a building.
> The GROUP THEATRE is a troupe, not of actors but of

Actors
Producers
Writers
Musicians
Painters
Technicians
etc, etc, and
AUDIENCE

Because you are not moving or speaking you are not therefore a
passenger.
If you are seeing and hearing you are co-operating.[4]

The manifesto unequivocally establishes 'seeing and hearing' as a
form of co-operation. As Peter McDonald illustrates in his 1997 essay
'Believing in the Thirties,' the decade's significance quickly came to
be presented in terms of 'the relation between the writer and society,
the individual and history, art and commitment.'[5] This commitment to
engagement—both social and political—as well as its formal implications for literature written during the 1930s is a central focus of this
chapter.

Auden's own literary career throughout the 1930s exhibited a visible
commitment to the views advanced in the manifesto and was, likewise, concerned with the relationships identified by McDonald and
other contributors to *Rewriting the Thirties* (1997). Auden routinely
collaborated with other artists and explored a variety of literary forms
with the express intent of engaging the active cooperation and response of his audience. This commitment is further demonstrated by
the diversity of artists with whom Auden worked over the course of
the decade. He wrote plays with Christopher Isherwood; poems and
travelogues with Louis MacNeice; collaborated with composer
Benjamin Britten on operas; and worked with filmmaker John
Grierson to create documentaries.

DOCUMENTARY MODERNISM

This list of collaborators represents artists associated with 1930s modernism and the emerging British documentary tradition, and as such,
two seemingly incompatible branches of creative activity are brought
into play. However, as recent work by Tyrus Miller and Bill Nichols
suggests, there is in fact a complementary relationship at work. In his
2002 article 'Documentary/Modernism: Convergence and Comple-
mentarity in the 1930s,' Miller argues modernism, 'formally innovative experimentalism,' and the documentary, 'naturalistic explorations
of everyday life,' 'were not so much opposed as instead complementary moments of a broader modernist poetics.' In short, the 1930s saw
the emergence of a poetics in which the documentary was as committed to verisimilitude as was stream-of-consciousness prose, and the
prose poem was as committed to technical coherence as was an avant-

garde inspired montage sequence in a documentary film.[6] Miller's position is grounded in the work of communist philosopher and literary critic Georg Lúkacs who differentiates between nineteenth-century realism and the naturalism of French novelist Émile Zola.[7] This differentiation encourages a reading of modern literature that is attuned to the 'basically *naturalistic* character of modernist literature.'[8] As guided by Lúkacs' reading of the naturalism-modernism continuum, Miller notes that both the documentary and modernism work by destroying the coherence of the world and, in turn,

> they reduce details to the level of mere particularity (once again, the connection between modernism and naturalism is plain). Detail, in its allegorical transferability, though brought into a direct, if paradoxical connection with transcendence, becomes an abstract function of the transcendence to which it points.[9]

Modernism and the documentary both rely on a commitment to the particular, and through this concentration on detail seek to reveal the previously unseen.

In a 1936 piece for the *Left Review*, Stephen Spender gives contemporary expression to Miller's retrospective yoking of documentary and modernism.[10] Spender engaged in an analysis of contemporary writers' stylistic options and then made the following observation about the recently completed Auden and Isherwood play *The Ascent of F6*:

> Perhaps the best feature of the Auden-Isherwood dramatic style in *The Ascent of F6* is the rhythmic contrast which the writers maintain between two entirely different methods of presentation: firstly, realistic scenes of political reportage; secondly, fables. There are two approaches to the contemporary political scene: the one is direct, or partially satiric, external presentation; the other is fantasy or allegory.[11]

The former is driven by the authority of fact, the latter by the authority of the imagination. Throughout the 1930s, more and more examples of straight documentary reportage—in film and prose—and creative works like *The Ascent of F6*—which effectively blended styles—appeared in print and on stage and screen.

As a mode of persuasion, the documentary works with what John Grierson called the raw materials of reality to generate the 'creative interpretation of actuality.' In this sense, Grierson and the staff in his General Post Office (GPO) Film Unit sought 'to make things known' and to expose viewers to what Soviet filmmaker Sergei Trekiakov called the 'biography of things.'[12] Of the films made while Grierson headed the GPO Film Unit, the best known is *Night Mail* (1936),

> partly because Auden and Benjamin Britten worked on it: but it merits its reputation as a whole and successful work of art, a genuinely collaborative effort [. . .] it is a poem of contrasts—the dark and empty landscape through which the [night mail

train from London to Glasgow] rushes, and the bright cheerful
interiors of the carriage, where the men work swiftly together
joking and talking as they work. That contrast makes it a film
about loneliness and companionship, for which the letters that
the train carries become symbols.[13]

Auden's 'Night Mail' poem anchors the final sequence of the documentary as a kind of metaphoric commentary complementing the
film's visuals. The visuals focus the viewers' attention on the train;
with this focus, Marsha Bryant suggests that, 'the film participates in
forming an *industrial unconscious* of Britain's "other" country by de-
picting a labour performed while most of Britain sleeps.'[14] The poem,
in contrast, grounds the audience in the city—in the world of the men
and women receiving the letters:

> The chatty, the catty, the boring, adoring,
> The cold and official and the heart's outpouring,
> Clever, stupid, short, long,
> The typed and the printed and the spelt all wrong.[15]

The art of the documentary—in this instance, the careful mixing of
shot and poem—emerges as what critic Samuel Hynes called 'an instrument for spreading political, sociological, and economic knowledge, and as a counter-force to the bourgeois, propaganda media—the
national newspapers, commercial entertainment, and public education.'[16] Hynes' 1976 reading of *Night Mail* is in harmony with
Spender's previously mentioned review of *The Ascent of F6*. Furthermore, Hynes is also of the view that among the best works of 1930s
documentary reportage are those in which the documentary method
and imaginative approach are evident in a single work—those which
make 'landscape and incident—the factual materials of *reportage*—do
the work of symbol and myth—the materials of *fable*.'[17] Taking our
lead from Hynes' comments, this chapter will examine W.H. Auden
and Christopher Isherwood's play *On the Frontier* (1938) and George
Orwell's political travelogue *Homage to Catalonia* (1938) as examples of two late modernist texts that work with the techniques and objectives of the documentary tradition so as to render fact fable.

In doing so, it will become apparent that modernism and the documentary do indeed share what Tyrus Miller characterizes as late modernism's defining features. In *Late Modernism: Politics, Fiction, and
the Arts Between the World Wars* (1999), Miller sets out those features:

> Taking their standpoint upon the shifting seismic plates of
> European society between two catastrophic wars, late modernist
> writers confronted no less an issue than the survival of individ-
> ual selves in a world of technological culture, mass politics, and
> shock experiences, both on the battlefield and in the cities of the
> intervening peace.[18]

Auden and Isherwood's poetic drama and Orwell's documentary travelogue explicitly explore the status of the individual in the 'world of technological culture, mass politics, and shock experiences.' While Orwell writes about the battlefields of the Spanish Civil War, Auden and Isherwood situate their play in an allegorical Europe's collapsing peace. These locations invite the reader to experience the pressing concerns of the 1930s writer who was grappling with the ways in which public life 'reopen[ed] the modernist enclosure of form onto the work's social and political environs, facilitating its more direct, polemical engagement with topical and popular discourses.'[19]

'MAKE ACTION URGENT'

Before moving into a discussion of *On the Frontier* and *Homage to Catalonia*, it is important to explore ways in which writers themselves were calling for direct engagement with the period's 'intense social, political, and economic pressures [that] increasingly threatened the efficacy of high modernist form.'[20] As suggested by Auden's 1935 birthday poem for Christopher Isherwood, the writing of the day reflects the escalating political turmoil of a nightmarish present:

> So in this hour of crisis and dismay,
> What better than your strict and adult pen
> Can warn us from the colours and consolations,
> The showy arid works, reveal
> The squalid shadow of academy and garden,
> Make action urgent and its nature clear?
> Who give us nearer insight to resist
> The expanding fear, the savaging disaster?[21]

In the language of the poem, an artist must be guided by his moral commitment and a strict sense of responsibility as 'all sway forward on the dangerous flood/Of history, that sleeps or dies,/And, held one moment, burns the hand.'[22] According to this conception, the artist must strive to make fellow citizens aware of the need for action in the hope that his insights 'give men strength to resist their enemies, without and within. This is more than simply a moral theory of literature, it asserts a direct relation between literature and action in the public world; writing becomes a mode of action.'[23]

In this 1935 poem, Auden is asking for something more difficult than simply engaging in political pamphleteering. It is a demand for affective writing explicitly concerned with the realities of the present moment. Auden is calling for the production of literature that has a moral role in a time of crisis: as Samuel Hynes notes, Auden is asking for 'alternative *worlds*, worlds of the imagination which would consist in new, significant forms, and through which literature could play a moral role.'[24] Hynes further observed that by 1935 Spender and Auden had explicitly turned to questions about the social aspects of literature: 'what is its relation to immediate history? how does it reflect the social background? what is its function in an unstable, perhaps a revolutionary society?'[25] During this period, as Spender argued in *The Destructive Element* (1935), it was no longer possible for people—writers, in particular—to be shaped by a 'personified ideal':

> 'we must serve with all our faculties some actual thing', Mr.
> Yeats has written in a recent preface. This seems to me to be
> true. The 'actual thing' is the true moral or widely political
> subject that must be realized by contemporary literature, if that
> literature itself is to be moral and true.[26]

For writers such as Spender, it was a given that a consideration of political content is unavoidable for the serious writer. *The Destructive Element*'s aim was 'to show that, apart from all the questions of tendency, there is, in our modern literature, a consistent tradition of writing that has a political-moral subject.'[27] In what was Spender's first major work, he defends writers who are 'in the widest sense political'—writers who seek 'to discover a system of values that are not purely subjective and individualistic, but objective and social.'[28] Noteworthy, however, even within this highly politicized framework is Spender's insistence that the writer's beliefs are of 'no literary interest . . . because art does not illustrate a point of view, it does not illustrate at all, it presents its subject in a new form.'[29]

The following year Woolf's essay 'Why Art Today Follows Politics,' first published in the *Daily Worker*, offered similar arguments.[30] Her short essay is a succinct meditation on the relationship between art and politics wherein she argues that the artist is 'in such close touch with human life that any agitation in it must change his angle of vision. Either he focuses his sight upon the immediate problem; or he brings his subject matter into relation with the present.'[31] The artist must comment—the artist must act—otherwise, the survival of art and the survival of culture are at risk. This is not to suggest that traditional literary considerations were no longer relevant for Woolf. The artfulness of a work of literature, technique and the workings of the imagination were still thought necessary elements for consideration when creating and evaluating art. Fears regarding the impact of pressures to be politically orthodox, to make art a class weapon, to abandon the traditional past, to simplify the complexities of art in the service of an urgent cause only accentuated the ongoing importance of aesthetic principles even in a moment of heightened political urgency.

THE SHAPE OF A DECADE

The ways in which Auden, Spender, Woolf, and others responded to this moment of urgency were both varied and impressive. Experiments in prose, poetry, and drama surfaced throughout the decade in compelling attempts to solve the problems posed by the dramatic social and political changes enveloping artists. If this widespread call for engagement is disregarded, the 1930s can look like a chaotic decade in which there is little unifying the literature that it produced. To take this view is to over-simplify and ignore the shared concerns of seemingly divergent works. In fact, a well established characterization of the 1930s—that this is a decade which ignored modernist revolutions in technique in favour of a return to realism or a turn towards polemical work—is insufficient on at least two counts.

First, an over-emphasis on the perceived return to realist modes or exclusively polemical work fails to acknowledge the impact that high modernism had in shaping the literary contours of the younger authors' work. An interesting example of one such author is Henry Green—a well regarded but little discussed English novelist—who published his second novel *Living* in 1929. Set in a Birmingham iron foundry, *Living* stresses and stretches its syntax, offering a taut and spare novel which explores the estranging grammar of the proletarian characters' West Midlands discourse:

> The inner shape of the novel [. . .] imitates our experience of
> living: it promises pattern then withholds it, insisting on a
> formless banality; it describes intensity, but as a part of grudg-
> ingly accepting monotony; it glimpses poetry, but only from the
> corner of its eye.[32]

In this linguistically self-conscious novel, Green is working firmly within the experimental limits of the modernist novel as established by Joyce and Woolf during the early 1920s, and he does so with the distinct concern for the social that likewise characterizes their work from the 1930s.

Second, many of the writers closely associated with the experiments of the previous decades continued to work well into the 1930s without abandoning formal experimentation as their primary mode of literary expression. James Joyce worked on *Finnegans Wake* (1939) throughout the 1930s and Virginia Woolf published *The Waves* in 1931. Although separated by almost an entire decade, *The Waves* and *Finnegans Wake* embody the sort of prose described in Woolf's speculative essay 'The Narrow Bridge of Art' where she wrote of a future in which 'prose will be used for purposes for which prose has never been used before. We shall be forced to invent new names for the different books which masquerade under this one heading.'[33] Fittingly, *The Waves* leaves readers questioning whether they have in fact read a novel; the book has variously been explored by critics as an example of elegiac writing and a prose poem. The names that readers might give *The Waves* are largely dependent on how they make sense of its highly stylized structure. The novel follows six characters—

three women and three men—from childhood to late adulthood in a kind of communal *bildungsroman*; to do so it employs a series of direct monologues grouped between anonymous italicized narrations describing the passage of the sun over the course of a single day. In each of the nine sections, the soliloquies are united through the repetition of phrases and a shared concern with identity, individuality, and the body. The reader is left to engage with and react to an impressionistic communally-produced portrait of group consciousness within a particular social milieu.

Similarly, *Finnegans Wake* is strikingly characterized by intense experimentation with structure, characterization, and language. The novel famously opens with the latter half of the closing sentence, thereby destabilizing more traditional understandings of what constitutes a beginning and an end. This circular view parallels Joyce's interest in the work of Italian philosopher Giambattista Vico (1668—1744) who conceived of history as a cycle of three ages—the mythic, the heroic, and the human era—followed by a period of renewal, which he called *ricorso*. *Finnegans Wake* follows a similar structure with a *ricorso* which 'brings us back to Howth Castle and Environs' where the novel opened. In its exploration of local and mythic history, the novel likewise explores characterization as a function of the particular and archetypal; the lead female character, for example, appears as herself Anna Livia Plurabelle (A.L.P.) and the River Liffey. The complexities of self-construction and public perception become entwined in both A.L.P. and her husband H.C.E. whose initials can variously stand for Humphrey Chimpden Earwicker, Here Comes Everybody, Howth Castle and Environs, and so forth. Joyce, like Woolf, is attending to the ways in which a personal and communal sense of history is shaped by the ways in which we use language—the ways in which we speak or dream ourselves into being. In turn, there is a sense in which the modernist novel as handled by Joyce and Woolf in the 1930s emerges as cyclical and never-ending.

Not only do established modernists continue to extend the boundaries of the genres with which they are most closely associated, there is also a shared impulse to experiment with new forms of literature, and these excursions into new genres often run parallel to the rise of documentary tradition and the call to action through politically and socially engaged writing. During this period, Woolf 'moved from the personal to the social, from individual intensity to group voices' and while doing so she began to explore the possibility of writing a novel as a kind of essay.[34] At first what eventually became *The Years* (1937) was structured 'to alternate fictional "extracts" from an imaginary longer novel about "a family called Pargiter," with essays commenting on the difficulties for the woman writer in dealing with such material.'[35] While ultimately her experiment resulted in two books—*Three*

Guineas and *The Years*—the motives animating the project in concert
with the majority of her essays written in this period attest to her keen
personal commitment to balance the political and aesthetic responsibilities of the artist—her struggle to keep out 'the pedagogic, the
didactic, the loudspeaker strain.'[36]

As Woolf was experimenting with the novel-essay, Auden and
Isherwood were refining Auden's earlier forays into verse drama—
excursions suggestively influenced by his readings of *The Waste Land*
as an undergraduate during the mid-1920s:

> From *The Waste Land* Auden learned that all utterances are
> transactions, oratorical performances with an end in view—that
> they are 'interested' rather than disinterested, intended to per-
> suade, whether as prophecy, indictment, seduction, conversion,
> greeting, insult, reproach, complaint, confession, or whatever.[37]

Like Eliot's, Auden's work draws on radio broadcasts, talk in waiting
rooms, the commands of armies, and snatched pleasures taken from a
complex mine of resources—Latin elegy, Anglo-Saxon alliterative
verse forms, dramatic monologues, Norse runes, music-hall songs,
blues, and jazz. With the plays, Auden mixed avant-garde elements
with popular forms in an attempt to attract a broad-based audience in
keeping with his view that drama is 'essentially a social art.'[38]

THE VERSE DRAMA—
POETIC ENGAGEMENT

W.H. Auden and Christopher Isherwood first met as boys at St
Edmund's Preparatory School. During the mid-1920s, while
Isherwood was at Cambridge and Auden was taking his degree at
Oxford, the young men renewed their earlier acquaintance. When the
two men collaborated on *The Enemies of the Bishop, or Die When I
Say When: A Morality Play in Four Acts* in 1929, they did not attempt
to publish or perform their initial creative effort. Within a few years,
however, they had collaborated on a series of plays, which appeared
on stage and in print.

Auden and Isherwood's three co-written plays are influenced by
German expressionist and epic theatre, the modern music hall, and the
cinema—its documentary and narrative traditions alike.[39] In
particular, the plays overtly draw attention to their ability to merge
distinct styles and genres to dramatic effect—an approach advocated
by German playwright Bertolt Brecht:

> So let us invite all the sister arts of the drama, not in order to
> create an 'integrated work of art' in which they all offer them-
> selves up and are lost, but so that together with the drama they
> may further the common task in their different ways; and their
> relations with one another consist in this: that they lead to mu-
> tual alienation.[40]

Brecht is a seminal figure in the history of twentieth-century explorations of drama as a forum for political ideas. He wanted his plays to identify and improve the principles governing social behaviour. In his use of theatrical montage, in which discrete separate scenes illuminate one another, he set out to expose the social dynamics of group action. Brecht's early work when set alongside Grierson's use of montage in his documentaries suggested a possible structure for Auden and Isherwood's political fables. All three plays boldly mixed symbolic quests with the disorienting shifts in perspective and sudden scenes associated with (avant-garde and documentary) montage to provocative effect. Brecht, Grierson, Auden, and Isherwood all strove to engage their audiences intellectually through the rejection of accepted theatrical and filmic conventions, and in doing so they sought to draw attention to the unexpressed or ignored. Working within this framework, Auden and Isherwood produced what William Stott has called vicarious documentary; this form of documentary 'gives facts indirectly, through an intermediary'—in other words, watching the events on stage gives the audience the sense of 'being there' and as such offers a 'representation of the actual in a way that makes it credible and vivid to people.'[41]

Auden and Isherwood's first successful stage collaboration, *The Dog Beneath the Skin*, was swiftly followed by a second highly topical play, *The Ascent of F6* (1936), which incorporated repeated direct references to contemporary media outlets. *The Ascent of F6* combined fable and reportage in its account of an allegorically-named mountaineer—Michael Ransom—caught between public and private ambitions. The British government asks Ransom to climb F6—a peak on the border between British Sudoland and Ostnian Sudoland—as it is thought that conquering the peak will help secure control of the region for whichever nation can scale the mountain first. Ransom initially declines the commission but then succumbs to the pleas from his mother to climb for her and his country. The romance of the solitary adventurer whose quests are appropriated for national glory would have registered powerfully with contemporary audiences for these were the years of the great Everest expeditions. Between 1920 and 1939, there were seven British attempts alone to scale Everest.[42] During the summer in which the play was written, there was a high-profile British–American expedition attempting to summit Nanda Devi on the India–Tibet border that received extensive, almost daily, attention in the press. As such, the action of the play parallels actual events and draws attention to the fact that 'press coverage of such a gesture of public heroism is itself a kind of myth-making, and so even reportage becomes fable.'[43]

The Ascent of F6 explores this process of reportage becoming fable through the incorporation of news broadcasts and newspaper headlines into the play. The first Act concludes with the cries of newsboys on a darkened stage announcing Ransom's decision to accept the commission:

> Evening Special! Evening Special!
> Ransom to lead Expedition!
> Famous Climber's Decision!
> *Evening Moon:* Late Night Final!
> Young English Climber's Daredevil Attempt!
> The Haunted Mountain: Full Story and Pictures!
> Monasteries in Sudoland: Amazing Revelations![44]

Driven by secret and private motives, Ransom accepts a contradictory public role: while Fleet Street and the Colonial Office pay his expenses, the public celebrates him as a symbol of romantic freedom. Ransom's inability to reconcile the public–private split is his tragedy regardless of which ending of the play any given reader or production privileges.[45]

ON THE FRONTIER

In March 1937, with *The Ascent of F6* on stage receiving warm reviews, Auden and Isherwood began to consider their next collaboration. Buoyed by the play's relative success—it filled the small Mercury Theatre for two months and then ran in the West End for five weeks—the men were encouraged to aim for a large commercial production of their next play. Taking Europe as their starting point, they drafted a new story in the spring of 1937 and wrote the dialogue that summer. The first version of the play was completed by September 1937 and a copy was sent to John Maynard Keynes who, after producing *The Ascent of F6* at the Arts Theatre, Cambridge in April 1937, wanted to continue working with Auden and Isherwood. Within weeks of reading the manuscript, Keynes agreed to back a Group Theatre production of *On the Frontier* at the Arts Theatre in Cambridge, to be followed by a further run in another provincial city or London. A substantially revised version of their third play eventually opened in Cambridge in November the following year.[46]

On the Frontier takes the theme of partings, boundaries, and divisions to the furthest extreme of the three plays. 1938 was the year during which Hitler flatly disregarded various European borders—Germany crossed the border to occupy Austria in March; six months later it demanded that it be allowed to annex the Czechoslovakian Sudetan, rich in coal, to the growing German nation; and with the signing of the Munich Agreement, this request was granted on 29 September 1938. It is thus fitting that borders dominate the play to the point of determining its title. With notable topicality, *On the Frontier* tackles the matter of rising hostilities between nations, the emergence of dubious leaders, and the inability of any one person to change the course of history. The plot traces the escalation of traditional hostilities between two European nations after what appears to be a staged terrorist attack on a frontier bridge leads to the outbreak of full-scale war.

On the Frontier does not apportion blame. Instead, it is an exposé of two European states drawing each other into war. The imaginary countries share responsibility for the conflict that engulfs them. Auden and Isherwood expose nationalism as a dangerous and corrosive sentiment that leads to violent armed conflict when a nation's citizens unthinkingly and unquestioningly adopt the rhetoric of their leaders. Until the final scenes of the play, Dr Thorvold—a middle-aged professor at a Westland university—is no exception. It is only when his son is in danger that he begins to consider the impact of his long uttered hollow words:

> I haven't tried to understand what made him act as he did. You
> see, I was brought up to think that a man's greatest privilege
> was to fight for his country; and it's hard to change one's ideas.
> Perhaps we were all wrong. War seems so beastly when it actu-
> ally happens! Perhaps 'country' and 'frontier' are old-fashioned
> words that don't mean anything now. What are we really fight-
> ing for?[47]

Even though this is a powerful instance of an individual meditating on his actions, the majority of the play's characters are caricatures without the ability or the will to shape the events in which they find themselves immersed.

The play is focused neither on individuals nor on an individual's agency, as is distressingly illustrated in the second act when the industrialist Valerian, his lieutenant Stahl, and the Westland Leader learn that war with their Ostnian neighbours is all but an accomplished fact. In response, the Leader undergoes a complete about-face in just a few lines. One minute he is radiantly proclaiming that he has

> withdrawn the Westland troops, unconditionally, ten miles from
> the frontier. [The world will hear tomorrow] that I have
> proposed to Ostnia a pact of non-aggression, guaranteeing the
> sanctity of the frontier for a thousand years.

A few lines later he cries,

> The die is cast! The name of Ostnia shall be blotted from the
> map of Europe for ever! . . . Confident in the justice of our
> cause, and determined to defend our sacred Westland
> homesteads to the last, we swear—.[48]

The curtain falls on Act II with the Leader still shouting—bombastically demonstrating his ability to adapt his rhetoric and posture to whatever position the moment requires.

Social commentary dominates regardless of which combination of characters is on stage. The audience is presented with 'an animated cartoon on the quarrels of international capitalists, the deceptions of the Press, the psychology of fascism, and the inner decay of democracies.'[49] The closest the play has to a villain is the fascist leader of Westland and the industrialists who exploit him. Nevertheless, as much as the industrialist Valerian may think that he is in control, he, too, will be destroyed by the end of the play. His self-perceived power and self-indulgent speeches are insufficient protection in this surreal but all too real world of hate and fear, prejudice and selfish desires. Valerian unwittingly comes closest to uttering the truth at the beginning of the play when he muses: 'Real political power is only made possible by electricity, double entry [bookkeeping] and high explosives.'[50] This insight is fleeting and he is ultimately no more secure than the Leader whom he indulges at the beginning of the play. Like the Leader, he too deals in platitudes and stock phrases. Valerian is unable to adapt to the rapidly changing world in which he finds himself after the bombing on the bridge when allegiances are no longer what they appeared at the beginning of the day. In the opening scene, the audience watched Valerian laughing dutifully, suppressing groans, and ignoring the Leader. Near the end of the play when Stahl is advocating that they flee and align themselves with South American industrialists, Valerian has become as irrelevant as the Leader of Westland.

The relevancy of individuals is further explored in the treatment of the two families caught up in the descent into war forming the action of *On the Frontier*. The impossibility of separating family life from public life is visually and aurally pressed upon the audience during scenes in the Ostnia–Westland room. The stage is divided in half—with Ostnia on one side and Westland on the other. As the play progresses, the actions that take place in each country are mirrored by similar actions in the other country—on the other side of the stage. For instance, the first scene of Act II begins with the Thorvolds (Westland) and the Vrodnys (Ostnia) huddled round their respective wireless sets waiting for the news. That an event of serious consequence has taken place is evident—an event for which Ostnia is blaming Westland and Westland is blaming Ostnia; for now, however, the audience must wait with the families to learn what has happened. The impossibility of determining and apportioning blame is made apparent the instant the radio broadcasts begin:

> WESTLAND RADIO: Maria Kinderheim, the six-year-old
> child injured in the bomb outrage at the Iron Bridge, died in the
> hospital this evening. This brings the number of the Westland
> dead up to nineteen.
> OSTNIAN RADIO: Peter Vollard, the eighty-year-old labourer
> injured in the bomb outrage at the Iron Bridge, died in the
> hospital this evening. This brings the number of the Ostnian
> dead up to twenty.

WESTLAND RADIO: The Minister for Propaganda and the
Minister for Air and Marine flew to Castle Tuborg this
afternoon to discuss with the Leader what steps should be taken.
. . . It is rumoured that the Ostnian Government is calling up the
nineteen-fourteen and nineteen-fifteen Classes.
OSTNIAN RADIO: An emergency meeting of the Cabinet was
called this evening to consider what steps should be taken. . . .
There are rumours that Westland will order general
mobilization.
WESTLAND RADIO: In view of the extreme gravity of the
situation . . .
OSTNIAN RADIO: In view of the extreme gravity of the
situation . . .
WESTLAND RADIO: The Leader . . .
OSTNIAN RADIO: His Majesty the King . . .
WESTLAND RADIO: Has decided . . .
OSTNIAN RADIO: Has decided . . . [51]

As the radio announcers' voices fill the stage with their clichés and
rhetoric, the audience is all too aware that the Thorvolds and Vrodnys
are listening to almost identical radio reports. Save for minor substi-
tutions—an elderly man for a small child, a king for a leader—they
are being told the same story. In turn, the two families respond with
similar degrees of unthinking condemnation of their enemies' actions.

Anna Thorvold is the only character on stage who articulates the
possibility of a compassionate response when she says, 'Some of them
were killed, too; weren't they, Mother.'[52] However, she absents
herself from the belligerent posturing on account of a headache—an
action mirrored by Eric Vrodny on the opposite side of the stage a few
lines later when he abruptly declares that he has a headache and
excuses himself from the stage. During the second radio broadcast in
which the Leader's and King's respective use of angry platitudes only
escalates, Anna and Eric are offstage, thereby emphasizing their desire
to separate themselves from the unthinking hatred espoused by their
families.

When the double broadcast justifying violent retribution and the un-
sheathing of swords concludes in Act II Scene I, Anna and Eric meet
in the middle of the stage. Their hopes and desires dissolve the frontier in an expressionistic dream scene symbolizing an alternative vision. The words exchanged by the young couple have a different
cadence and rhythm from those fired off by their elders.   Alternating
between feelings of hope and despair, Anna and Eric attempt to
imagine a different kind of future for themselves—a future in a 'good
place': 'Where the air is not filled with screams of hatred/Nor words
of great and good men twisted/To flatter conceit and justify murder.'[53]
This desire to conceive of a 'good place' must be brokered in language other than that which is being used to incite people into further
cycles of violence and destruction. Anna and Eric's use of poetry sig-

nals an attempt to employ language that is not stale and worn, in order to reject the blindness and pride associated with those who would drive Love and Truth underground.

The final act, which takes place nine months after the opening act, is one of intensified chaos. Total war has erupted between Ostnia and Westland. Eric is in prison. Anna is nursing the injured. Like a time-signal, a voice tonelessly repeats 'Kill, Kill, Kill, Kill, Kill!' on Westland Radio while Anna weeps for the suffering on both sides of the frontier.[54] On the frontier itself, soldiers express their disgust with the war and are exposed as the pawns of their commanding officers; they fight because they are so commanded and not out of any deep abiding conviction in their superiors or love of nation. The effect of the short and kaleidoscopic final act is that of seeing 'a series of melodramatic cartoons . . . like a number of escaped posters and photographs blown by the wind in one's face.'[55]

The play's fourth and final interlude reinforces this reading. The stage directions call for five male members of the chorus to stand before the curtain as representatives of five English newspapers:

> They should be dressed according to their shades of political opinion. Thus, the FIRST READER has a conservative, highly respectable government paper, the SECOND a violently reactionary, more popular paper, with pictures, the THIRD a liberal paper, the FOURTH a communist paper. The FIFTH READER, who is trembling all over, is studying one of those sensational and alarming news-letters which give the 'low-down' on the international situation. Each reader is seated. A spotlight rests on each in turn, as he reads his passage aloud.[56]

The mutually contradictory English newspapers highlight the fractiousness that divides England and exposes the audience to the inability of even English papers to make sense of current events. The papers can agree on no more than the ultimate consequences of the events in Europe: war. The snippets of articles read to the audience represent positions as divergent as that occupied by Lady Corker, a 'well-known local right-wing socialite,'[57] who is directly implicated in the events because she entertains the Westland Ambassador, through to an insular disavowal of responsibility as expressed by the first paper's overly simplistic critique of the events in Europe:

> There is an increasing danger to Europe of splitting into two irreconcilable camps. To this, the Englishman, with his love of liberty and his distrust of cast-iron ideologies, is tempted to retort, in the words of our national poet: 'A plague on both your houses!'[58]

With the invocation of Shakespeare via a line from *Romeo and Juliet*, the feuding houses of Ostnia and Westland are left to condemn their children to death. The newspaper chorus gives way to the final scene in which Anna and Eric die, sacrificed to the quarrel between their countries.

Anna and Eric die asserting that their real enemies are not those whom they have been called upon to fight but rather the passive acceptance of the circumstances in which Europe finds itself entangled. Eric, a pacifist, who came to fight on the barricades in an attempted revolution, utters the main moral of the play:

> Believing it was wrong to kill,
> I went to prison, seeing myself
> As the sane and innocent student
> Aloof among practical and violent madmen,
> But I was wrong. We cannot choose our world,
> Our time, our class. None are innocent, none.
> Causes of violence lie so deep in all our lives
> It touches every act.
> Certain it is for all we do
> We shall pay dearly. . . .
> Yet we must kill and suffer and know why.
> All errors are not equal.[59]

And so a play about how wars begin ends by deflecting 'our attention from parties and causes, from Left versus Right and Choruses of Red Prisoners, to a theme beyond politics, the human effort to create the Just Place.'[60] It deflects the audience's attention from the spectacle that has been laid before them, and instead demands that they meditate upon the place of the individual within this Europe that 'lies in the dark.'[61]

ON THE PENINSULA

George Orwell's *Homage to Catalonia* (1938) 'lies in the dark' that settled on the Iberian Peninsula after the outbreak of the Spanish Civil War. The three-year war has been described by the Spanish historian Francisco Salvadó as a brutal attempt to use military conflict to solve 'a host of social and political issues that divided Spaniards for generations.'[62] Conflicting views regarding land reform, calls for increased regional autonomy, and the role of the church and military in modern Spain had plagued successive ruling parties since the Restoration of the Bourbon Monarchy after the fall of the First Spanish Republic in 1874. When General Franco and his supporters met resistance in response to their attempted military coup in July 1936, a bloody fratricidal struggle between Franco's Nationalists and the Republicans ensued.[63]

What transpired was not simply a civil war; the conflict in Spain roused the interest of people throughout the world and elicited direct intervention on the part of various European nations—namely Hitler's Germany, Mussolini's Italy, and Stalin's Soviet Union—that unquestionably influenced the outcome of the war. The USSR entered the fray on the Republican side in an attempt to build an alliance against Fascism as opposed to being guided by a strong sense of ideological sympathy with the Republicans. In contrast, countries like Britain and France—in keeping with the policy of appeasement—chose to disregard building evidence of the Fascist powers' blatant involvement in Spain even after the mass bombing of cities and the sinking of merchant ships.[64]

When their governments did not take action, individuals began to step forward in support of the Republicans—in support of a fight against Fascism. European volunteers primarily aligned themselves with the International Brigades, while many Americans fought in the Abraham Lincoln Battalion. Six months into the conflict, Orwell began to make arrangements to leave England for Spain and join the International Brigade in Madrid. His intention was to fight and to write. Refused assistance by the British Communists, Orwell went to Spain in late 1936 with a letter of introduction from the Independent Labour Party (ILP). This fact of history took Orwell to 'Barcelona instead of Madrid, and so into the heart of the sectarian struggles that played a part in destroying the Republican cause.'[65] As such, *Homage to Catalonia* in large part emerges as one man's account of the subterfuge and deceit—the war of words and lies—that swiftly enveloped the Spanish Civil War. By May 1937, Orwell was writing to his then publisher Victor Gollancz of his hope that he would 'get a chance to write the truth about what [he had] seen. The stuff appearing in the English papers is largely the most appalling lies.'[66]

At a personal level, the full consequences of these 'most appalling lies' would not become apparent until his return to England after six months in Spain. Orwell's account of the events in which he participated was not in harmony with the British Left's position on the war. In particular, his association with POUM (*Partit Obrer d'Unificació Marxista*)—the anti-Stalinist Spanish communist party formed in 1935 by Andrés Nin and Joaquím Maurín—and his hostility to Communists was not acceptable to many back in Britain, including Gollancz, the publisher of his highly successful previous book *The Road to Wigan Pier* (1937). Gollancz ran the Left Book Club, which at its height had some 50,000 members, and without Gollancz's support *Homage to Catalonia* floundered after being published by Frederic Warburg—a publisher committed to printing books by the dissident left and socialists hostile to Stalinist communism.

Two months after Warburg released *Homage to Catalonia*, Orwell published a short essay entitled 'Why I Joined the Independent Labour Party' in the *New Leader*—the ILP's print organ. He opened with the declaration: 'I am a writer. The impulse of every writer is to "keep out of politics". What he wants is to be left alone so that he can go on writing.'[67] Unfortunately, as Orwell well knew, by 1938 it was no longer possible to keep out of politics and this tension accounts for much that is compelling about *Homage to Catalonia*. Orwell gestures towards this tension in a 1938 letter to Stephen Spender written as he was completing his Spain book:

> I hate writing that kind of stuff [the two chapters on Catalan politics] and I am much more interested in my own experiences, but unfortunately in this bloody period we are living in one's only experiences *are* being mixed up in controversies, intrigues, etc.[68]

Homage to Catalonia is then a record of Orwell's attempt to write truthfully without violating his literary instincts in a moment when the limitations of the writer and the press were being openly acknowledged.

It was with these limitations in mind that many of the book's first reviewers engaged with it. Geoffrey Gorer, for example, devoted his *Time and Tide* review to a detailed overview of Orwell's account of the Barcelona street fights from May 1937 and the ensuing events, out of the conviction that 'they will either be distorted or ignored in the greater part of the press':

> Emphatically, this is a book to read; politically and as literature it is a work of first-class importance. It will probably be abused by both Conservatives and Communists; anyone interested in the political situation (whatever their own views) or in literature would be foolish to neglect it.[69]

Gorer privileges *Homage to Catalonia* as a political document and an aesthetic object; there is no sense that the text must belong to any one single category, no sense that personal and public testimony are incompatible, no sense the book is compromised by its dual function.

Likewise, Philip Mairet's review in *New English Weekly* emphasized the value of the nuanced perspective on offer in *Homage to Catalonia*. He praised Orwell's attempts to be little more than 'a highly conscious and interested observer'—a difficult task in an atmosphere 'dense with rumours, lying propaganda and local feuds.'[70] For Mairet, Orwell's value as a commentator on the Spanish Civil War is tied directly to his distance from the press—local and foreign—committed as it is to mendacity 'in any matter connected with the present ideological war.' Unlike the content of the mainstream press as conceived by Mairet, *Homage to Catalonia* is characterized by:

> Its frank individuality of outlook, combined with a certain political naïveté, [which] gives internal evidence of its freedom from political obscurantism, for what bias it has is named and wholly unashamed. Its literary quality, which is of a high order, is of the kind that springs from a well-extraverted attention and spontaneous reaction, so that the observations are reliable and convincingly communicated.[71]

In short, the narrative persona assumed by Orwell in *Homage to Catalonia* is of fundamental importance in understanding why reviewers like Gorer and Mairet as well as later readers have so positively valued his autobiographical and unavoidably political account of the Spanish Civil War.

The narrator refuses to assume a dominant, authoritarian point of view. Instead, from the outset there is an awareness of the difficulty inherent in striving to represent the conflict discursively. Orwell recognizes that by arriving when he has—six long months after the attempted coup—he has entered into events midstream and he is also aware that his ability to fully comprehend what he is witnessing is hampered by the limits of his own position:

> The Anarchists were still in virtual control of Catalonia and the
> revolution was still in full swing. To anyone who had been
> there since the beginning it probably seemed even in December
> or January that the revolutionary period was ending; but when
> one came straight from England the aspect of Barcelona was
> something startling and overwhelming. It was the first time that
> I had ever been in a town where the working class was in the
> saddle.

Nevertheless, Orwell's frank and unabashed wonder and pleasure in a Barcelona covered in revolutionary posters and draped in flags emerges as the retrospective impetus for his book and personal recognition that this was a 'state of affairs worth fighting for.' His belief in the possibility of democratic socialism as fostered by his experiences in Spain demands that he write this account of his months serving as a militiaman on the Aragón front. In the end, his narrative can do little more than record and acknowledge the discrepancies found in competing accounts of the war as noted and experienced by Orwell: 'beware of my partisanship, my mistakes of fact and the distortion caused by my having seen only one corner of events. And beware of exactly the same things when you read any other book on this period of the Spanish Civil War.'[72] This proviso helps to forge an atmosphere of deceptively simple trust between the reader and writer that only unravels upon close reading.

Orwell's gently coercive narrative style such as is found in Appendix II may even pass unnoticed by a thoroughly won-over reader, on first pass.[73] Here, with an almost apologetic air, Orwell turns to his account of the Barcelona street fighting that occurred when internecine tensions swelled in violence, and the attendant political controversies, with the suggestion that the disinterested reader may want to skip ahead: 'It is a horrible thing to have to enter into the details of inter-party polemics; it is like diving into a cesspool. But it is necessary to try and establish the truth, so far as it is possible.'

With that said, Orwell goes on to establish why this interruption is necessary:

> It will never be possible to get a completely accurate and unbiased account of the Barcelona fighting, because the records do not exist. Future historians will have nothing to go upon except a mass of accusations and party propaganda. I myself have little data beyond what I saw with my own eyes and what I have learned from other eyewitnesses whom I believe to be reliable. I can, however, contradict some of the more flagrant lies and help to get the affair into some kind of perspective.[74]

The reader's willingness to trust in Orwell's eyewitness testimony is further aided by his unflinching recognition that what he sees—what he witnesses—is always and unavoidably transfigured by his changing allegiances. After recovering from a gunshot wound to his throat, which he received on the front three days after the Barcelona fighting ended, Orwell travels to the POUM headquarters in Siétamo for his discharge papers. With his discharge notice in hand, Orwell becomes aware of a shift in perspective: he is no longer seeing as a soldier, and the city of Barbastro, which 'had seemed to [him] simply a part of the war—a grey, muddy, cold place, full of roaring lorries and shabby troops,' now appeared changed:

> With my discharge papers in my pocket I felt like a human being again, and also a little like a tourist. For almost the first time I felt that I was really in Spain, in a country that I had longed all my life to visit. In the quiet back streets of Lérida and Barbastro I seemed to catch a momentary glimpse, a sort of far-off rumour of the Spain that dwells in everyone's imagination.[75]

Within one observer multiple versions of Spain emerge and with this deft weaving of documentary reportage, political commentary, and personal memoir, *Homage to Catalonia* solidifies its position as an important modern text drawing attention to just how intensely problematic the representation of events had become four decades into the new century.

The reader is made conscious of the shifting barrier between mythic and reliable representations of place (and conflict) as well as the degree to which our own impressions and convictions colour what we want to see and hear. A certain truth emerges in Orwell's own failure to meet an impossible standard of neutrality and he urges the reader to distrust his own account: 'I believe that on such an issue as this no one is or can be completely truthful. It is difficult to be certain about anything except what you have seen with your own eyes, and consciously or unconsciously everyone writes as a partisan.'[76] In this sense, *Homage to Catalonia* is an extended meditation on 'what it is to be certain' and the documentary method.[77] Orwell's observations draw attention to the formal concerns of documentary literature in its commitment to presenting (or representing) actual facts in contrast with imaginative writing. As such, the politics of (documentary) form and its ability to shape political consciousness must necessarily be considered in any readings of *Homage to Catalonia*.

By working in a manner analogous to Soviet filmmakers and John Grierson in Britain, Orwell's Spanish example of literary documentary reportage offered readers aesthetically innovative interpretations of reality. Where filmmakers edited factual footage to make unexpected—or previously unexposed—connections through non-discursive montage, Orwell exposed hidden events and perspectives through his combination of the hard facts of observation with the artifice and self-conscious use of language characteristic of modernist aesthetics. Keith Williams suggests that reportage as practised by Orwell is then partly a reaction against modernism's self-analysis and experimentation without simplistically returning to nineteenth-century realism's unquestioned mimesis. From this perspective, *Homage to Catalonia* offers a paradoxical—and arguably late modernist—solution with objective art reproducing reality as soberly and authentically as possible, while simultaneously baring its own devices in an anti-illusionistic manner.[78]

In turn, a few short years on from Orwell's *Homage to Catalonia*, a desire and willingness to debunk communally-held illusions playfully and deftly weaves its way into Virginia Woolf's final novel *Between the Acts* (1941). The novel takes the public and private—the 'orts, scraps and fragments' of everyone's lives—to relay the story of a village pageant on a warm summer's day at an English country house shortly before the beginning of the World War II.[79] Just as the pageant's audience finds itself essential to the conclusion of the performance, so too were the first readers invited into the text. Gillian Beer's 'Introduction' to a recent Penguin edition of the novel observes that for the novel's earliest readers much of its force lay in its often ironic negotiation of the diminishing space between peace and war and the mingling of fact and fiction: 'The work itself humorously, sometimes sardonically, interleaves literature, gossip, and communal events actually occurring in the world beyond fiction. It dwells on objects and emptiness, skews (and skewers) perceptions through puns and rhymes.'[80] With a provocative admixture of outside sources and an account of the public performance of a pageant as well as the private interludes between the acts, Woolf offers up a novelistic experiment in sympathy with the documentary tradition as adapted by Orwell, Auden, and Isherwood.[81] By way of Woolf's last novel and the poetry of H.D. and T.S. Eliot, our final chapter will trace the ways in which the political and aesthetic ambitions of the 1930s coalesce in three works published during World War II. In opening with *Between the Acts*, we will consider the novel as Woolf's reply to the social necessity of producing art that speaks to the contemporary moment and strives to negotiate the thin line between barbarism and civilization, between ignorance and accountability, between public and private.

FOR FURTHER CONSIDERATION: SUGGESTED READING

The 1930s

Baxendale, John, and Christopher Pawling. *Narrating the Thirties*. London: Palgrave Macmillan, 1995.

Bergonzi, Bernard. *Reading the Thirties*. London: Macmillan, 1978.

Carter, Ronald (ed.). *Thirties Poets: The Auden Group*. London: Macmillan, 1984.

Cunningham, Valentine. *British Writers of the Thirties*. Oxford: Oxford University Press, 1988.

Deane, Patrick (ed.). *History in Our Hands: A Critical Anthology of Writings on Literature, Culture and Politics from the 1930s*. Leicester: Leicester University Press, 1998.

Hynes, Samuel. *The Auden Generation: Literature and Politics in England in the 1930s*. London: Bodley Head, 1976.

Miller, Tyrus. *Late Modernism: Politics, Fiction, and the Arts Between the World Wars*. Berkeley: University of California Press, 1999.

Muggeridge, Malcolm. *The Thirties*. London: Hamish Hamilton, 1940.

Shuttleworth, Antony (ed.). *And In Our Time: Vision, Revision, and British Writing of the 1930s*. London: Associated University Press, 2003.

Spender, Stephen. *The Thirties and After: Poetry, Politics, People*. London: Fontana, 1978.

Williams, Keith and Steven Matthews (eds). *Rewriting the Thirties*. London: Longman, 1997.

W.H. Auden

Bahlke George (ed.). *Critical Essays on W.H. Auden*. New York: G. K. Hall, 1991.

Bell, Kathleen. 'Auden, Isherwood, and the Censors,' *W.H. Auden Society Newsletter* 10.11 (1993): 15–21.

Hynes, Samuel. *The Auden Generation: Literature and Politics in England in the 1930s*. New York: Viking, 1977.

McDiarmid, Lucy. *Saving Civilization: Yeats, Eliot, and Auden Between the Wars*. Cambridge: Cambridge University Press, 1984.

Rainer, Emig. *W.H. Auden: Towards a Postmodern Poetics*. London: Macmillan, 2000.

Documentary

Aitken, Ian. *Film and Reform: John Grierson and the Documentary Film Movement*. London: Routledge, 1990.

Bryant, Marsha. *Auden and Documentary in the 1930s*. Charlottesville: University of Virginia Press, 1997.

Grierson, John. *Grierson on Documentary.* Forsyth Hardy (ed.). London: Faber, 1966.

MacDonald, Kevin and Mark Cousins (eds). *Imagining Reality: The Faber Book of the Documentary.* London: Faber, 1998.

Nichols, Bill. 'Documentary Film and the Modernist Avant-Garde,' *Critical Inquiry* 27 (Summer 2001) 580–610.

Drama

Innes, C. D. *Modern British Drama.* Cambridge: Cambridge University Press, 2002.

Willet, John (ed.). *Brecht on Theatre.* London: Methuen, 1964.

George Orwell

Bluemel, Kristin. *George Orwell and the Radical Eccentrics: Intermodernism in Literary London.* New York: Palgrave Macmillan, 2004.

Cushman, Thomas and John Rodden. *George Orwell: Into the Twenty-first Century.* Boulder CO: Paradigm, 2004

Laity, Paul (ed.). *Left Book Club: Anthology.* London: Gollancz, 2001.

Orwell, George. *Orwell in Spain.* Peter Davison (ed.). London: Penguin, 2001.

NOTES

1 Oswald Mosley began his political career as a Conservative MP for Harrow in 1918, crossing the floor to sit as an Independent, then joining the Labour Party in 1924. He was well connected to the British establishment socially—his first wife was Lady Cynthia Curzon, the daughter of a Viceroy of India—their 1920 wedding had been the social event of the season. She died in 1933, and Mosley married his long time mistress Diana Guinness, one of the famous Mitford sisters, at the home of Josef Goebbels in 1936 with Adolf Hitler in attendance as an honoured guest. As a member of parliament and through his marriages, Mosley had access to the elite British social and political circles of the day and the impact of his activities within these circles has long been the subject of considerable speculation.

2 Auden recommended writers and plays from a wide historical cross-section: classical—Aeschylus and Aristophanes; medieval—the Wakefield Nativity Plays and *Everyman*; Elizabethan—Christopher Marlowe and Ben Jonson; eighteenth century—George Lillo; nineteenth century—Henrik Ibsen; and modern—Bertolt Brecht and Jean Cocteau. See Edward Mendelson's *Plays and Other Dramatic Writings by W.H. Auden, 1928–1938* (Princeton: Princeton University Press, 1988) 495–6 for a complete list of materials recommended by Auden.

3 The *Criterion* was published between 1921 and 1938. For background on Eliot's influential publication see Jason Harding's *The 'Criterion': Cultural Politics and Periodical Networks in Interwar Britain* (Oxford: Oxford University Press, 2002).

4 As quoted in M.J. Sidnell, 'Auden and the Group Theatre,' in *Plays and Other Dramatic Writings by W.H. Auden,* 491–2.

5 Peter McDonald, 'Believing in the Thirties,' in Keith Williams and Steven Matthews (eds), *Rewriting the Thirties: Modernism and After* (London: Longman, 1997) 71.

6 Tyrus Miller, *Late Modernism: Politics, Fiction, and the Arts Between the World Wars* (Berkeley: University of California Press, 1999) 226. See also Bill Nichols, 'Documentary Film and the Modernist Avant-Garde,' *Critical Inquiry* 27 (Summer 2001) 580–610. Montage is a technique used primarily in film, but also in the visual arts and literature, in which the artist combines existing images to form a larger, unified picture. The technique is closely associated with the Russian filmmaker Sergei Eisenstein (1898–1948), best known for the silent films *Battleship Potemkin* (1925) and *Oktober* (1927).

7 The term Realism was first used in France during the 1850s to describe novels that represented the world as it is rather than as it ought to be. Realist novels and plays are recognizable by verisimilitude of setting, coherence of characters, contemporary problems, and use of prosaic dialogue. Naturalism refers to the scientifically based extension of realism advocated by Émile Zola in the late 1870s. Naturalist writers incorporate scientific theories into their readings of human character and social interactions. The individual's struggle to adapt to historically determined circumstances is the central concern of naturalistic fiction and drama. In contradistinction to realist drama, naturalistic drama takes a more explicit interest in environment, not merely as setting, but as an element of action. Swedish playwright August Strindberg gave his naturalistic plays a psychological basis, and examined his characters' innermost workings at a level of symbolic elemental action. *Miss Julie* (1888) mixes an emphasis on heredity and environment with vacillating characters and meandering dialogue in order to draw attention to schematic patterns and mythic references that take the literal into the realm of the symbolic. Strindberg's later plays (*The Burned House*, 1907, and *The Ghost Sonata*, 1907) moved away from an expressly naturalist framework and influenced the development of expressionist and absurdist theatre in the early twentieth century.

8 Georg Lúkacs, 'The Ideology of Modernism,' in E. San Juan, Jr. (ed.), *Marxism and Human Liberation* (New York: Delta Books, 1973) 294–5.

9 Lúkacs 304.

10 First published in 1934, *Left Review* was the official organ of the British Writers' International.

11 Stephen Spender, 'Fable and Reportage,' *Left Review* 2 (November 1936) 782.

12 As quoted in Keith Williams, 'Post/Modern Documentary: Orwell, Agee and the New Reportage,' in *Rewriting the Thirties: Modernism and After* 166. Auden made six films with the GPO Film Unit: *Coal Face* (1935), *Beside the Sea Side* (1935), *Night Mail* (1936), *The Way to the Sea* (1937), *The Londoners* (1939), and *God's Chillun* (1939).

13 Samuel Hynes, *The Auden Generation: Literature and Politics in the 1930s* (London: Faber, 1979) 214.

14 Marsha Bryant, *Auden and the Documentary in the 1930s* (Charlottesville: University Press of Virginia, 1997) 48.

15 Auden, *Plays and Other Dramatic Writings* 423.

16 Hynes 212–13.

17 Hynes 228.

18 Tyrus Miller, *Late Modernism* 24.

19 Miller 20.

20 Miller 20

21 W.H. Auden, 'XXIV' in Edward Mendelson (ed.), *The English Auden* (London: Faber, 1977) 157. Auden did not give titles to most of his early poems; instead he gave them numbers. Critics typically refer to these numbered poems by their first lines, in lieu of a title. The first line of this poem is 'August for the people and their favourite islands.'

22 Auden, *The English Auden* 157.

23 Hynes 13.

24 Hynes 13.

25 Hynes 160.

26 Stephen Spender, 'Writers and Manifestos,' *Left Review* (February 1935) 145.

27 Stephen Spender, *The Destructive Element* (London: Cape, 1935) 278.

28 Spender 223.

29 Spender 279.

30 This short piece was written at the request of the Artists' International Association, which had been founded in 1933 in order to promote united action among artists and designers on social and political issues. They supported the Republican side in the Spanish Civil War, and contributed to the Artists' Refugee Committee through exhibitions and other fund-raising activities.

31 Woolf, 'The Crowded Dance of Modern Life,' Rachel Bowlby (ed.), *The Crowded Dance of Modern Life* (London: Penguin, 1993) 133.

32 Sebastian Faulks, 'Caught in the Web,' *Guardian* 24 September 2005.

33 Virginia Woolf, 'The Narrow Bridge of Art,' *Collected Essays II* (New York: Harcourt, 1967) 224.

34 Hermione Lee, *Virginia Woolf* (London: Chatto & Windus, 1996) 638.

35 Lee 638.

36 Virginia Woolf, 'The Leaning Tower,' *Collected Essays II* 175.

37 Stan Smith, 'Remembering Bryden's Bill: Modernism from Eliot to Auden,' *Rewriting the Thirties* 55.

38 Auden, *Plays and Other Dramatic Writings* xiv.

39 Expressionism was a continental rejection of realism in the arts and literature, based in Germany and Central Europe. Expressionist theatre was at its most vital between the first decade of the twentieth century and the mid-1920s. Expressionist playwrights sought to verbalize emotions as opposed to dramatizing conflicts. Character development is frequently less important than the construction of schematized types that capture the play's emotional tone and primary themes. The plays took up subjects as varied as conflict between the sexes, different classes and generations as well as taboo topics such as incest and patricide. As befits a movement indebted to the visual arts, expressionist plays make use of bold lighting, innovative stage design and blocking, garish colours, and distorted architecture. Epic theatre, in turn, is best described as a reaction against the expressionist focus on emotion. The essential point of epic theatre was that it appealed less to feelings than to the audience's reason. The following stage devices are associated with epic theatre: half-curtain, half-masks, summary projections, limited use of props, visible stage-machinery, songs punctuating the action, and 'cool' or estranged acting.

40 Bertolt Brecht, *Brecht on Theatre*, John Willet (ed.) (London: Methuen, 1964) 204. The alienation effect was a key element in Brecht's theory of drama; according to Brecht, the audience and actors should preserve a state of critical detachment from the play and its presentation in performance. The alienation

effect requires that the audience be reminded that they are watching a play and should therefore control their identification with the characters and action. Likewise, the actors should keep a kind of distance from the parts that they are interpreting. The ensuing sensation of estrangement arguably allows the audience to better follow the work's didactic effect.

41 William Stott, *Documentary Expression and Thirties America* (Oxford: Oxford University Press, 1973) 33, 14.

42 On 29 May 1953 New Zealander Sir Edmund Hillary and Sherpa Tenzing Norgay became the first men to successfully summit Mt Everest.

43 Hynes 237.

44 Auden, *Plays and Other Dramatic Writings* 314.

45 The early versions of the play emphasize that Ransom and his followers die as victims of their pride and ambition. The revised ending—written after the outbreak of the Spanish Civil War—implies that Ransom's fate is less his own responsibility than the result of being driven by his followers and victimized by the lies of government officials.

46 The play was published on 27 October 1938. Keynes' production opened on 14 November 1938 for a limited run of one week. Rupert Doone directed. Benjamin Britten composed the music. On 12 February 1939, the production moved to London for a single Sunday performance at the Globe Theatre.

47 W.H. Auden and Christopher Isherwood, *The Ascent of F6 and On the Frontier* (London: Faber, 1958) 166–7.

48 Auden and Isherwood 161.

49 Richard Hoggart, 'An Introductory Essay on *The Ascent of F6* and *On the Frontier*,' in George W. Bahlke (ed.), *Critical Essays on W.H. Auden* (New York: G.K. Hall, 1991) 66.

50 Auden and Isherwood 117.

51 Auden and Isherwood 142–3.

52 Auden and Isherwood 143.

53 Auden and Isherwood 150.

54 Auden and Isherwood 170.

55 Louis MacNeice, 'The Theatre,' *Spectator* (18 November 1938) 858.

56 Auden and Isherwood 186.

57 When writing *On the Frontier*, Auden and Isherwood would have been aware of Lady Diana Mitford—mistress and later wife of British Fascist leader Sir Oswald Mosley—and her sister Unity—who later attempted suicide when Britain declared war on Germany in 1939. The sisters were well–known for their friendship with Hitler and involvement in right-wing political causes.

58 Auden and Isherwood 187.

59 Auden and Isherwood 189.

60 Hynes, *The Auden Generation* 310–11.

61 Auden and Isherwood 190.

62 Francisco J. Romero Salvadó, *The Spanish Civil War* (London: Palgrave, 2005) ix.

63 The Nationalist supporters included monarchists, Carlists, Falangists (Fascists) and the Catholic church. The Republic side was primarily composed of socialists, communists, anarchists, Catalan and Basque nationalists, and moderates.

64 The aerial attack on the Basque city of Guernica on 26 April 1937 by the Condor Legion of the German Luftwaffe is one of the many bombings and battles associated with the Spanish Civil War. It is among the best known largely on account of Pablo Picasso's 1937 mural condemning the destruction of the city. The large mural—commissioned by the Republicans—was initially displayed in the Spanish Pavilion at the 1937 Paris International Exposition.

65 Julian Symons, 'Introduction,' *Homage to Catalonia*, Peter Davison (ed.) (London: Penguin, 1989) vi.

66 George Orwell, 'Letter to Victor Gollancz,' *Collected Essays, Journalism and Letters of George Orwell* vol. 1, Sonia Orwell and Ian Angus (eds) (New York: Harcourt Brace, 1968) 267.

67 George Orwell, 'Why I Joined the Independent Labour Party,' *Collected Essays* 336.

68 George Orwell, 'Letter to Stephen Spender,' *Collected Essays* 311.

69 Geoffrey Gorer, rev. of *Homage to Catalonia* in *Time and Tide* 30 April 1938 (599–600) 599.

70 Philip Mariet as reprinted in Jeffrey Meyers (ed.), *George Orwell: The Critical Heritage* (London: Routledge, 1975) 127.

71 Mairet 128.

72 George Orwell, *Homage to Catalonia*, Peter Davison (ed.) (London: Penguin, 2000) 2, 3, 186.

73 Appendix II was originally Chapter XI. Not without controversy, Peter Davison's 1986 edition of *Homage to Catalonia* revises the book according to the notes that Orwell left his Literary Executor just before he died in January 1950. The most significant changes are the removal of chapters V and XI from the book for repositioning as appendixes at the end of the book, where—according to Davison—Orwell considered it more appropriate to place a historical and political discussion of what otherwise was a personal account of his experiences. This arrangement has not been adopted in subsequent American editions of *Homage to Catalonia*.

74 Orwell, *Homage to Catalonia* 216.

75 Orwell, *Homage to Catalonia* 156, 157.

76 Orwell, *Homage to Catalonia* 186.

77 Antony Shuttleworth, 'The Real George Orwell: Dis-simulation in *Homage to Catalonia* and *Coming Up for Air*,' in Antony Shuttleworth (ed.), *And In Our Time: Vision, Revision, and British Writing of the 1930s* (London: Associated University Press, 2003) 208.

78 Keith Williams, 'Post/Modern Documentary: Orwell, Agee and the New Reportage,' in *Rewriting the Thirties: Modernism and After* 165.

79 Britain declared war on Germany on 3 September 1939.

80 Gillian Beer, 'Introduction,' *Between the Acts* by Virginia Woolf (London: Penguin, 1992) x. The pageant is intended to raise funds for the illumination of the village church; ironically, however, as readers in the 1940s would have known, the blackout was just about to be imposed and fittingly the novel ends 'in the heart of darkness, in the fields of night' (129).

81 For further insight into Woolf's incorporation of actual newspaper clippings see Karin E. Westman, '"For her generation the newspaper was a book": Media, Mediation, and Oscillation in Virginia Woolf's *Between the Acts*,' *Journal of Modern Literature* 29: 2 (Winter 2006) 1–18.

A LITERARY CODA

IN THE MIDST OF WAR

A Modernist Chronology—1940–5

Arts & Literature	Historical Events
1940 W.H. Auden, *Another Time* T.S. Eliot, 'East Coker' Graham Greene, *The Power and the Glory*	Chamberlain resigns and Churchill becomes Prime Minister Hitler invades France Channel Islands occupied by Germany Battle of Britain fought in the skies of southern England The Blitz begins
1941 W.H. Auden, *Three Songs for St Cecilia's Day* T.S. Eliot, 'The Dry Salvages' Virginia Woolf, *Between the Acts*	*Daily Worker* banned Scottish cities bombed Hitler invades the Soviet Union Japanese bomb Pearl Harbor and invade Hong Kong and Malaya United States enters the war
1942 T.S. Eliot, 'Little Gidding'	Singapore falls to Japan Britain fights the Germans and Italians in North Africa for control of the Eastern Mediterranean, oil, and the Suez Canal
1943 Henry Green, *Caught*	Tunis falls to Allies ending the North African campaign RAF 'dambusters' breach Ruhr dams Sicily invaded by Allies RAF raids on Hamburg kill thousands of civilians
1944 W.H. Auden, *For the Time Being* H.D., *The Walls Do Not Fall* T.S. Eliot, *Four Quartets* Somerset Maugham, *The Razor's Edge*	Allies enter Rome D-Day landings in Normandy De Gaulle enters Paris Allies recognize De Gaulle's administration as the official French government
1945 Bertolt Brecht, *The Caucasian Chalk Circle* Benjamin Britten, *Peter Grimes* H.D., *Tribute to the Angels* Henry Green, *Loving* George Orwell, *Animal Farm*	British troops liberate Belsen concentration camp Yalta conference between Churchill, Roosevelt, and Stalin V-E Day celebrations on 8 May mark official end of war in Europe Atomic bombs dropped on Hiroshima and Nagasaki V-J Day celebrations on 15 August mark official end of war in the Pacific

As the 1940s began, the anxieties of the '20s and '30s about the likelihood of another war were justified, as Europe was engulfed in the twentieth century's second world war. This was a war unlike the Great War, however, since modern technology meant that civilians were caught up in the conflict in never imagined ways. Nightly bombing raids took place on both sides of the English Channel; the bombs made no distinctions between military and civilian targets, and many civilians spent their nights in bomb shelters and the mornings after digging through rubble to find survivors or the dead. For the first years of the war, the British fought almost alone against Hitler and his allies, bearing the brunt of the war—economically as well as in terms of casualties and the destruction of British infrastructure. However, the tide turned in 1941 when Germany's ally Japan bombed Pearl Harbor in Hawaii, drawing the United States into the conflict. From that point onward, the two nations and their allies worked in tandem to defeat Hitler and his allies.

Victory came in Europe in May 1945 and in the Pacific in August 1945. But victory came at a steep price—the war in the Pacific had ended after the dropping of atomic bombs on Hiroshima and Nagasaki, bringing warfare to an unimagined level of barbarity. Britain, which had begun the century as the pre-eminent world power, would find itself at the conclusion of World War II in a much-diminished position. The costs of rebuilding the nation's infrastructure that had been heavily damaged during the six years of conflict would prove a significant postwar challenge. India, its largest colony, was, after continued bloodshed and political infighting, to declare independence in 1947. The sub-continent was divided along religious lines—Hindu India and Muslim Pakistan—thus sowing the seeds of future sectarian conflict. Other colonies were also to gain independence in the next few decades. Though commentators declared the beginning of a new Elizabethan era when Elizabeth II ascended the throne in 1952, the realm over which she was to reign was significantly different from the realm over which her great grandmother Queen Victoria had reigned some fifty years previously.

The war years saw the deaths of several leading modernists—W.B. Yeats in 1939; James Joyce in January of 1941; and Virginia Woolf in March of 1941. However, other first-generation modernists produced important work in the 1940s—Eliot's *Four Quartets* and H.D.'s *Trilogy*, for example. Some second-generation modernists, such as W.H. Auden and George Orwell, were actively involved in the war effort, while others, such as Christopher Isherwood, proclaimed pacifist views.[1] Most of the second-generation modernists continued to write throughout the '40s, with Auden's output including his Pulitzer Prize winning *The Age of Anxiety* (1947). Despite the upheaval of the war, then, modernists continued to write and continued to challenge themselves and their readers. This chapter will look at what form that writing took. It will then look beyond the modernists themselves to the ways in which the literature they produced and the movement they proclaimed have been analyzed, debated, and canonized by three generations of critics.

MODERNISM'S JANUS FACE

In his 1863 essay 'The Painter of Modern Life,' Charles Baudelaire infamously celebrated 'the painter of the passing moment and of all the suggestions of eternity that it contains.' He went on to declare that by modernity he meant 'the ephemeral, the fugitive, the contingent, the half of art whose other half is the eternal and the immutable.'[2] The Janus-faced proclivities of the modern writer are evident in the three works under scrutiny in the Coda with their profoundly intimate interest in the moment of composition as grounded in contemporary history and the wider status of a work of art during times of conflict. Under the searchlights of a Britain at war, Virginia Woolf wrote her final novel—*Between the Acts* (1941); T.S. Eliot his last poem—*Four Quartets* (1943); and H.D. her epic masterpiece—*Trilogy* (1944–1946).[3] However, shortly before Europe plunged back into war, there was a less momentous event that—in its own way—signalled another Janus-faced moment of relevance to the story of modernism. During the summer of 1938, T.S. Eliot announced that the *Criterion* would no longer be published. First published in 1921, Eliot's literary review had swiftly established itself as an important force in the inter-war literary critical scene. In retrospect, this announcement formally marked the end of an era and set it against a new note in modernism variously labelled late, blitz or war modernism.

Terminology aside, this phase in the history of British modernism emerges as a moment during which three writers closely identified with high modernist experimentation engage in sustained meditations on history, tradition, and the role of the creator or artist. To engage with the 'war' work of H.D., Eliot, and Woolf is to examine these three writers' highly individual responses to a conflict from which none of them chose to absent themselves. Instead all three writers remained in the south of England during the war and, in turn, experienced the very real dangers that this presented to civilians. Throughout this chapter, we will explore how the commitment to social commentary and political engagement evident in the critical and creative work of the 1930s finds continued expression in the mature works of Woolf, Eliot, and H.D.

THE CURTAIN ROSE

Woolf's final novel *Between the Acts* (1941) does not offer conclusions. There is no one lesson learned, no one moral illustrated, in this

163

story of a village pageant held on a warm summer's afternoon weeks before the beginning of World War II. The pageant ends, the audience disperses, the playwright Miss La Trobe contemplates her next piece of work, and the day with which the novel began comes to a close in an inconclusive evening scene: 'The curtain rose. They spoke.'[4] It little matters that we do not know what Giles and Isa Oliver are about to say to each other. What matters is that they are speaking. In this sense, the novel is an exploration of the dialogic nature of ritual, repetition, and renewal—a form of patterning central to H.D.'s war epic *Trilogy* and T.S. Eliot's long poem *Four Quartets*.

In keeping with Woolf's own experiments throughout the 1930s and the work of other writers examined in Chapter 4, *Between the Acts* breaks down boundaries between genres—novel and pageant—as well as the boundary between audience and actor. Or as one of the pageant goers puts it, 'Our part . . . is to be the audience. And a very important part too.'[5] In this sense, it is a richly inclusive novel into which the reader enters: audience and actors play an equal part as the novel moves between the scenes on the stage and all that takes place off stage where there is almost as much acting and performing as there is in Miss La Trobe's pageant. The cornerstone of *Between the Acts* is its mix of dramatic pageantry and poetic prose—a combination through which Woolf rejects the individual in favour of the communal.

A 1938 journal entry described the novel as the story of 'we' not 'I' wherein we is 'composed of many different things . . . we [is] all life, all art, all waifs and strays—a rambling capricious but somehow unified whole.'[6] As befits a novel that declines to account for a single unified consciousness, *Between the Acts* playfully and mischievously borrows from a variety of genres and traditions—stretching and testing the formal limits of not only the genre of the novel, but also of genre itself:

> Woolf's mingling of genres, aspiration towards a plural narrator, and detailed attention to forms of laughter occur, significantly, in a novel about a village pageant, a survival of a folk carnival form. Woolf's search for plural and anonymous narrators, in this novel and the uncompleted 'Anon,' represents a departure from the modernist emphasis on individual consciousness.[7]

Like Auden and Isherwood who similarly adapted a wide array of literary traditions in order to explore the complexity of the communal voice, Woolf does not draft a portrait of the modern soul in isolation. Indeed, Woolf is writing at a point in European history during which it is highly difficult to ignore the roles of different communities in the perpetuation of culture *and* violence. In kind, *Between the Acts* refuses simple binaries like right and wrong, good and evil, English and German.

Woolf began writing *Between the Acts* during the final months of a peace that most Europeans had long expected to be shattered. Even with the advent of war, she refused to consider conflict from an exclusively English perspective in which the Germans and Italians were irretrievably evil and the Allies were righteous defenders of goodness. This ambivalent treatment of warring nations has much in common with the sentiments expressed in *On the Frontier* (1938) in its portrait of warring Ostnia and Westland and their equally obtuse and blinkered citizens and Orwell's anger regarding the lies and misinformation offered up in the English media's reports on the Spanish Civil War. Written in 1940, Woolf's essay 'Thoughts on Peace in an Air Raid' poses a simple but powerful question: 'what is the use of freeing the young Englishman' from the shackles of war 'if the young German and the young Italian remain slaves' to the ideology and blood lust that unquestioningly accepts the inevitability of war in the quest for power and wealth? Woolf was convinced that no one person, no one country, could stand alone:

> The Germans were over this house last night and the night
> before that. Here they are again. It is a queer experience, lying
> in the dark and listening to the zoom of a hornet which may at
> any moment sting you to death. Yet it is a sound—far more
> than prayers and anthems—that should compel one to think
> about peace. Unless we can think peace into existence we—not
> this one body in this one bed but millions of bodies yet to be
> born—will lie in the same darkness and hear the same death
> rattle overhead.[8]

Woolf frames thinking peace into existence as a task that must be undertaken communally: 'Unless *we* can think peace into existence. . . *we* will lie in the same darkness and hear the same death rattle overhead.'[9] A few paragraphs later she affirms what the reader has likely intuited, 'we' does not exclusively refer to generation upon generation of English citizens willing a new mode of being in existence—'we' must also include Germans:

> One of the pilots landed safe in a field near here the other day.
> He said to his captors, speaking fairly good English, 'How glad
> I am that the fight is over!' Then an Englishman gave him a
> cigarette, and an Englishwoman made him a cup of tea. That
> would seem to show that if you can free the man from the
> machine, the seed does not fall upon altogether stony ground.
> The seed may be fertile.[10]

Woolf asks that the readers conceive of the enemy as a person. She also demands that we conceive of this man as capable of allegiance to constructs other than fighting. Here, as in much of Woolf's work, there is no one single method by which any one person or community can be categorized or interpreted. Freed of the instruments of war and removed from the arena of combat, a soldier is a man capable of expressing relief.

As a result, although critics have read *Between the Acts* as a straightforward political text occupied with familiar binaries such as public and private, professional and domestic, male and female, to do so runs the risk of judging the novel on its ability to negotiate such (false) divisions. Woolf is writing against the impulse to focus on a 'single fundamental political purpose or psychological (or transcendental) effect of narratives, whether it be to reflect reality or to supplement it, to reinforce ruling ideologies or to subvert them.'[11] Or as Andrew Miller argues, '*Between the Acts* cannot be adequately described in terms of repression or subversion, affirmation or negation, revolution or reaction.'[12] The novel draws attention to the degree that Woolf's critique of society rests on a willingness to abandon 'the possibility of a cultural history with a destination.'[13] She resists grand narratives and refuses to ascribe any kind of privilege to one historical period, character, or reader.

For example, in the village pageant around which *Between the Acts* revolves, era after era gives way to yet another. However, the novel refuses to celebrate the age in which the pageant is situated as the triumphant realization of all man's progress. Woolf does away with the finale in which the Grand Ensemble takes the stage to celebrate the nation's economic might, military power, and cultural superiority as was customary in Empire Day pageants. Instead, Woolf presents history as 'a cycle of which the audience is the end, and, as the last page indicates, the beginning as well.'[14] The reader is also made well aware of a double focus on history and audience: there is history and audience as depicted within the novel, which, in turn, are further framed by history and audience as negotiated outside the narrative. While the story recounted within the novel takes place in a twenty-four hour period, its force emanates from the double focus and its ability to invoke all time stretching back to when the busy streets of Piccadilly were crowded with massive rhododendron forests and

> when the entire continent, not then, [Lucy] understood, divided
> by a channel, was all one; populated, she understood, by
> elephant-bodied, seal-necked, heaving, surging, slowly
> writhing, and, she supposed, barking monsters; the iguanodon,
> the mammoth, and the mastodon; from whom presumably, she
> thought, jerking the window open, we descend.[15]

Whether by way of Lucy Swithin's imaginative acts of reading or the pageant itself, *Between the Acts* explores how we read the present into our evolving view of history.

Isa Oliver can remember seven pageants—one for each year of her marriage to Giles Oliver. However, the tradition of a village pageant extends into a past well beyond what Isa can recollect; this is made plain by the nearby Roman road that 'you could still see, plainly marked' along with 'the scars made by the Britons; by the Romans; by the Elizabethan manor house; and by plough, when they ploughed the hill to grow wheat in the Napoleonic wars.'[16] The English pageant tradition evolved out of rituals adopted during the Roman occupation of Britain—a history that also suggests the form has long been associated with political will and tyranny. In medieval times, pageants were incorporated into the Church calendar as ecclesiastical officials became increasingly attuned to the power of shared and regularly repeated rituals. In turn, pageants celebrating civic duty and the state became increasingly commonplace in the Renaissance with coronations and investitures celebrated on a spectacular scale. Elizabeth I, in particular, did much to advance Tudor political pageantry with her spectacular coronation celebrations in 1559.

Importantly, pageants can be readily adapted for political purposes on account of their largely plotless form and dependence on ritualistic symbols and music to express unifying moralistic (or nationalistic) themes. A pageant affirms the place of an audience within a specific community; in bearing witness to the spectacle, the audience is invited to consume tradition as conceived by the authorities sanctioning and backing the event. Year after year, audiences are gathered to affirm the importance of shared values and beliefs or individuals elevated by the proceedings, whether the unifying force is a young Tudor monarch or the German National Socialist party in the 1930s. Hitler, like centuries of rulers—dictators, monarchs, and popes—before him, took advantage of the propaganda power of pageantry: 'To achieve the goal of creating the [Fascist] folk community (identified with structure), the Third Reich redefined every occasion which used to offer the people a taste of *communitas*, or release them from official structure: folk celebrations, religious ritual and art' for their own purposes.[17]

Marlowe Miller has convincingly argued that Virginia and Leonard Woolf were acutely aware of the parallels between British historical pageants and modern day fascist spectacles. In 1931, Leonard wrote of the great political dangers stemming from 'the psychology of modern patriotism'—that is, from the psychological error of identifying 'not [with] a community of individuals' but instead with 'a communal abstraction—one's country.'[18] *Between the Acts*, in turn, subverts the pageant tradition in order to draw attention to the hollow abstractions upon which the present's understanding of the past and contemporary reality are founded. The violence of the past and the latest looming conflict invade the pastoral present through a montage of shadows and scars from the past, snippets of newspaper reports, the roar of planes overhead, and the actions of the characters themselves. By choosing to frame the novel within the events of a single day, Woolf can write a condensed and anything but conventional history pageant.

Woolf's Miss La Trobe is a playwright in the manner of Auden and Isherwood who likewise were of the conviction that their responsibilities as playwrights were limited to jarring the audience into action as opposed to prescribing the actions they should take in response to their call. If any one theme can be assigned to the pageant, it is the repeated insistence on refusing and frustrating pageant conventions and audience expectations. There is no celebration of the glory of England or the sovereign. Once the pageant has begun, the audience initially settles in comfortably when they recognize 'Queen Elizabeth.' The pageant begins by deliberately tugging on common sentiment and a 'pride of nationality in the first place; also of religious pride, college pride, school pride, family pride, sex pride and those unreal loyalties that spring from them.'[19] But Miss La Trobe refuses to let her audience become too comfortable 'celebrating familiar symbols like the "Virgin Queen" or "Merry England" because the pageant reveals instead the labour and the lives that sustain these symbols, both literally and figuratively.'

In this way, La Trobe's pageant performs the same function for which Woolf praises Chaucer: both Chaucer's poetry and La Trobe's pageant wrap their 'doctrines in flesh and blood and make a complete model of the world without excluding the bad or laying stress upon the good. We do not have a simple symbol in Eliza/Elizabeth, but a message in "flesh and blood".'[20] The audience sees the stage figure as both Queen Elizabeth and 'Eliza Clark, licensed to sell tobacco.' Queen Elizabeth's prestige, in part, was advanced by the wealth of her colonies, which included the tobacco-rich plantations of the Virginias.[21] Over the centuries, the contributions of 'Eliza Clarks' throughout the kingdom and empire have ensured the continuing glory of England and the monarchy—a reliance exposed by Miss La Trobe's casting and costuming that does not mask the player beyond recognition. The audience asks, 'Who was she? What did she represent? . . . England was she? Queen Anne was she? Who was she?'[22]

The impossibility of answering these questions is evident by way of the narrative's insistence that no one character has a stable true self but rather all have selves which change depending on the context and angle of vision. Early in the novel, Isa is seated in front of her 'three-folded mirror' in which she can 'see three separate versions of her rather heavy, yet handsome face.' Correspondingly, for each version of her face, there is a separate version of love: 'in love,' or inner love, 'in the eyes' which corresponds with her feelings for the gentleman farmer Rupert Haines; there is outer lover 'on the dressing table' which corresponds with her home and the role of wife as expressed by her marriage to Giles Oliver; and then there is that third 'feeling . . . that stirred in her now when . . . she saw coming across the lawn the perambulator . . . and her little boy George.'[23] Isa is not the only person capable of assessing these subtle shifts. Woolf takes care to illustrate the (potential) transparency of such shifts, as is evident when William Dodge watches Isa during the intermission:

> [H]e saw her face change, as if she had got out of one dress and put on another. A small boy battled his way through the crowd, striking against shirts and trousers as if he were swimming blindly. . . . He made a bee-line for her. He was her little boy, apparently, her son, her George. She gave him cake; then a mug of milk. Then Nurse came up. Then again she changed her dress. This time, from the expression in her eyes it was apparently something in the nature of a strait waistcoat. Hirsute, handsome, virile, the young man in the blue jacket and brass buttons, standing in a beam of dusty light, was her husband. And she was his wife. Their relations, as he had noted at lunch, were as people say in novels 'strained'. As he had noted at the play, her bare arm had raised itself nervously to her shoulder when she turned—looking for whom?[24]

Mother. Wife. In love. William notes the 'three-folded' changes—interrelated yet separate self-identifications that Isa so easily and almost unconsciously performs as George, Giles, and Rupert move in and out of her consciousness.

As Christopher Ames suggests, the entire novel is characterized by an overarching interest in change of all kinds:

> Were [the fish] a bit whiffy? Mrs. Sands held them to her nose. The cat rubbed itself this way, that way against the table legs, against her legs. She would save a slice for Sunny—his drawing-room name Sung-Yen had undergone a kitchen change into Sunny. She took them, the cat attendant, to the larder, and laid them on a plate in that semi-ecclesiastical apartment. For the house before the Reformation, like so many houses in that neighbourhood, had a chapel; and the chapel had become a larder, changing like a cat's name, as religion changed. The Master (his drawing-room name; in the kitchen they called him Bartie) would bring gentlemen sometimes to see the larder— often when cook wasn't dressed.[25]

The passage encompasses linguistic change, historical change, religious change, and the alterations of perspective attendant on changes in social class: '[a]ll of these changes are figured in the pageant as well, where workers impersonate clergy and royalty, and secularization advances through the Restoration and Victorian playlets.'[26]

Even the audience is forced to entertain change. The pageant goers watch the stage expectantly with the assumption that their beliefs and views will be affirmed and upheld by the play. Colonel Mayhew and his wife anticipate that the Army, Navy, Union Jack, and the Church—the markers by which they have lived—will be foregrounded throughout the pageant. Their expectations, however, are thwarted and the colonel, baffled by the choice of scenes, wonders, 'Why leave out the British Army? What's history without the Army, eh?'[27] History as told through the national corporate identity offers a clear-cut identity to which an individual can attach himself, especially a man such as Colonel Mayhew whose adult life has been devoted to the military. His search for the army in each vignette exposes the correlation between nationalism and war. Colonel Mayhew has much in common with 'the red-nosed Turtons and Burtons'—the Anglo-Indian governing class—who must unquestioningly believe in the British administration of India in order to remain secure and confident in their purpose. *A Passage to India* and *Between the Acts* both expose the limits of monologic discourse, and instead favour endings that insist upon the value of diversity and exchange. In the absence of a pageant with pious themes and battles, the audience cannot complacently consume the pageant. The very structure of the pageant forces the audience to make meaning for themselves by way of responding to their bewilderment and discomfort.

The pageant climaxes when Miss La Trobe plunges her unprepared audience into the glaring dazzling flashing present. The spectacle before them is no longer the past, but instead the present before they have the opportunity to assume their customary parts. Suddenly, the reality of their own unhappiness and confused responses to Miss La Trobe's pageant is on offer as opposed to the anticipated celebration of transcendent values around which a nation can rally. The desire for such an ending renders the audience complicit with the tyrannies that a conventional pageant reinforces. Waiting expectantly 'their nerves … on edge,' the audience sits 'exposed' never anticipating how their anxiety shall be answered. The stage becomes a sea of glass:

> Mopping, mowing, whisking, frisking, the looking glasses
> darted, flashed, exposed. . . . And Lord! the jangle and the din!
> The very cows joined in. Walloping, tail lashing, the reticence
> of nature was undone, and the barriers which should divide Man
> the Master from the Brute were dissolved.[28]

The division between man and nature is undone in the fragmented view offered by the sea of hand glasses, tin cans, scraps of scullery glass, harness room glass, and heavily embossed silver mirrors held up towards the audience by the cast. The different means by which the reflections themselves are created draw yet further attention to competing forms of vision—kitchen implements versus lady's boudoir versus stable block: these conventional boundaries are destabilized by the art of the play. Her one concession to convention occurs when the silence and discomfort of an audience unsure as how best to act their part are broken by an anonymous voice: 'But before they had come to any common conclusions, a voice asserted itself. Whose voice it was no one knew. It came from the bushes—a megaphonic, anonymous, loud-speaking affirmation.'[29]

The anonymous voice suggests the tyranny of mass communication, but what the voice begs of the audience is that it ceases to unthinkingly accept the self-identifications that it has come to accept so passively from various media outlets. The voice asks that the audience 'break the rhythm and forget the rhyme. And calmly consider ourselves.'[30] The voice includes itself in the call not to hide behind accepted 'truths'—such as the 'virtue in those that have grown white hairs'—and instead

> [c]onsider the gun slayers, bomb droppers here or there. They do openly what we do slyly. . . . O we're all the same. Take myself now. Do I escape my own reprobation, simulating indignation, in the bush, among the leaves? There's a rhyme, to suggest, in spite of protestation and the desire for immolation, I too have had some, what's called education. . . . Look at ourselves, ladies and gentlemen![31]

The voice vows that no one can offer statements—or solutions—that lie outside personal, social, or political bias. The pageant asks, why not look and ask questions yourself? In the end, Miss La Trobe's take on a village pageant is a critique of unquestioning acceptance—a critique of passivity: the pageant explores 'the art of making meaning, an act which is so fraught and so necessary, that this novel exhorts us all to engage in.'[32]

Although when thanking Miss La Trobe, the Rev. G.W. Streathfield struggles to make sense of what he has just watched, she is not a failed playwright. Her actors are reluctant to leave the terrace, and the dispersing audience responds to the beauty of the scene before them:

> Each still acted the unacted part conferred on them by their clothes. Beauty was on them. Beauty revealed them. Was it the light that did it?—the tender, the fading, the uninquisitive but searching light of evening that reveals depths in water and makes even the red brick bungalow radiant?

The snippets of conversation suggest flickerings of understanding in amongst the incomprehension: 'I thought it brilliantly clever . . . O my dear, I thought it utter bosh. Did *you* understand the meaning? Well, he said she meant we all act all parts . . . He said, too, if I caught his meaning, Nature takes part . . . .'[33] William Dodge pauses to thank her in the company of Mrs Swithin who had exclaimed pleasure in the play's ability to stir in her her 'unacted part' during the interval.[34] Her play 'can be judged a success if we think not of what she has taught the community but of how she has stimulated them to think.'[35] And Miss La Trobe, in spite of her initial doubts, finds future inspiration in the words of the cross-section of society who made up her cast when she sits in the village pub after the performance:

> She raised her glass to her lips. And drank. And listened. Words of one syllable sank down into the mud. She drowsed; she

> nodded. The mud became fertile. Words rose above the
> intolerably laden dumb oxen plodding through the mud. Words
> without meaning – wonderful words.[36]

She begins to imagine her next play: '[t]here was the high ground at midnight; there the rock; and two scarcely perceptible figures. Suddenly the tree was pelted with starlings. She set down her glass. She heard the first words.'[37]

A few hours later after dark, at the end of the day, Isa frets, 'Love and hate—how they tore her asunder! Surely it was time someone invented a new plot, or that the author came out of the bushes.'[38] But neither Miss La Trobe nor Virginia Woolf will come out from under the bushes. Miss La Trobe, like Woolf, works by dispersal. In the final pages of the novel, the stage is gradually cleared of other actors, leaving Isa and Giles alone together as the particularities of a June day slip away into a timeless repetition of enmity and love. Isa and Giles lose their individuality and become the dog fox and vixen 'in the heart of darkness' as they enact the beginning Miss La Trobe is contemplating in the pub: the house 'lost its shelter. It was night before roads were made, or houses. It was the night that dwellers in caves had watched from some high place among rocks. Then the curtain rose. They spoke.'[39] The next act is begun. Each story begets another and so assaults the spectre of a future in which the telling of stories has become impossible. Within the framework of the novel, Woolf's actors and her playwright continue to enter into communicative acts.

THE POET AS WAR CORRESPONDENT

H.D.'s poem *Trilogy* is a 'war poem' in the sense that *Between the Acts* is a 'war novel.' The poem is written both against the war and against the backdrop of the war. Expanding the terrain of Rebecca West's novel *The Return of the Soldier* (1918)—a non-combatant's response to World War I—H.D. and Woolf are writing during a moment in history when the non-combatant is more intimately and dangerously positioned within the lines of battle than ever before. As examples of what Marina MacKay has described as 'blitz modernism,' H.D. and Woolf make use of a modified documentary montage as they move between a factual and imaginative response to the historical moment in which they are located.[40] With *Trilogy*, in particular, the reader is intensely aware of the stress and strain of the physical realities in which the writer is entwined.

Trilogy marks all three sections of the book-length poem with an indication of the time and place of composition. From the opening line, the experience of living in London during the Blitz is registered throughout. The first book, 'The Walls Do Not Fall,' is dated London 1942—a period during the war where there was little or no sense of a possible victory or peace. In contrast, the second book, 'Tribute to the

Angels,' dated 17–31 May 1944, has been read as a putative peace poem. While the end of the war was not in sight, there was a sense of the Allies beginning to make ground against Nazi Germany. This reading is further strengthened by our retrospective recognition that the D-Day landings took place the week after H.D. completed 'Tribute to the Angels.' The third book, 'The Flowering of the Rod,' is dated 18–31 December 1944.[41] A Christmas poem of sorts, 'The Flowering of the Rod' is the least explicitly embedded in the physical reality of the war experience. It instead takes its thematic centre in images of transcendence and renewal. Sarah H.S. Graham argues that:

> By including these specific dates, H.D. suggests to the readers—significantly, at the end of their reading—that what they have experienced is not the war mediated by H.D.'s particular response, but the war itself, with H.D. merely as its conduit. Readers are thus reminded that this poetry is not concerned with the conventional notions of speaking to posterity from the enclaves of high art: this is the poet as war correspondent, reporting back from the civilian front line.[42]

The civilian front lines are woven into in the opening lines of 'The Walls Do Not Fall':

> An incident here and there,
> and rails gone (for guns)
> from your (and my) old town square.[43]

By invoking the shared experience and the indiscriminate reach of the bombings 'here and there,' H.D.'s epic poem begins with the invitation to understand that what follows is relevant to the readers themselves. The landscape of their daily lives has been transformed by war and, in turn, her poem speaks to this very experience at an immediate and trans-historical level. She puts the reader at the centre of the epic. By doing so, she distinctively reworks the epic tradition for her own purposes in much the same fashion that Woolf has disrupted the conventions associated with the pageant.

Traditionally, an epic is defined as a long narrative poem written in an elevated style recounting the exploits of legendary or divine characters and in doing so it centres on events of a cultural or national significance. The earliest epics were based on legends and stories preserved in oral traditions and later written down, such as Homer's *Illiad* and the Old English epic *Beowulf*. Modern epics are a written variant of the traditional form—the best-known example in English being Milton's *Paradise Lost* (1667). Here ten books of blank verse tell the story of the Fall of Man. Conventionally, epics begin with a statement of the poem's argument or subject matter, proceed to an invocation of a muse or divine source of inspiration, and then return to the central narrative. The opening lines in the first poem, 'The Walls Do Not Fall,' function in a similar fashion as they introduce the violence of

World War II and the historical cycles of destruction and ruin as the poem's subject:

> there, as here, ruin opens
> the tomb, the temple; enter,
> there as here, there are no doors:
>
> the shrine lies open to the sky,
> the rain falls, here, there
> sand drifts; eternity endures[44]

In a letter to Norman Holmes Pearson, she glossed the parallels between the London and Egypt at the beginning of 'The Walls Do Not Fall':

> The parallel between ancient Egypt and 'ancient' London is obvious. In [Section] 1 the 'fallen roof leaves the sealed room open to the air' is of course true of our own house of life—outer violence touching the deepest hidden subconscious terrors, etc., and we see so much of our past 'on show,' as it were 'another sliced wall where poor utensils show like rare objects in a museum.' Egypt? London? Mystery, majic [sic]—that I have found in London![45]

With the expansive terrain of the poem established, the speaker then moves on to the invocation of a divine source of inspiration:

> so, through our desolation
> thoughts stir, inspiration stalks us
> through gloom:
> unaware, Spirit announces the Presence;[46]

In full view of this divine presence, the poem returns to the central narrative—or more correctly, the central question—which animates the quest at the core of *Trilogy*: for what purpose has the 'bone-frame,' the 'skeleton,' withstood the 'terror' of war-time destruction:

> the flesh? it was melted away,
> the heart burnt out, dead ember,
> tendons, muscles shattered, outer husk dismembered
>
> yet the frame held:
> we passed the flame: we wonder
> what saved us? what for?[47]

Trilogy's three books emerge as a complex response to the deceptively simple question posed at the outset.

In striving to answer this question, H.D. offers her readers more than a personal response to World War II; she provides a visionary example of synthesis through which hope and resurrection might arise out of the Apocalypse:

> In no wise is the pillar-of-fire
> that went before

different from the pillar-of-fire
that comes after;

chasm, schism in consciousness
must be bridged over;[48]

With this call, H.D.'s double invocation of the 'pillar-of-fire' in Exodus and Revelation reminds readers that the Old and New Testament draw from a series of shared symbols; the New Testament reworks and modifies the stories of the Old Testament in symbolic expansion of meaning. In its evocation of a Judeo-Christian tradition alongside Egyptian and Greek pagan traditions, the entire poem functions as a 'palimpsest' in which it is possible to see the old writing—the old stories—under the new and expose 'what words conceal.'[49] The poem is, however, in no way prescriptive; instead, there is an overriding sense of deferring to a syncretic method and to whatever the work in its totality comes to suggest, as is signalled in the final section of 'The Walls Do Not Fall':

we know no rule
of procedure,

we are voyagers, discovers
of the not-known,

the unrecorded;
we have no map;

possibly we will reach haven,
heaven.[50]

With the repetition of the first book's closing couplet on 'Tribute to the Angels' dedication page, H.D. elegantly re-inscribes her thematic interest in continuity, survival, renewal, and the sacred as she opens the second section of the poem.

Leaving behind the 'Christos-image' 'most difficult to disentangle,' 'Tribute to the Angels' moves to reclaim 'what the new-church spat upon/and broke and shattered' and with these shattered shards of 'splintered glass' 'melt down and integrate,/re-involve, re-create/opal, onyx, obsidian.'[51] With this process of re-creation, H.D. embraces a feminine creative principle which suffuses the poem in order to restore the 'mother-father' and move beyond an impoverished spirituality of broken halves and 'unsatisfied duality.'[52] In order for the possibility of restoration to be explored in the third book, 'Tribute to the Angels' shares the poet's vision of the feminine—the poet's vision of the primal mother.

Throughout the second book, there are three dominant manifestations of the feminine creative principle: the 'bitter, bitter jewel' in the crucible that is 'melted' in 'mer, mere, mere, mater, Maia, Mary,/Star

of the Sea,/Mother'; the 'ordinary' charred yet flowering may-tree—
'in an old garden-square'; and the vision of the Lady herself with all
the power of 'Psyche, the butterfly,/out of the cocoon.'[53] With this
focus, 'Tribute to the Angels' emerges as an affirmation of historically
devalued female creative principles—an affirmation of the maternal
force essential to human creation. In its celebration of the 'new Eve'
who 'brings the Book of Life,' 'Tribute to the Angels' offers a sacred
vision which brings forth the possibility of pausing '*to give/thanks
that we rise again from death and live.*'

This reading of *Trilogy*—or conception of the poem as sacred—is
paralleled in Aliki Barnstone's 'Introduction' to the New Directions
edition of the poem, which argues that structurally and thematically
Trilogy establishes H.D. as a major poet among other modernists:

> Like T.S. Eliot's *The Waste Land*, William Carlos Williams'
> *Paterson*, and Erza Pound's *Cantos*, *Trilogy* is an epic poem
> that takes the reader on the poet's political, spiritual,
> philosophical, and artistic quest. Each poet, like their precursors
> Milton, Whitman, and Baudelaire, has composed a personal
> bible; *Trilogy* is H.D.'s multi-layered sacred text.[54]

Given Barnstone's reading, fittingly 'The Flowering of the Rod'—the
third book—is the least overtly engaged with the immediate physical
experience of living in war-torn London. It leaves behind the overt
double references to 'may-tree or apple' found in 'Tribute to the
Angels,' which conjure the scarred yet living tree blooming in a burnt-
out square as spotted by H.D. from atop a London bus, and the symbolic weight of the spiritual associations with Christ's crown of thorns
and those of fruitfulness, immortality, and magic.[55] This pairing
persuasively affirms H.D.'s desire to write a poem that insists upon
the possibility of seeing and, in turn, acknowledging the sacred as embodied in the everyday: 'it was an ordinary tree/in an old garden
square' and yet it was 'blossoming/this is the flowering of the
rood/this is the flowering of the wood.'[56] Instead, the third book desires an amplification of the poet's commitment to the visionary—to
the as-of-yet-unimagined.

If the dominant image of 'Tribute to the Angels' is the blossoming
vision of the Lady carrying 'a book [that] is not/the tome of ancient
wisdom' but instead 'the unwritten volume of the new,' then 'The
Flowering of the Rod' is the story of receiving the promise of this vision. The story, in H.D.'s telling of it, includes the very difficulty of
being able to accept this gift.[57] H.D. depicts this dynamic through a
series of poems centred on Kaspar—the third wise man—who must
transcend the 'hedges and fortresses of the mind' in order to recognize
Mary—the Lady—and see 'the whole scope and plan/of our and his
civilization on this, his and our earth, before Adam.'[58] In coming to an
acceptance of an unexpected vision—'*it is unseemly that a*

woman/appear at all'—he can act: he can deliver 'the other' jar of myrrh.[59] And with this deliverance, H.D. closes the poem with the recreation of a nativity scene in which the feminine creative principle is uncompromisingly incorporated into the vision 'of all flowering things together.'[60]

'AND THE FIRE AND THE ROSE ARE ONE'

Written in 1942, the final section of Eliot's fourth quartet 'Little Gidding' opens with lines that H.D. could have employed as an epigraph for *Trilogy*:

> What we call the beginning is often the end
> And to make an end is to make a beginning.
> The end is where we start from . . .[61]

In moving from *Trilogy* to *Four Quartets*, we become aware of a shared method in both poets' elegant mining of sacred and literary traditions, in their communication of a mature and powerfully realized poetic vision. The vision of both poets depends heavily on their ability and willingness to move forward and backward between past and present, or as H.D. writes in 'The Flowering of the Rod':

> I am the first or the last to renounce
> iron, steel, metal;
>
> I have gone forward,
> I have gone backward,
>
> I have gone onward from bronze and iron,
> into the Golden Age.[62]

Likewise, the last stanza of 'Little Gidding' reads:

> We shall not cease from exploration
> And the end of all our exploring
> Will be to arrive where we started
> And know the place for the first time.[63]

Helen Gardner's 1949 suggestion—in an appropriately circular study of Eliot's poetry which begins and ends with *Four Quartets*—that 'in *Four Quartets* a more richly complex experience finds richer and more varied expression; the range of feeling and the range of the instrument is greater than before' could have as easily been written of *Trilogy*. The two poems read convincingly as 'the mature achievement' of the poets.[64] In part, this achievement lies in their shared willingness to begin writing with a visible incorporation of the personal not evident in their earlier work.

The early work of H.D., *Imagiste*, is as associated with a cool impersonality as that of Eliot at the time he published *The Waste Land*. Over two decades later, however, *Four Quartets* is carefully grounded in Eliot's personal geography and in the experience of his 1927 conversion to Anglo-Catholicism. Mary Ann Gillies has argued that *Four Quartets* can be 'read as a re-enactment of Eliot's own spiritual struggle and as a paradigm of the struggle that Eliot believes we all must undergo before we can understand ourselves and our world.'[65] For Eliot, religion emerges as a means of answering the questions that we cannot answer ourselves. Where in 'The Flowering of the Rod' Kaspar must come to trust in his unexpected vision, the speaker of *Four Quartets* must come to accept the paradox embedded in the first quartet 'Burnt Norton':

> Time present and time past
> Are both perhaps present in time future
> And time future continued in time past.
> If all time is eternally present
> All time is unredeemable.
> What might have been is an abstraction
> Remaining a perpetual possibility
> Only in a world of speculation.[66]

The private—or personal—quality of the poem is further emphasized when the history of the poem's composition and titles of each quartet are also taken into consideration. *Four Quartets*, like *Trilogy*, is now read as a unified sequence even though all four poems were originally written and published separately. The first poem in the sequence, 'Burnt Norton,' was composed in 1935 and is set in the garden of a country house in the Cotswolds of the same name, which he had visited the previous summer with Emily Hale. 'Burnt Norton' first appeared in Eliot's *Collected Poems 1909–1935* (1936). This positioning leaves the later reader with the retrospective recognition that the first quartet—in a physical sense—marks a beginning and an end: it is the first of the sequence of four poems that was to become his mature masterpiece *Four Quartets*; yet it also marks the beginning of the end of Eliot's career as an active poet since *Four Quartets*, in its completed form—with the exception of *Old Possum's Book of Practical Cats* (1939)—is Eliot's last poem.

Written over a two-year period during World War II, the final three quartets are similar in tone to 'Burnt Norton' and share its five-part structure. The second quartet, 'East Coker,' takes its name from the village that was home to Eliot's Puritan ancestors who left for America in the 1660s. 'East Coker' was first published by Faber in September 1940, and five months later Faber made available the first separate edition of 'Burnt Norton.' 'The Dry Salvages,' marked by its similarly personal association with the Massachusetts coast of Eliot's childhood, appeared in autumn 1941. The final poem, 'Little Gidding,' with its vivid references to the war, was published in

December 1942.[67] In England, the poems were first published as a sequence by Faber in 1944.[68]

When the poems are read as a sequence, the intricate patterning and superb bridging structure become apparent. And the title itself of course gestures towards the complex and rewarding interplay of four instruments united in the presentation of one work. Here within the poem in its entirety and within each quartet, voices embodying a range of tones come into play. As the poem moves back and forth between the reflective and the visionary, the lyrical and meditative, a dynamic coherence emerges between the pieces and moves the poem towards an ending that 'neither inform[s] nor instructs, but establish[es] a certain orientation . . . towards "God's holy fire".' The poem is directed towards a discovery of the spiritual—of the ineffable. With this orientation towards the intangible, *Four Quartets*—like *A Passage to India* in Chapter 3—explores the limits of language and communicative acts

> because the spiritual sense is beyond any sense which words
> can make, the art has to work in a mainly negative way,
> creating space for "the dumb spirit" by excluding whatever is
> not in accord with it. The art, at its finest, is necessarily an art of
> alienation and negation. [69]

With the use of negative definitions—'not this,' 'not that'—the first quartet edges towards its conclusion as 'Words strain,/Crack and sometimes break, under the burden/Under the tension, slip, slide, perish.'[70]

The rose-garden memories of light and laughter in 'Burnt Norton' are supplanted by autumnal imagery in 'East Coker' with the diminished light of November long since stripped of summer heat. The second quartet with its ruminations on concrete and abstract time—the historical and trans-historical—is awash in darkness, or a sort of weariness, that is paradoxically imbued with a sense of awakening renewal. With this intensifying sense of the poet's engagement with the personal, it is difficult to read the fifth stanza of 'East Coker' without conjuring up the middle-aged Eliot himself as he writes in the middle of this latest war:

> So here I am, in the middle way, having had twenty years –
> Twenty years largely wasted, the year of *l'entre deux guerres* –
> Trying to learn to use words, and every attempt
> Is a wholly new start, and a different kind of failure
> Because one has only learnt to get the better of words

Here the poem is moving towards a recognition of the power in accepting inarticulacy and—as in *Trilogy*—there is a simple expression of the only need being the need to 'fight to recover what has been lost/And found and lost again and again: and now, under conditions/That seem unpropitious.'[71] Within this need, there is purpose and an acceptance that:

> Here and there does not matter
> We must be still and still moving
> Into another intensity
> For a further union, a deeper communion
> Through the dark cold and the empty desolation,
> The wave cry, the wind cry, the vast waters
> Of the petrel and the porpoise. In my end is my beginning.[72]

'The Dry Salvages' takes the reader to yet another specific locale that resonates with Eliot's personal experience and it also immerses us fully in the timeless realm of the universal. Eliot's title refers to a small group of rocks, with a beacon, off the North East coast of Cape Ann, Massachusetts, an area that Eliot knew well as a child and young man, having spent summers with his family nearby. Eliot's invocation of a place that has personal significance for him is juxtaposed with the opening lines of this quartet that stress the universal:

> I do not know much about gods; but I think that the river
> Is a strong brown god—sullen, untamed and intractable,
> Patient to some degree, at first recognised as a frontier;
> Useful, untrustworthy, as a conveyor of commerce;
> Then only a problem confronting the builder of bridges.
> The problem once solved, the brown god is almost forgotten
> By the dwellers in cities—ever, however, implacable.
> Keeping his seasons and rages, destroyer, reminder
> Of what men choose to forget. Unhonoured, unpropitiated
> By worshippers of the machine, but waiting, watching and
> waiting.[73]

This 'sullen, untamed and intractable' 'strong brown god' is not the white God that had stood at the centre of Eliot's childhood. Though critics have often suggested that the river in these lines is the Mississippi, which runs through St Louis, the city of Eliot's birth, the river could just as easily be the Ganges that flows through Forster's *A Passage to India* given the emphasis on the universal evident here. The next few lines underscore the difference between human consciousness and nature: the river is 'at first recognised as a frontier;' it is a 'conveyer of commerce;' and it is 'only a problem confronting the builder of bridges.' Though the 'brown god is almost forgotten' by 'the dwellers in cities,' who now worship 'the machine' instead of the river, it keeps 'his seasons and rages' and is always 'waiting, watching and waiting.' Humanity names, uses, and discards objects such as the river; nature is immutable, its rhythms and existence governed only by the changing seasons and physical conditions. A few lines later, Eliot makes explicit what this third quartet will treat: 'The river is within us, the sea is all about us;' and 'The sea has many voices,/Many gods and many voices.'[74] The individual is connected inevitably to the communal whole—the river flows to the sea. Moreover, the many possibilities embodied in the communal whole—the many voices and many gods—call into question the very nature of how individuals come to understand the world around them. In short, the opening movement of 'The Dry Salvages' announces that it will explore the ways in which belief or meaning is fashioned and refashioned over time and in various places.

The human need to believe in something—a doctrine, a divinity, even a dictator—is acute in times of turmoil. The lines of the poem suggest that need for something to hold onto has changed little over the centuries. Nevertheless, the need to question the beliefs one inherits, to search for new doctrines or gods to take the place of the old ones, is also central to this poem. The following lines evoke the sense of crisis that is brought about when what one believed in no longer serves its purpose:

> There is the final addition, the failing
> Pride or resentment at failing powers,
> The unattached devotion which might pass for devotionless,
> In a drifting boat with a slow leakage,
> The silent listening to the undeniable
> Clamour of the bell of the last annunciation.[75]

As bombs rain down upon London, humanity struggles to find meaning where there appears to be none. The awareness that one reaches is:

> That the past experience revived in the meaning
> Is not the experience of one life only
> But of many generations[76]

The individual search for meaning is thus joined with the communal search for meaning. Eliot's speaker here comes to the awareness that:

> For most of us, there is only the unattended
> Moment, the moment in and out of time,
> The distraction fit, lost in a shaft of sunlight,
> The wild thyme unseen, or the winter lightning
> Or the waterfall, or music heard so deeply
> That it is not heard at all, but you are the music
> While the music lasts. These are only hints and guesses,
> Hints followed by guesses; and the rest
> Is prayer, observance, discipline, thought and action.
> The hint half guessed, the gift half understood, is Incarnation.[77]

What you believe in is less important than the awareness that you must find something in which to believe: art, music, nature, God, or a 'strong brown god' will all do. Yet, there is a hint here that the search for meaning outside one's self is not the answer—'but you are the music/While the music lasts'—and this hint takes us into the fourth and final quartet.

'Little Gidding' repeats the same structure as the previous three quartets: the title situates the poem in a specific location—in this case a village in Huntingdonshire, where Nicholas Ferrar established an Anglican community in the seventeenth century. There are five movements that pivot around a series of themes introduced in the opening few lines of the first movement. The final few lines of the fifth movement circle back to the opening lines, revisiting the opening themes but in a deeper more complex manner. Since this quartet is also the final in the sequence of four, the themes, images, metaphors, and symbols working throughout it also refer back to the earlier quartets. As a result, though 'Little Gidding' can stand alone as a wonderful piece of poetry, the full measure of this richly complex and allusive poem depends on the reader's knowledge of what has come before. In fashioning his final poem in this manner, Eliot underscored the central theme of *Four Quartets* as a whole—the relation of the individual to the communal.

The opening lines of 'Little Gidding' describe a bleak world, a place where the land and the heart are both frozen:

> Midwinter spring is its own season
> Sempiternal though sodden towards sundown,
> Suspended in time, between pole and tropic.
> When the short day is brightest, with frost and fire,
> The brief sun flames the ice, on pond and ditches,
> In windless cold that is the heart's heat,
> Reflecting in a watery mirror
> A glare that is blindness in the early afternoon.[78]

The speaker provides instruction for those who walk this frozen landscape, seeking for meaning:

> If you came at night like a broken king,
> If you came by day not knowing what you came for,
> It would be the same, when you leave the rough road
> And turn behind the pig-sty to the dull façade
> And the tombstone. And what you thought you came for
> Is only a shell, a husk of meaning
> From which the purpose breaks only when it is fulfilled
> If at all. Either you had no purpose
> Or the purpose is beyond the end you figured
> And is altered in fulfilment. There are other places
> Which also are the world's end, some at the sea jaws,
> Or over a dark lake, in a desert or a city—
> But this is the nearest, in place and time,
> Now and in England.[79]

These lines unite various times, places, and individuals in a communal search for meaning. Though the opening section of this movement suggests that those who are searching stop at Little Gidding, the place that 'is the nearest, in place and time,/Now and in England,' the first movement actually ends with the following lines: 'Here, the intersection of the timeless moment/Is England and nowhere. Never and always.' These lines suggest that the search for meaning is an unending one—it takes place at the intersection of the present moment and the timeless moment—and those who set out on the path will find that meaning in the immediate location—England—and in no location. The opening movement of this quartet is thus a meditation on the very nature of meaning or belief and the absolute need for humanity to search for it, even though the search will never result in a final answer.

The rest of 'Little Gidding' explores these themes, weaving into them meditations on the nature of art, religion, Eliot's own search for meaning, and the reality of life in London during the Blitz. The poem's quest for meaning is most frequently read in Christian terms, and certainly this reading is supported by the many Christian allusions found throughout this quartet in particular. The poem's final image,

> When the tongues of flame are in-folded
> Into the crowned knot of fire
> And the fire and the rose are one[80]

is conventionally read as explicitly Christian with the fire, especially 'the tongues of flame,' symbolizing the Holy Spirit as it descended on the Apostles at Pentecost and the rose symbolizing completion or perfection—in this case, the completion of the search by finding meaning in a Christian God. In fact, by choosing to use 'Little Gidding' as the title, Eliot directs his readers towards just such a reading because of the association of the village with Nicholas Ferrar's Christian monastery.

Yet given the fact that the earlier quartets, as well as the opening lines of this one, have emphasized the universal nature of this search for meaning, it is just as likely that other religious, philosophical, or ideological systems can supply the meaning that humans seek. In fact, the final stanza of the poem opens with lines that suggest that the search cannot end by adopting a set of beliefs and thereafter adhering to them. To search for meaning is, in the end, unending because it is the search for one's self:

> We shall not cease from exploration
> And the end of all our exploring
> Will be to arrive where we started
> And know the place for the first time.
> Through the unknown, unremembered gate
> When the last of earth left to discover
> Is that which was the beginning;
> At the source of the longest river
> The voice of the hidden waterfall
> And the children in the apple-tree
> Not known, because not looked for
> But heard, half-heard, in the stillness
> Between two waves of the sea.[81]

What we discover 'Between two waves of the sea' and what leads to the union of the 'fire and the rose' is the awareness that what we need to find is inside us all along—our very existence provides the meaning for which we search, just as the very existence of the river provides its own meaning. But we can make sense of that existence only when we can unite the river—our own existence—to the sea—the communal world that includes all times and all cultures.

Though we have only scratched the surface of Eliot's masterful meditation on the nature of human experience, it is clear that in the writing of *Four Quartets* he was engaged in the same kind of soul searching that Woolf and H.D. were undertaking in their own work. The world appeared to be on the brink of destruction and it is not surprising that questions of meaning or faith feature prominently in the prose and poetry that they composed at this time. Yet this was not the first time that war had dominated these writers' horizons—they had all lived through World War I; however, this time their experience of war was significantly different. In the first place, this war had an immediate impact on their lives in ways that World War I did not. Woolf lost both of her London homes to bombing raids and German planes passed over her country home in Sussex on their nightly raids.[82] H.D. remained in London throughout the war, enduring the bombing raids and the fear that they invoked. Eliot was an Air Raid Warden, and as a result he was intimately aware of the death and destruction wrought by German bombs. In the second place, they had spent twenty more years honing their skills and learning their craft. Though we can spot some of the themes or techniques that are central to *Four Quartets* in *The Waste Land*—the multiple voices, literary allusions, or use of complex symbols, for example—they are deployed with greater assurance and at the service of a more complex and deeper presentation of human nature. Thus, while it is true that in the post World War II world, modernism ceased to be the force it had been, it is nonetheless the case that during the war, these three modernists created some of the most important and memorable works of their careers.

THE MODERNIST CANON AND RECENT SCHOLARSHIP

As these readings of Woolf, H.D. and Eliot remind us, the ways in which we as readers come to form a relationship with a literary period and its representative texts is highly dependent on the critical framework within which we are positioned. Through this chapter's insistence on examining how three modernist writers responded to World War II with reference to their evolving creative visions, a very specific version of late modernism is presented. And with this presentation also comes the acknowledgement that the history of modernism's reception is also the history of changing critical fashions. As the objectives of literary scholarship and classroom practices change, so too do the reputations of individual texts and writers.

Joseph Kelly's 1998 study *Our Joyce: From Outcast to Icon* is an engaging and thorough example of scholarship explicitly interested in exploring the politics and machinations of canon formation in relation to individual literary reputations. Kelly begins by establishing his scholarly debt to the recent sociological orientation of textual criticism as practised by Jerome McGann and the late D.F. McKenzie, both of whom 'directed attention to the social character of a literary work throughout its entire life.'[83] In particular, Jerome McGann has proposed the consideration of literature as a social event:

> [s]pecific poetic utterances—specific poems—are human acts occupying social space; as such, they most certainly are involved with extra-poetic operations. For poetry is itself one form of social activity, and no proper understanding of the nature of poetry can be made if the poem is abstracted from the experience of the poem, either at its point of origin or at any subsequent period.[84]

McGann is advocating the division of a work into two periods: first, its point of origin and, second, the moment when a work 'passes entirely beyond the purposive control of the author.'[85] With this approach in mind, Kelly tells the changing story of Joyce's literary reputation.

The book's five sections explore distinct phases in the construction of Joyce's reputation. Chapter 1 considers Joyce's earliest intentions—as distinct from his later persona—as suggested by what Kelly describes as Joyce's 'uncompromising, unromantic, hard-featured realism.'[86] Chapter 2 explores how Ezra Pound, T.S. Eliot, and their readers as found in *The Egoist* and the *Criterion* collaborated to canonize Joyce as an avant-garde, cosmopolitan writer—a tradition perpetuated by Richard Ellmann's 1959 biography of Joyce and in Hugh Kenner's *The Pound Era*. In Chapter 3, Kelly introduces readers to Morris Ernst's Joyce. Ernst, lawyer for Radclyffe Hall's *The Well of Loneliness* (1928), defended *Ulysses* during its 1930s obscenity trials. Kelly illustrates how the direction that Ernst felt necessary to take in court—namely, 'elevated, isolated, geniuses were incapable of obscenity'—came to ensure the perpetuation of the narrow and inaccurate view that *Ulysses* was 'incomprehensible except to a safe coterie of educated and wealthy readers.'[87] Chapter 4 examines the enduring influence of Richard Ellmann's *James Joyce* and, in turn, Chapter 5 assesses the academy's attraction to 'Joyce the Genius' as privileged by Eliot, Pound, and Ellmann. Kelly's study itself emerges as a sort of de facto Chapter 6 that points to the recent developments in Joyce scholarship with the current academic interest in textual and cultural studies seen in modernist scholarship.

A similar project could be undertaken for British modernism, and indeed a comprehensive analysis of modernism along these lines would be a fitting subject for an entire book. Here instead we will limit ourselves to a brief overview of the movement's critical reception within the context of English-language scholarship. The introduction to *Rereading the New: A Backward Glance at Modernism* (1992), an anthology of essays edited by Kevin J.H. Dettmar, is suggestive in this regard with its discussion of first, second, and third generation critics of modernism. Dettmar's first generation is the reviewers (and—indirectly—the publishers) who did not respond favourably to the early works—a point of frustration among many writers as seen earlier with discussion of Joyce's open letter to the press in Chapter 1. Pound—with his impresario streak—understood better than anyone the value (and the critical importance) of writers 'filling the roles of both publisher and critic.'[88] His career is as much about his own poetry as it is about his work as contributing editor to others' periodicals (*The Dial*, *Poetry*, and *The Egoist*) and overseeing the production of his own publications (*Blast* and *Little Review*). Pound's literary critical work, supplemented by essays and reviews written by the likes of T.S. Eliot and Virginia Woolf—both of whom had their own publishing organs by way of the *Criterion* and the Hogarth Press—did much to convince a second generation of critics of the value in reading and favourably promoting the new writers' work.

In turn, second-generation modernist critics advanced a definition of modernism and a critical standard that was very much in harmony with the aesthetic ideals held by Pound and Eliot. The work of the second generation was to create and disseminate strategies for reading. *The Modern Novel* (1926) by Elizabeth Drew and *James Joyce and the Plain Reader—An Essay* (1932) by Charles Duff were careful yet accessible literary guidebooks that helped advance a view of modernism that celebrated technical innovation.[89] The literary criticism of this school, which Pound praised, was described as 'very nearly an impersonal criticism, and comes from the sharpened desire for, or even insistence on, greater accuracy of expression, which is shared by more than a half-dozen writers.'[90] With this kind of sustained critical attention, modernism 'slowly assumed coherence, as aesthetic concepts received new formulation, as those concepts were worked into doctrine.'[91] This doctrine was closely associated with the work of I.A. Richards in England and New Criticism as advanced by critics like W.K. Wimsatt and Cleanth Brooks in the United States, who favoured 'impersonality, craftsmanship, objectivity, hardness and clarity of a kind, a union of emotion with verbal object, a norm of inclusiveness and reconciliation and hence a close interdependence of drama, irony, ambiguity, and metaphor or the near equivalent of these four . . . .'[92]

Unsurprisingly, with critical order imposed on modernist experimentation as guided by the pre-eminent writer-critics themselves, the view of Pound, Eliot, and Joyce as the triumvirate who best exemplified the nature of modernism flourished for decades. After World War II, the mythologizing force of the aforementioned Richard Ellmann Joyce biography and Hugh Kenner's celebratory *Pound Era* insisted upon a very narrow view of modernism as practised by male high modernist priests. Even Woolf, whose reputation was favourable in her lifetime, languished with little or no critical attention paid to her work in the decades immediately after the war.

With the rise of what Dettmar refers to as the third generation of modernist critics, scholarship enters into a new phase with a community of critics interested in leaving aside readings of modernism that celebrate a narrow cult of genius. Instead there is a preference for discovering what has been effaced—what has been ignored—in homogeneous readings of the movement that downplay what an early critic complainingly described as modernism's tendency towards a 'general impression [that] is momentary; there are moods and emotions, but no steady current of ideas behind them.'[93] With this widening of perspective, four critical approaches in particular have made exciting contributions to the expansion of modernist studies: feminist literary criticism, New Historicist/textual criticism, cultural studies, and postcolonial studies.

Second-wave feminist literary criticism in the 1970s is strongly associated with Sandra Gilbert and Susan Gubar's *The Madwoman in the Attic: The Woman Writer and the Nineteenth-Century Literary Imagination* (1979), which was then followed by the three-volume *No Man's Land: The Place of the Woman Writer in the Twentieth Century* (1988–1994). While more recent developments in queer theory and postcolonial studies, for example, have led to yet more diverse and nuanced approaches to feminist scholarship, Gilbert and Gubar's work drew attention to the many women writers whose reputations had suffered during the years of consolidation when the shape of modernism narrowed in keeping with New Criticism's highly formalized understanding of modernist aesthetics. During the 1980s and '90s, there was an exciting explosion of reprints, anthologies, and critical works which continued to undermine the view of modernism as the exclusive province of male genius. Titles exploring modernism as consisting of not just one, but many strands—for example, Ann Ardis, *New Women, New Novels: Feminism and Early Modernism* (1990); Shari Benstock, *The Women of the Left Bank* (1985); Rita Felski, *The Gender of Modernity* (1995); Gilbert and Gubar, *The Female Imagination and the Modernist Aesthetic* (1986); and Bonnie Kime Scott, *The Gender of Modernism* (1990)—were accompanied by studies of individual writers as diverse as Djuna Barnes, H.D., Katherine Mansfield,

Dorothy Richardson, Rebecca West, and Virginia Woolf. This foundational work has continued to inspire those interested in the intersection between feminism, gender, and modernism as illustrated by recent books: *Irrational Modernism: A Neurasthenic History of New York* (2004) by Alison Jones, examining the intersection between the international Dada movement and the Baroness Elsa von Freytag-Loringhoven; and *Gender, Desire and Sexuality in T.S. Eliot* (2004), edited by Cassandra Laity and Nancy K. Gish, which points to new directions in Eliot studies.

The republication of out-of-print books by female writers by publishers like Virago and academic presses indirectly draws attention to a second important strand of modernist scholarship in recent decades. The wider critical interest in the social and material conditions of production as advanced by New Historicism and materialist or textual approaches to criticism influenced a return to the archive and the historical record that has provocatively transfigured our sense of the 'making of modernism.' Peter Bürger's *Theory of the Avant-garde* (1974), which was translated into English in 1984, emphasized the value of exploring both 'the productive and distributive apparatus' supporting cultural productions and the 'ideas about art that prevail at a given time . . . that determine the reception of works.'[94] Evidence of this kind of approach in English-language scholarship became apparent in the early 1980s. Michael Levenson's *A Genealogy of Modernism: A Study of English Literary Doctrine, 1908–1922* (1984) maps the networks that brought together writers like Ezra Pound, T.E. Hulme, Ford Madox Ford, Wyndham Lewis, and T.S. Eliot as well as the various sub-movements with which the men were associated— Impressionism, Imagism, Vorticism, and Classicism. Levenson argues that the post-1922 critical hegemony of the *Criterion* worked to efface the factionalism that in fact characterizes modernism; his argument initiates debate about the necessity for a more broadly defined conception of modernism. Five years later, Lawrence Rainey's essay 'The Price of Modernism' offered a detailed examination of the financial negotiations, backroom deal-making, and posturing that took place in the months preceding the publication of *The Waste Land* in *The Dial* and the *Criterion*. Here Rainey draws attention to the uses to which individuals and cultures put art. Even before *The Waste Land* had been published Pound was pitching it to interested parties based on the poem's representational qualities—based on his declaration that it was indeed 'the justification of the "movement," of our modern experiment since 1900.'[95] The history sketched by Rainey exposes modernist writers as anything but self-sacrificing formalists disinterested in the reception of their work—an approach that was expanded in his 1998 book *Institutions of Modernism: Literary Elites and Public Culture*. Rainey's scholarship has been complemented by Joseph

Kelly's previously discussed work on Joyce and scholarship from writers such as Jayne E. Marek, Stephen Watt, Joyce Piell Wexler, and Ian Willison who have looked at everything from 'little magazines' to the cultural politics of limited editions in modernist canon formation.[96]

The expansion of scope characteristic in the work of modernist critics interested in the institutional politics of literature is paralleled in the arena of cultural studies. As literary theory has encouraged a continual questioning of categories and distinctions, so too have wider distinctions between scholarly categories been questioned by a generation of academics. In the past decade, there has been an intensification of interest in literary history that actively explores the intersections between literature and other histories—be that race relations, popular culture, consumerism, politics, economics, or geography, to name a few areas of recent focus. This strand of modernist scholarship is linked to the history of cultural studies in England as traced through Raymond Williams and Stuart Hall and in the United States by way of John Guillory. Through the adoption of an interdisciplinary approach, unexpected and powerful insights are offered into modernism as a broad-based aesthetic movement in a variety of disciplines—music, painting, photography, dance, film, theatre, and architecture.

For example, Michael North's *Reading 1922: A Return to the Scene of the Modern* (1999) maps the cultural topography of the original audience for *The Waste Land*, *Ulysses*, and *Jacob's Room*. In his reading of the conversation between *The Waste Land*, Tutankhamen, and Howard Carter, the British archaeologist who discovered the tomb in 1922, North demonstrates that on anecdotal ground alone it is possible to undermine any remaining impulse to separate modernism from its popular analogues:

> The common dichotomies by which literary modernism of 1922 is distinguished from the larger culture of the time cannot be maintained against the evidence that the very terms those dichotomies depend on were redefined by literature and culture in concert. The modern itself is obviously an unstable category when the new, in literature and in fashion, comes into being in such close association with the ancient.[97]

North's conclusion calls for an ongoing commitment to the excavation of the sociology of modernism—a call that has continued to be ably and suggestively answered in the early years of the twentieth century with new books from Joshua Esty, Douglas Mao and Rebecca L. Walkowitz, and Andrew Thacker.[98] It is worth briefly mentioning the introduction to Thacker's book *Moving Through Modernity* (2003) because it draws attention to the centrality of postcolonial theory and criticism in explorations of how writers produce texts that cognitively map empire. This affords Thacker the opportunity to put modernist constructions of 'space' into conversation with the more familiar associations between modernism and 'time.' For us, however, it suggests the importance of exploring a final strand in recent scholarship: the place of the postcolonial studies in modernist scholarship.

If the transformation of 'modernism' into 'modernisms' was begun by feminist scholars, then it was extended by postcolonial critics. A conception of modernism that moves beyond the borders of London and other metropolitan centres to include more diverse settings for modernist experimentation finds its articulation in modernist scholarship that incorporates postcolonial theory. Whether writing about Katherine Mansfield, William Faulkner, or the Harlem Renaissance, a view of modernism not exclusively committed to a homogenous evocation of privileged urban alienation comes into focus. Instead, suddenly there is New Zealand. The American South. The long city blocks of Harlem to the north of Manhattan's Central Park. Likewise, books like Elizabeth Podnieks' *Daily Modernism: The Literary Diaries of Virginia Woolf, Antonia White, Elizabeth Smart, and Anaïs Nin* (2000) and Stefan Meyer's *The Experimental Arabic Novel: Postcolonial Modernism in the Levant* (2000) respectively offer up geographically unexpected combinations of writers and, in turn, under-examined regions. Not only does a postcolonial perspective invite readers to look at literature from other geographical regions—Africa, Asia, Australia, Canada, Caribbean, and South America—but it also invites us to look at Anglo-American and European modernists through the lens of imperial conquest and colonization. *Ulysses*, *A Passage to India* and *The Last September* are all opened to new interpretations when the history of Irish subjugation and the colonization of India become the analytical framework for a critical reading of the respective texts. Edna Duffy's *Subaltern Ulysses* (1994) is but one example, as are the many postcolonial readings of *A Passage to India* including Peter Morey's *Fictions of India: Narrative and Power* (2000).[99]

The resulting scholarship paints portraits of modernism that would in many cases have been unrecognizable to the first generation of critics, let alone to the modernists themselves. Yet this is just our point. Any piece of art or literature, any literary movement, is at the mercy of those read and write about it. Their concerns—whether aesthetic, political, or ideological—are as important as the concerns that fuelled the writing of the modernist text itself. As the angle of approach alters over time, so too does the shape of the movement. At the core, however, we will always find the art—the stories, poems, plays, and novels composed during the first forty or so years of the twentieth century. The fact that a diverse group of scholars and critics are still engaged in defining and debating modernism attests to the continuing currency and power of modernist literature. We close this book with a question to you as a reader—what does modernism mean to you?

FOR FURTHER CONSIDERATION: SUGGESTED READING

H.D.

Edmunds, Susan. *Out of Line: History, Psychoanalysis, and Montage in H.D.'s Long Poems.* Stanford: Stanford University Press, 1994.

Sword, Helen. *Engendering Inspiration: Visionary Strategies in Rilke, Lawrence, and H.D.* Ann Arbor: University of Michigan Press, 1995.

Taylor, Georgina. *H.D. and the Public Sphere of Modernist Women Writers, 1913–1946: Talking Women.* Oxford: Clarendon Press, 2001.

T.S. Eliot

Bergonzi, Bernard (ed.). *T.S. Eliot's Four Quartets: A Casebook.* London: Macmillan, 1969.

Cooper, John Xiros. *T.S. Eliot and the Ideology of Four Quartets.* Cambridge: Cambridge University Press, 1995.

Gardner, Helen. *The Art of T.S. Eliot.* London: Faber, 1949.

Moody, A. David. *The Cambridge Companion to T.S. Eliot.* Cambridge: Cambridge University Press, 1994.

Virginia Woolf

Busse, Kristina. 'Reflecting the Subject in History: The Return of the Real in *Between the Acts*,' *Woolf Studies Annual* 7 (2001): 75–101.

Cramer, Patricia. 'Virginia Woolf's Matriarchal Family of Origins in *Between the Acts*,' *Twentieth-Century Literature* 39.2 (1993): 166–84.

Daughtery, Beth Rigel, and Eileen Barrett (eds). *Virginia Woolf: Texts and Contexts.* New York: Pace University Press, 1996.

Flint, Kate. 'Reading Uncommonly: Virginia Woolf and the Practice of Reading,' *Yearbook of English Studies* 26 (1996): 187–98.

Hussey, Mark (ed.). *Virginia Woolf and War: Fiction, Reality and Myth.* Syracuse: Syracuse University Press, 1991.

Jones, Suzanne W. (ed.). *Writing the Woman Artist: Essays on Poetics, Politics, and Portraiture.* Philadelphia: University of Pennsylvania Press, 1991.

Miller, Andrew John. '"Our Representative, Our Spokesman": Modernity, Professionalism, and Representation in Virginia Woolf's *Between the Acts*,' *Studies in the Novel* 33.1 (2001): 34–50.

Pridmore-Brown, Michele. 'Virginia Woolf and the BBC: Public and Private Voices,' *Virginia Woolf Miscellany* 56 (2000): 3–4.

Roe, Sue, and Susan Sellers (eds). *The Cambridge Companion to Virginia Woolf.* Cambridge: Cambridge University Press, 2000.

Modernism: Critical Consolidations

Cultural Studies

Esty, Joshua. *A Shrinking Island: Modernism and National Culture in England*. Princeton: Princeton University Press, 2004.

Mao, Douglas, and Rebecca L. Walkowitz (eds). *Bad Modernisms*. Durham: Duke University Press, 2006.

North, Michael. *Reading 1922: A Return to the Scene of the Modern*. Oxford: Oxford University Press, 1999.

Rado, Lisa. *Modernism, Gender, and Culture: A Cultural Studies Approach*. New York: Garland, 1997.

Thacker, Andrew. *Moving Through Modernity*. Manchester: Manchester University Press, 2003.

Feminist Studies

Benstock, Shari. *Women of the Left Bank: Paris 1900–1940*. Austin: University of Texas Press, 1986.

Elliott, Bridget and Jo-Ann Wallace. *Woman Artists and Writers: Modernist (Im)Positionings*. London: Routledge, 1994.

Felski, Rita. *The Gender of Modernity*. Cambridge MA: Harvard University Press, 1995.

Gilbert, Sandra M., and Susan Gubar, *No Man's Land: The Place of the Woman Writer in the Twentieth Century*. 3 vols. New Haven CT: Yale University Press, 1988–94.

Rado, Lisa (ed.). *Rereading Modernism: New Directions for Feminist Criticism*. New York: Garland, 1994.

Scott, Bonnie Kime. *The Gender of Modernism: A Critical Anthology*. Bloomington: Indiana University Press, 1990.

Scott, Bonnie Kime. *Refiguring Modernism*. 2 vols. Bloomington: Indiana University Press, 1995.

Foundational Texts and New Criticism

Bradbury, Malcolm and James McFarlane. *Modernism: 1890-1930*. London: Penguin, 1983.

Ellmann, Richard. *James Joyce*. Oxford: Oxford University Press, 1959.

Howe, Irving. *Modern Literary Criticism*. Boston: Beacon Press, 1958.

Kenner, Hugh. *The Pound Era*. Berkeley: University of California, 1971.

Spender, Stephen. *The Struggle of the Modern*. Berkeley: University of California, 1963.

New Historicism and Textual Criticism

Dettmar, Kevin (ed.). *Rereading the New: A Backward Glance at Modernism*. Ann Arbor: University of Michigan Press, 1992.

Kelly, Joseph. *Our Joyce: From Outcast to Icon*. Austin: University of Texas Press, 1998.

Kiely, Robert (ed.). *Modernism Reconsidered*. Cambridge MA: Harvard University Press, 1983.

Levenson, Michael. *The Genealogy of Modernism: A Study of English Literary Doctrine, 1908–1922*. Cambridge: Cambridge University Press, 1984.

Willison, Ian, et al. (eds). *Modernist Writers and the Marketplace*. London: Macmillan, 1996.

Post Colonial Studies of Modernism
Coyle, Michael. *Ezra Pound and African American Modernism*. Orono ME: National Poetry Foundation, 2001.

Doyle, Laura, and Laura Winkiel (eds). *Geomodernisms: Race, Modernism, Modernity*. Bloomington: Indiana University Press, 2005.

Duffy, Edna. *The Subaltern Ulysses*. Minneapolis: University of Minnesota Press, 1994.

Morey, Peter. *Fictions of India: Narrative and Power*. Edinburgh: Edinburgh University Press, 2000.

Pollard, Charles W. *New World Modernisms: T.S. Eliot, Derek Walcott, and Kamau Brathwaite*. Charlottesville: University of Virginia Press, 2004.

NOTES

1 Auden was given a special commission as a Major in the Intelligence branch of the US Army. His job was to report on the psychological effects of bombing on the German civilian population. Orwell had opposed the war against Germany, but during it he served as a sergeant in the Home Guard. Isherwood settled in California during the war, where he worked as a teacher and wrote Hollywood film scripts. In 1941–42 he worked at a Quaker hostel in Pennsylvania with refugees from Europe. In 1943 he became a follower of Swami Prabhavananda, producing several works on Indian Vedānta in the following decades.

2 Charles Baudelaire, *The Painter of Modern Life and Other Essays*. Trans. Jonathan Mayne (London: Phaidon, 1964) 4–5, 13.

3 H.D. published the three long poems that comprise *Trilogy* individually during the war—*The Walls Do Not Fall* (1944); *Tribute to the Angels* (1945); *The Flowering of the Rod* (1946). The three were revised and combined into a one-volume edition and published as *Trilogy* in 1973.

4 Virginia Woolf, *Between the Acts* (London: Penguin, 1992) 130.

5 Woolf, *Between the Acts* 37.

6 Virginia Woolf, *Diary* V (London: Hogarth Press, 1977–84) 135.

7 Christopher Ames, 'Carnivalesque Comedy in *Between the Acts*,' *Twentieth-Century Literature* Winter 44 (4) 395.

8 Virginia Woolf, 'Thoughts on Peace in an Air Raid,' Rachel Bowlby (ed.), *The Crowded Dance of Modern Life* (London: Penguin, 1992) 168.

9 Woolf, 'Thoughts on Peace in an Air Raid' 168.

10 Woolf, 'Thoughts on Peace in an Air Raid' 171.

11 Barbara Herrnstein Smith, 'Narrative Versions, Narrative Theories,' *On Narrative*, W.J.T. Mitchell (ed.), (Chicago: University of Chicago Press, 1981) 231.

12 Andrew Miller, '"Our Representative, Our Spokesman": Modernity, Professionalism, And Representation in Virginia Woolf's *Between the Acts*,' *Studies in the Novel* 33 (Spring 2001) 35.

13 Rachel Bowlby, *Feminist Destinations and Further Essays on Virginia Woolf* (Edinburgh: Edinburgh University Press, 1997) 136.

14 Northrop Frye, *Anatomy of Criticism* (Princeton: Princeton University Press, 1957) 203.

15 Woolf, *Between the Acts* 8.

16 Woolf, *Between the Acts* 5.

17 Patricia Klindienst Joplin, 'The Authority of Illusion: Feminism and Fascism in Virginia Woolf's *Between the Acts*,' *South Central Review* 6 (1989) 93. Pageantry by no means disappeared in twentieth-century Britain; royal coronations, weddings, and births continued to be cause for public parades and celebrations of considerable magnitude. In *Between the Acts*, the barn—the site of afternoon tea—is still decorated with 'festoons of paper roses, left from the Coronation, drooped from the rafters' (Woolf 61). More recent examples of state processions include Princess Diana's funeral cortege in 1997 and the 2002 Golden Jubilee celebrations in honour of Queen Elizabeth's fiftieth year on the throne. For a German example see Leni Riefenstahl's *Triumph of the Will* (1935); a visually innovative documentary chronicling the pageantry of the 1934 National Socialist Party Congress in Nuremberg, it is also a powerful propaganda piece.

18 Leonard Woolf, *After the Deluge: A Study of Communal Psychology* (London: Hogarth Press, 1931) 260, 295.

19 Virginia Woolf, *Three Guineas* (London: Blackwell, 2001) 75.

20 Marlowe A. Miller, 'Unveiling "The Dialectic of Culture and Barbarism" in British Pageantry: Virginia Woolf's *Between the Acts*,' *Papers on Language and Literature* 1998 Spring 34 (2) 151.

21 Tobacco was the first commodity to be introduced to England as a direct result of imperial expansion.

22 Woolf, *Between the Acts* 75.

23 Woolf, *Between the Acts* 11.

24 Woolf, *Between the Acts* 65.

25 Woolf, *Between the Acts* 22.

26 Ames, 'Carnivalesque Comedy' 406.

27 Woolf, *Between the Acts* 94.

28 Woolf, *Between the Acts* 110.

29 Woolf, *Between the Acts* 111.

30 Woolf, *Between the Acts* 111.

31 Woolf, *Between the Acts* 111.

32 Miller, 'Unveiling' 160. In another playful rejection of passivity, *Three Guineas* (1938) includes the recommendation that the daughters of educated men should read 'three dailies, and three weeklies' because only by 'compar[ing] at least three different versions of the same fact' can one arrive 'in the end at your own conclusion' (*Three Guineas* 95). Woolf herself collected clippings from *The Daily Herald*, *The Daily Telegraph*, the *Evening Standard*, *The Listener*, *The New Statesman and Nation*, the *Observer*, and *The Times*. See Brenda Silver's *Virginia Woolf's Reading Notebooks* (Princeton: Princeton University Press, 1983).

33 Woolf, *Between the Acts* 117.

34 Woolf, *Between the Acts* 122.

35 Melba Cuddy-Keane, 'The Politics of Comic Modes in Virginia Woolf's *Between the Acts,*' *PMLA* 105 (1995) 279.

36 Woolf, *Between the Acts* 125.

37 Woolf, *Between the Acts* 125–6.

38 Woolf, *Between the Acts* 126–7.

39 Woolf, *Between the Acts* 129, 130.

40 See Marina MacKay, 'Putting the House in Order: Virginia Woolf and Blitz Modernism,' *Modern Language Quarterly* 66: 2 (June 2005) 227–52.

41 Twelve years after H.D.'s death in 1961, New Directions published all three books together for the first time in 1973 with the title *Trilogy*.

42 Sarah H. S. Graham, '"We have a secret. We are alive": H.D.'s *Trilogy* as a Response to War,' *Texas Studies in Literature and Language* 44:2 (Summer 2002) 162. With the exception of 'The Walls Do Not Fall' where the date appears at the beginning in the form of a dedication to Bryher, the dates do appear – as stated by Graham – at the end of each book.

43 H.D., 'The Walls Do Not Fall,' *Trilogy* (New York: New Directions, 1998) 3. 'Incident' was the preferred euphemism in British newspapers when reporting on air strikes over Britain during World War II.

44 H.D., 'The Walls Do Not Fall,' 3.

45 Norman Holmes Pearson (ed.), 'Introduction,' *Trilogy* (New York: New Directions, 1973) vii.

46 H.D., 'The Walls Do Not Fall,' 3.

47 H.D., 'The Walls Do Not Fall' 4.

48 H.D., 'The Walls Do Not Fall' 49.

49 H.D., 'The Walls Do Not Fall' 6, 14.

50 H.D., 'The Walls Do Not Fall' 59.

51 H.D., 'The Walls Do Not Fall' 27 and 'Tribute to the Angels' 63.

52 H.D., 'Tribute to the Angels' 72.

53 H.D., 'Tribute to the Angels' 71, 83, 103.

54 Aliki Barnstone (ed.), 'Introduction,' *Trilogy* (New York: New Directions, 1998) vii.

55 H.D., 'Tribute to the Angels' 82, 87.

56 H.D., 'Tribute to the Angels' 83, 87.

57 H.D., 'Tribute to the Angels' 103.

58 H.D., 'The Flowering of the Rod' 158, 154.

59 H.D., 'The Flowering of the Rod' 158, 169.

60 H.D., 'The Flowering of the Rod' 172.

61 T.S. Eliot, 'Little Gidding,' *Four Quartets* in *The Complete Poems and Plays: 1909–1950* (New York: Harcourt Brace, 1962) 144.

62 H.D., 'The Flowering of the Rod,' *Trilogy* 124.

63 Eliot , 'Little Gidding' 145.

64 Helen Gardner, *The Art of T.S. Eliot* (London: Cresset Press, 1968) 2.

65 Mary Ann Gillies, *Henri Bergson and British Modernism* (Montreal and Kingston: McGill-Queen's University Press, 1996) 96.

66 Eliot, 'Burnt Norton' 117.

67 Little Gidding, near Cambridge, was the site of an Anglican religious community founded by Nicholas Ferrar in 1636 that blended Roman Catholic and Puritan faiths. The community's association with Catholic priests and provision of refuge to Charles I led to the destruction of the village church by Puritan troops.

68 The first American edition of *Four Quartets* was published a year earlier in May 1943 by the New York firm Harcourt Brace.

69 A. David Moody, '*Four Quartets*: Music, Word, Meaning and Value,' *The Cambridge Companion to T.S. Eliot* (Cambridge: Cambridge University Press, 1994) 151.

70 Eliot, 'Burnt Norton' 121.

71 Eliot, 'East Coker' 128.

72 Eliot, 'East Coker' 129.

73 Eliot, 'The Dry Salvages' 130.

74 Eliot, 'The Dry Salvages' 130.

75 Eliot, 'The Dry Salvages' 132.

76 Eliot, 'The Dry Salvages' 133.

77 Eliot, 'The Dry Salvages' 136.

78 Eliot, 'Little Gidding' 138.

79 Eliot, 'Little Gidding' 138–9.

80 Eliot, 'Little Gidding' 145.

81 Eliot, 'Little Gidding' 145.

82 Woolf committed suicide on 28 March 1941 at the height of Germany's success in the war. The reasons for her suicide have been widely debated, but in the end there can be little doubt that the effects of nightly bombing raids on Woolf's always fragile psyche must have been a contributing factor.

83 Joseph Kelly, *Our Joyce: From Outcast to Icon* (Austin: University of Texas Press, 1998) 2.

84 Jerome McGann, *The Beauty of Inflections* (Oxford: Clarendon Press, 1985) 21.

85 McGann, 24.

86 Kelly, 9.

87 Kelly, 10

88 Kevin Dettmar (ed.), *Rereading the New: A Backward Glance at Modernism* (Ann Arbor: University of Michigan Press, 1992) 6.

89 Elizabeth Drew published books on modern literature through to the 1960s, often with titles along the lines of *Poetry: A Modern Guide to Its Understanding and Enjoyment* (1959), *Discovering Drama* (1968) or *Discovering Modern Poetry* (1961), suggesting an ongoing commitment to the critical business of explicating modernist writing to non-specialist readers.

90 Ezra Pound, 'Manifesto,' *Poetry* (October 1932) 40–41.

91 Michael Levenson, *A Genealogy of Modernism: A Study of English Literary Doctrine, 1908–1922* (Cambridge: Cambridge University Press, 1984) viii.

92 W.K. Wimsatt and Cleanth Brooks, *Literary Criticism: A Short History* (Chicago: University of Chicago Press, 1957) 2: 730–1.

93 Michael Grant (ed.), *T.S. Eliot: The Critical Heritage* (London: Routledge) 1: 69.

94 Peter Bürger, *Theory of the Avant-Garde*, trans. Michael Shaw (Minneapolis: University of Minnesota Press, 1984) 22.

95 Lawrence Rainey, 'The Price of Modernism: Reconsidering the Publication of *The Waste Land,*' *Critical Quarterly* 31 (1989) 24.

96 See Kevin J. Dettmar and Stephen Watt (eds), *Marketing Modernisms: Self-Promotion, Canonisation and Rereading* (Ann Arbor: University of Michigan Press, 1996); Jayne E. Marek, *Women Editing Modernism: Little Magazines and Literary History* (Lexington: University Press of Kentucky, 1995); Joyce Piell Wexler, *Who Paid for Modernism? Art, Money, and the Fiction of Conrad, Joyce, and Lawrence* (Fayetteville: University of Arkansas Press, 1997); and Ian R. Willison et al. (eds), *Modernist Writers and the Marketplace* (London: Macmillan, 1996).

97 Michael North, *Reading 1922: A Return to the Scene of the Modern* (Oxford: Oxford University Press, 1999) 29.

98 See Joshua Esty, *A Shrinking Island: Modernism and National Culture in England* (Princeton: Princeton University Press, 2004); Douglas Mao and Rebecca L. Walkowitz (eds), *Bad Modernisms* (Durham: Duke University Press, 2006); and Andrew Thacker, *Moving Through Modernity* (Manchester: Manchester University Press, 2003).

99 See Edna Duffy, *The Subaltern Ulysses* (Minneapolis: University of Minnesota Press, 1994) and Peter Morey, *Fictions of India: Narrative and Power* (Edinburgh: Edinburgh University Press, 2000).

BIBLIOGRAPHY

PRIMARY SOURCES

Allen, Grant. *Falling in Love, with other Essays on More Exact Branches of Science*. London: Smith, Elder, & Co., 1889.

Auden, W.H., and Christopher Isherwood. *The Ascent of F6 and On the Frontier*. London: Faber, 1958.

Baudelaire, Charles. *The Painter of Modern Life and Other Essays*. Trans. Jonathan Mayne. London: Phaidon, 1964.

Blast (20 June 1914).

Bowen, Elizabeth. 'Preface,' *The Last September*. New York: Knopf, 1964.

Bowen, Elizabeth. *The Last September*. London: Penguin, 1987.

Brooke, Rupert. 'The Soldier,' *The Collected Poems of Rupert Brooke*. New York: Dodd, Mead, & Company, 1931.

Des Imagistes, An Anthology. London: The Poetry Bookshop, 1914.

Eliot, T.S. *Four Quartets* in *The Complete Poems and Plays: 1909–1950* New York: Harcourt Brace, 1962.

Eliot, T.S. 'Preludes,' *Blast* (July 1915): 48–9.

Eliot, T.S. '*Ulysses*, Order and Myth,' *Dial* (November 1923): 483.

Flint, F.S. 'History of Imagism,' *Egoist* 2 (1 May 1915): 70–1.

Flint, F.S. 'Imagisme,' *Poetry* (March 1913): 199.

Forster, E.M. *Aspects of the Novel*. New York: Harcourt Brace, 1927.

Forster, E.M. *A Passage to India*. New York: Harcourt Brace, 1984.

Grand, Sarah. 'The New Aspect of the Woman Question,' *A New Woman Reader: Fiction, Articles, Drama of the 1890s*. Ed. Carolyn Christensen Nelson. Peterborough ON: Broadview, 2001.

Graves, Robert. *Good–bye to All That*. 1929. New York: Anchor, 1998.

H. D. *Collected Poems*. Manchester: Carcanet, 1984.

H.D. 'Oread,' *Egoist* 1 (February 1914): 54–5.

H.D. *Trilogy*. 1973. New York: New Directions, 1998.

Hulme, T.E. *Further Speculations*. Ed. Samuel Hynes. Minneapolis: University of Minnesota Press, 1955.

Hulme, T.E. *Speculations*. Ed. Herbert Read. London: Routledge & Kegan Paul, 1924.

Huxley, Aldous. *Point Counter Point*. 1928. London: Flamingo, 1994.

Joyce, James. *Dubliners*. 1914. London: Vintage, 1993.

Lawrence, D.H. *The Prussian Officer and Other Stories*. Ed. John Worthen. Cambridge: Cambridge University Press, 1983.

Lewis, Wyndham. *Wyndham Lewis on Art: Collected Writings 1913–1956*. Eds Walter Michael and C. J. Fox. London: Thames and Hudson, 1969.

MacNeice, Louis. 'The Theatre,' *Spectator* (18 November 1938): 858.

Mansfield, Katherine. *In a German Pension*. London: Penguin, 1964.

Orwell, George. *Collected Essays, Journalism and Letters of George Orwell*, vol. 1. Eds Sonia Orwell and Ian Angus. New York: Harcourt Brace, 1968.

Orwell, George. *Homage to Catalonia*. Ed. Peter Davison. 1938. London: Penguin, 2000.

Orwell, George. *Orwell in Spain*. Ed. Peter Davison. London: Penguin, 2001.

Owen, Wilfred. 'Preface,' *The War Poems of Wilfred Owen*. Ed. Jon Silkin. London: Sinclair-Stevenson, 1994.

Pound, Ezra. *Personae: The Shorter Poems of Ezra Pound*. New York: New Directions, 1990.

Pound, Ezra. *The Letters of Ezra Pound*. Ed. D.D. Paige. London: Faber, 1951.

Pound, Ezra. *Literary Essays of Ezra Pound*. Ed. T.S. Eliot. London: Faber, 1968.

Pound, Ezra. 'Manifesto,' *Poetry* (October 1932): 40–1.

Pound, Ezra. 'Vortex,' *Blast* (20 June 1914): 153.

Pound, Ezra. 'Vorticism,' *Fortnightly Review, XCVI, n.s.* (1 September 1914): 469.

Sassoon, Siegfried. *Collected Poems 1908–1956*. London: Faber, 1961.

Sassoon, Siegfried. *Memoirs of an Infantry Officer*. London: Faber, 1930.

Somerville, E.O., and Martin Ross. *Some Experiences of an Irish R.M.* Nashville: J. Sanders & Co, 1998.

Spender, Stephen. *The Destructive Element*. London: Cape, 1935.

Spender, Stephen. 'Fable and Reportage,' *Left Review* 2 (November 1936): 782.

Spender, Stephen. 'Writers and Manifestos,' *Left Review* (February 1935): 145.

Whitman, Walt. *Leaves of Grass*. New York: Aventine Press, 1931.

Woolf, Leonard. *After the Deluge: A Study of Communal Psychology*. London: Hogarth Press, 1931.

Woolf, Virginia. *Between the Acts*. 1941. London: Penguin, 1992.

Woolf, Virginia. *Collected Essays*, vol. 2. New York: Harcourt, 1967.

Woolf, Virginia. *The Crowded Dance of Modern Life*. Ed. Rachel Bowlby. London: Penguin, 1992.

Woolf, Virginia. *The Diary of Virginia Woolf*, vol. 5. Ed. Anne Oliver Bell. London: Hogarth Press, 1977–1984.

Woolf, Virginia. *Three Guineas*. 1938. London: Blackwell, 2001

Woolf, Virginia. *A Woman's Essays*. Ed. Rachel Bowlby. London: Penguin, 1992.

SECONDARY SOURCES

Abrams, M.H. *A Glossary of Literary Terms*. 1957. New York: Holt, Rinehart, and Winston, 1988.

Adorno, Theodor. *Prisms*. Trans. Samuel and Shierry Weber. Cambridge MA: MIT Press, 1981.

Aitken, Ian. *Film and Reform: John Grierson and the Documentary Film Movement*. London: Routledge, 1990.

Allen, Nicholas. *George Russell and the New Ireland, 1905–1930*. Dublin: Four Courts, 2003.

Ames, Christopher. 'Carnivalesque Comedy in *Between the Acts*,' *Twentieth-Century Literature* Winter 44 (4): 394–408.

Armstrong, Paul B. 'Reading India: E.M. Forster and the Politics of Interpretation,' *Twentieth-Century Literature* 38 (1992): 365–85.

Attridge, Derek, ed. *The Cambridge Companion to James Joyce*. Cambridge: Cambridge University Press, 1990.

Ayers, David. *English Literature of the 1920s*. Edinburgh: Edinburgh University Press, 1999.

Bahlke George, ed. *Critical Essays on W. H. Auden*. New York: G. K. Hall, 1991.

Barnstone, Aliki, ed. 'Introduction,' *Trilogy*. New York: New Directions, 1998.

Baxendale, John, and Christopher Pawling. *Narrating the Thirties*. London: Palgrave Macmillan, 1995.

Bayley, John. *The Short Story: Henry James to Elizabeth Bowen*. Brighton: Harvester Press, 1988.

Beckson, Karl, and Arthur Ganz. *Literary Terms: A Dictionary* New York: Noonday, 1989.

Beer, Gillian. 'Introduction,' *Between the Acts*. London: Penguin, 1992.

Beer, Gillian. 'Negation in *A Passage to India*,' *A Passage To India: Essays in Interpretation*. London: Macmillan, 1985, 44–58.

Beer, John, ed. *A Passage to India: Essays in Interpretation*. London: Macmillan, 1985.

Bell, Kathleen. 'Auden, Isherwood, and the Censors,' *W.H. Auden Society Newsletter* 10.11 (1993): 15–21.

Bell, Michael, ed. *The Context of English Literature 1900–1930*. London: Methuen, 1980.

Bennett, Andrew, and Nicholas Royle. *Elizabeth Bowen and the Dissolution of the Novel: Still Lives*. New York: St. Martin's, 1995.

Benstock, Shari. *Women of the Left Bank: Paris 1900–1940*. Austin: University of Texas Press, 1986.

Bergonzi, Bernard, ed. *T.S. Eliot's Four Quartets: A Casebook*. London: Macmillan, 1969.

Bergonzi, Bernard. *Reading the Thirties*. London: Macmillan, 1978.

Black, Michael. *D.H. Lawrence–The Early Fiction*. London: Macmillan, 1986.

Blake, Ann, ed. *England Through Colonial Eyes in Twentieth-Century Fiction*. New York: Palgrave, 2001.

Bluemel, Kristin. *George Orwell and the Radical Eccentrics: Intermodernism in Literary London*. New York: Palgrave Macmillan, 2004.

Bornstein, George. *Material Modernism: The Politics of the Page*. Cambridge: Cambridge University Press, 2001.

Bowlby, Rachel. *Feminist Destinations and Further Essays on Virginia Woolf*. Edinburgh: Edinburgh University Press, 1997.

Bradbury, Malcolm, and James McFarlane, eds. *Modernism: 1890–1930*. 1976. London: Penguin, 1983.

Brannigan, John, Geoff Ward, and Julian Wolfreys, eds. *Re:Joyce: Text, Culture, Politics*. New York: St. Martin's, 1998.

Brown, E.K. *Rhythm in the Novel*. Toronto: University of Toronto Press, 1950.

Bryant Jordan, Heather. *How Will the Heart Endure: Elizabeth Bowen and the Landscape of War*. Ann Arbor: University of Michigan Press, 1992.

Bryant, Marsha. *Auden and Documentary in the 1930s*. Charlottesville: University of Virginia Press, 1997.

Bürger, Peter. *Theory of the Avant-Garde*. Trans. Michael Shaw. Minneapolis: University of Minnesota Press, 1984.

Busse, Kristina. 'Reflecting the Subject in History: The Return of the Real in *Between the Acts*,' *Woolf Studies Annual* 7 (2001): 75–101.

Cahalan, James M. *Double Visions: Women and Men in Modern and Contemporary Irish Fiction*. Syracuse: Syracuse University Press, 1999.

Campbell, Patrick. *Siegfried Sassoon: A Study of the War Poetry*. London: McFarland, 1999.

Carpenter, Humphry. *W.H. Auden: A Biography*. London: George, Allen & Unwin, 1981.

Carter, Ronald, ed. *Thirties Poets: The Auden Group*. London: Macmillan, 1984.

Caserio, Robert. *The Novel in England, 1900–1950*. New York: Twayne, 1999.

Chekhov, Anton. *Letters on the Short Story, the Drama and other Literary Topics*. Ed. Louis S. Friedland. New York: B. Blom, 1964.

Collecott, Diana. *H.D. and Sapphic Modernism 1910–1950*. Cambridge: Cambridge University Press, 1999.

Cooper, John Xiros. *T.S. Eliot and the Ideology of Four Quartets*. Cambridge: Cambridge University Press, 1995.

Corcoran, Marlena, and Jolanta Wawrzycka, eds. *Gender in Joyce*. Gainesville: University Press of Florida, 1997.

Corcoran, Neil. 'Discovery of a Lack: History and Ellipsis in Elizabeth Bowen's *The Last September*,' *Irish University Review: A Journal of Irish Studies* 2001 Autumn–Winter 31 (2): 315–33.

Coyle, Michael. *Erza Pound and African American Modernism*. Orono ME: National Poetry Foundation, 2001.

Cramer, Patricia. 'Virginia Woolf's Matriarchal Family of Origins in *Between the Acts*,' *Twentieth-Century Literature* 39.2 (1993): 166–84.

Cuddon, J.A. *Dictionary of Literary Terms and Literary Theory*. 4th ed. London: Penguin, 2004.

Cuddy-Keane, Melba. 'The Politics of Comic Modes in Virginia Woolf's *Between the Acts*,' *PMLA* 105 (1995): 273–85.

Cunningham, Valentine. *British Writers of the Thirties*. Oxford: Oxford University Press, 1988.

Cushman, Thomas, and John Rodden. *George Orwell: Into the Twenty-first Century*. Boulder CO: Paradigm, 2004.

Das, G.K. '*A Passage to India*: A Socio-Historical Study,' *A Passage to India: Essays in Interpretation*. ed. John Beer. London: Macmillan, 1985, 1–15.

Daughtery, Beth Rigel, and Eileen Barrett, eds. *Virginia Woolf: Texts and Contexts*. New York: Pace University Press, 1996.

Davies, Tony, ed. 'Introduction,' *A Passage to India*. Buckingham: Open University Press, 1994.

Deane, Patrick, ed. *History in Our Hands: A Critical Anthology of Writings on Literature, Culture and Politics from the 1930s*. Leicester: Leicester University Press, 1998.

Dettmar, Kevin, ed. *Rereading the New: A Backward Glance at Modernism*. Ann Arbor: University of Michigan Press, 1992.

Dettmar, Kevin and Jennifer Wicke, eds. *The Twentieth Century*. vol. 2c. *The Longman Anthology of British Literature*. Ed. David Damrosch. New York: Longman, 2003.

Dettmar, Kevin J. and Stephen Watt, eds. *Marketing Modernisms: Self-Promotion, Canonisation and Rereading*. Ann Arbor: University of Michigan Press, 1996.

DiBattista, Maria, and Lucy McDiarmid. *High and Low Moderns: Literature and Culture, 1889–1939*. Oxford: Oxford University Press, 1996.

Doyle, Laura, and Laura Winkiel, eds. *Geomodernisms: Race, Modernism, Modernity*. Bloomington: Indiana University Press, 2005.

Drew, Elizabeth. *The Modern Novel*. London: Jonathan Cape, 1926.

Duff, Charles. *James Joyce and the Plain Reader—An Essay*. London: Desmond Harmsworth, 1932.

Duffy, Edna. *The Subaltern Ulysses*. Minneapolis: University of Minnesota Press, 1994.

Dunn, Maggie, and Ann Morris. *The Composite Novel: The Short Story Cycle in Transition*. Toronto: Macmillan, 1995.

Eagleton, Terry, and Drew Milne. *Marxist Literary Theory*. Oxford: Blackwell, 1996.

Edmunds, Susan. *Out of Line: History, Psychoanalysis, and Montage in H.D.'s Long Poems*. Stanford: Stanford University Press, 1994.

Elliott, Bridget, and Jo-Ann Wallace. *Woman Artists and Writers: Modernist (Im)Positionings*. London: Routledge, 1994.

Ellman, Richard. *James Joyce*. Oxford: Oxford University Press, 1959.

Esty, Joshua. *A Shrinking Island: Modernism and National Culture in England*. Princeton: Princeton University Press, 2004.

'Fashions of the Mind,' *Vogue* (Early February. 1924) 49.

Faulks, Sebastian. 'Caught in the Web,' *Guardian* 24 September 2005.

Felski, Rita. *The Gender of Modernity*. Cambridge MA: Harvard University Press, 1995.

Ferguson, Robert. *The Short Sharp Life of T.E. Hulme*. London: Allen Lane, 2002.

Fernihough, Anne, ed. *The Cambridge Companion to D.H. Lawrence*. Cambridge: Cambridge University Press, 2001.

Fernihough, Anne. 'Introduction,' *In a German Pension*. London: Penguin, 1999.

Finney, Michael. 'Why Gretta Falls Asleep: A Postmodern Sugarplum,' *Studies in Short Fiction*. 1995 Summer 32 (3): 475–81.

Flint, Kate. 'Reading Uncommonly: Virginia Woolf and the Practice of Reading,' *Yearbook of English Studies* 26 (1996): 187–98.

Flora, Joseph M. *The English Short Story, 1880–1945*. Boston: Twayne, 1985.

Frye, Northrop. *Anatomy of Criticism*. Princeton: Princeton University Press, 1957.

Gardener, Philip, ed. *E.M. Forster: The Critical Heritage*. London: Routledge & Kegan Paul, 1973.

Gardner, Helen. *The Art of T.S. Eliot*. London: Faber, 1949.

Gardner, Helen. *The Art of T.S. Eliot*. London: Cresset, 1968.

Giddens, Anthony. *The Consequences of Modernity*. Stanford: Stanford University Press, 1990.

Gilbert, Sandra M., and Susan Gubar. *No Man's Land: The Place of the Woman Writer in the Twentieth Century*. 3 vols. New Haven CT: Yale University Press, 1988–94.

Gillies, Mary Ann. *Henri Bergson and British Modernism*. Montreal and Kingston: McGill-Queen's University Press, 1996.

Gorer, Geoffrey. Review of *Homage to Catalonia* in *Time and Tide* 30 April 1938 (599–600): 599.

Graham, Sarah H.S. '"We have a secret. We are alive": H.D.'s *Trilogy* as a Response to War,' *Texas Studies in Literature and Language*, 44: 2 (Summer 2002): 162.

Grant, Michael, ed. *T.S. Eliot: The Critical Heritage*. London: Routledge, 1982.

Grierson, John. *Grierson on Documentary*. Ed. Forsyth Hardy. London: Faber, 1966.

Griest, Guinevere L. *Mudie's Circulating Library and the Victorian Novel*. Bloomington: Indiana University Press, 1970.

Hanson, Clare. *Short Stories and Short Fictions, 1880–1980*. London: Macmillan, 1985.

Hapgood, Lynne, and Nancy Paxton. *Outside Modernism: In Pursuit of the English Novel, 1900–30*. New York: St. Martin's, 2000.

Harding, Jason. *The 'Criterion': Cultural Politics and Periodical Networks in Interwar Britain*. Oxford: Oxford University Press, 2002.

Harris, Wendell. 'Vision and Form: The English Novel and the Emergence of the Short Story,' *Victorian Newsletter* 47 (1975): 8–12.

Head, Dominic. *The Modernist Short Story: A Study in Theory and Practice*. Cambridge: Cambridge University Press, 1992.

Herrnstein Smith, Barbara. 'Narrative Versions, Narrative Theories,' *On Narrative*. Ed. W.J.T. Mitchell. Chicago: University of Chicago Press, 1981, 213–36.

Hoggart, Richard. 'An Introductory Essay on *The Ascent of F6* and *On the Frontier*,' in *Critical Essays on W.H. Auden*. Ed. George W. Bahlke. New York: G.K. Hall, 1991, 64–9.

Howe, Irving. *Modern Literary Criticism*. Boston: Beacon Press, 1958.

Howes, Marjorie. 'Tradition, Gender and Migration in "The Dead," or: How Many People Has Gretta Conroy Killed?' *Yale Journal of Criticism: Interpretation in the Humanities* 2002 Spring 15 (1): 149–71.

Hussey, Mark, ed. *Virginia Woolf and War: Fiction, Reality and Myth*. Syracuse: Syracuse University Press, 1991.

Hynes, Samuel. *The Auden Generation Literature and Politics in England in the 1930s*. London: Bodley Head, 1976.

Innes, C.D. *Modern British Drama*. Cambridge: Cambridge University Press, 2002.

James, Henry. 'Preface' to 'The Lessons of the Master,' *The Art of the Novel: Critical Prefaces*. New York: C. Scribner's Sons, 1962.

Jauss, Hans Robert. *Towards an Aesthetic of Reception*. Minneapolis: University of Minnesota Press, 1982.

Johnson, Josephine. *Florence Farr: Bernard Shaw's 'New Woman'*. Totawa NJ: Rowman and Littlefield, 1975.

Jones, Suzanne W. ed. *Writing the Man Artist: Essays on Poetics, Politics and Portraiture*. Philadelphia: University of Pennsylvania Press, 1991

Kalnins, Maria. 'D.H. Lawrence's "Two Marriages" and "Daughters of the Vicar",' *Ariel* 7 (January 1976): 32–49.

Kaplan, Sydney. *Katherine Mansfield and the Origins of Modernist Fiction.* Ithaca: Cornell University Press, 1991.

Kelly, Aaron, and Alan Gillis, eds. *Critical Ireland: New Essays in Literature and Culture.* Dublin: Four Courts, 2001.

Kelly, Joseph. 'Joyce's Marriage Cycle,' *Studies in Short Fiction* 1995 Summer 32 (3): 367–78.

Kelly, Joseph. *Our Joyce: From Outcast to Icon.* Austin: University of Texas Press, 1998.

Kenner, Hugh. *The Pound Era.* Berkeley: University of California Press, 1973.

Kiely, Robert, eds. *Modernism Reconsidered.* Cambridge MA: Harvard University Press, 1983.

Klindienst Joplin, Patricia. 'The Authority of Illusion: Feminism and Fascism in Virginia Woolf's *Between the Acts,' South Central Review* 6 (1989): 88–104.

Kreilkamp, Vera. *The Anglo-Irish Novel and the Big House.* Syracuse: Syracuse University Press, 1998.

Laird, Holly. *Women Coauthors.* Urbana: University of Illinois Press, 2000.

Laity, Paul, ed. *Left Book Club: Anthology.* London: Gollancz, 2001.

Lane, Arthur. *An Adequate Response: The War Poetry of Wilfred Owen and Siegfried Sassoon.* Detroit: Wayne State University Press, 1972.

Ledger, Sally. *The New Woman: Fiction and Feminism at the Fin de Siècle.* Manchester: Manchester University Press, 1997.

Lee, Hermione. *Virginia Woolf.* London: Chatto & Windus, 1996.

Leonard, Garry. *Reading Dubliners Again: A Lacanian Perspective.* Syracuse: Syracuse University Press, 1993.

Levenson, Michael. *The Genealogy of Modernism: A Study of English Literary Doctrine, 1908–1922.* Cambridge: Cambridge University Press, 1984.

Lúkacs, Georg. 'The Ideology of Modernism,' *Marxism and Human Liberation.* Ed. E. San Juan, Jr. New York: Delta Books, 1973.

MacDonald, Kevin, and Mark Cousins, eds. *Imagining Reality: The Faber Book of the Documentary.* London: Faber, 1998.

MacKay, Marina. 'Putting the House in Order: Virginia Woolf and Blitz Modernism,' *Modern Language Quarterly* 66: 2 (June 2005): 227–52.

Mao, Douglas, and Rebecca L. Walkowitz, eds. *Bad Modernisms.* Durham: Duke University Press, 2006.

Marek, Jayne E. *Women Editing Modernism: Little Magazines and Literary History.* Lexington: University Press of Kentucky, 1995.

Mariet, Philip. Review of *Homage to Catalonia* as reprinted in Jeffrey Meyers, ed. *George Orwell: The Critical Heritage.* London: Routledge, 1975

Marks, Patricia. *Bicycles, Bangs and Bloomers: The New Woman in the Popular Press.* Lexington: University of Kentucky Press, 1990.

Martz, Louis. 'Introduction,' *H.D. Collected Poems, 1912–1944.* Ed. Louis Martz. Manchester: Carcanet, 1984.

May, Charles. *The Short Story: The Reality of Artifice.* Toronto: Macmillan, 1995.

McDiarmid, Lucy. *Saving Civilization: Yeats, Eliot, and Auden Between the Wars*. Cambridge: Cambridge University Press, 1984.

McDonald, Peter. 'Believing in the Thirties,' in Keith Williams and Steven Matthews, eds. *Rewriting the Thirties: Modernism and After* London: Longman, 1997, 71–90.

McGann, Jerome. *The Beauty of Inflections*. Oxford: Clarendon Press, 1985.

Mendelson, Edward, ed. *Plays and Other Dramatic Writings by W.H. Auden, 1928–1938*. Princeton: Princeton University Press, 1988.

Miller, Andrew John. '"Our Representative, Our Spokesman": Modernity, Professionalism, and Representation in Virginia Woolf's *Between the Acts*.' *Studies in the Novel* 33.1 (2001): 34–50.

Miller, Marlowe A. 'Unveiling "The Dialectic of Culture and Barbarism" in British Pageantry: Virginia Woolf's *Between the Acts*,' *Papers on Language and Literature* 1998 Spring 34 (2):134–61.

Miller, Tyrus. *Late Modernism: Politics, Fiction, and the Arts Between the World Wars*. Berkeley: University of California Press, 1999.

Moeyes, Paul. S*iegfried Sassoon, Scorched Glory: A Critical Study*. New York: St. Martin's, 1997.

Moody, A. David. '*Four Quartets*: Music, Word, Meaning and Value,' *The Cambridge Companion to T.S. Eliot*. Ed. A. David Moody. Cambridge: Cambridge University Press, 1994, 142–57.

Moody, A. David, ed. *The Cambridge Companion to T.S. Eliot*. Cambridge: Cambridge University Press, 1994.

Moran, Patricia. *Word of Mouth: Body Language in Katherine Mansfield and Virginia Woolf*. Charlottesville: University Press of Virginia, 1996.

Morey, Peter. *Fictions of India: Narrative and Power*. Edinburgh: Edinburgh University Press, 2000.

Muggeridge, Malcolm. *The Thirties*. London: Hamish Hamilton, 1940.

Nelson, Carolyn Christensen, ed. *A New Woman Reader: Fiction, Articles, and Drama of the 1890s*. Peterborough ON: Broadview Press, 2001.

Nicholls, Peter. *Modernisms: A Literary Guide*. London: Macmillan, 1995.

Nichols, Bill. 'Documentary Film and the Modernist Avant-Garde,' *Critical Inquiry* 27 (Summer 2001): 580–610.

North, Michael. *Reading 1922: A Return to the Scene of the Modern*. Oxford: Oxford University Press, 1999.

Osteen, Mark. '"A Splendid Bazaar": The Shopper's Guide to the New *Dubliners*,' *Studies in Short Fiction* 1995 Summer 32 (3): 483–96.

Parsons, Deborah L. *Streetwalking the Metropolis: Women, The City and Modernity*. Oxford: Oxford University Press, 2000.

Pearson, Norman Holmes, ed. 'Introduction,' *Trilogy*. New York: New Directions, 1973.

Poe, Edgar Allan. 'Review of Nathaniel Hawthorne's *Twice-Told Tales*,' in *The Complete Works of Edgar Allan Poe*. vol. 11. ed. James A. Harrison. 1902. New York: T.Y. Crowell, 1965.

Pollard, Charles W. *New World Modernisms: T.S. Eliot, Derek Walcott, and Kamau Brathwaite*. Charlottesville: University of Virginia Press, 2004.

Pondrom, Cyrena N., ed. 'Selected Letters from H.D. to F.S. Flint: A Commentary on the Imagist Period,' *Contemporary Literature* 10.4 (1969): 557–86.

Porcel-Garcia, Maria Isabel. 'Gretta Conroy: The Dead Woman/The Dead One?' *Papers on Joyce*, 1999 (5): 51–65.

Pratt, William. 'Introduction,' *The Imagist Poem: Modern Poetry In Miniature*. Ashland OR: Story Line, 2001.

Pridmore-Brown, Michele. 'Virginia Woolf and the BBC: Public and Private Voices,' *Virginia Woolf Miscellany* 56 (2000): 3–4.

Rado, Lisa. *Modernism, Gender, and Culture: A Cultural Studies Approach.* New York: Garland, 1997.

Rado, Lisa, ed. *Rereading Modernism: New Directions for Feminist Criticism.* New York: Garland, 1994.

Rae, Patricia. *The Practical Muse: Pragmatist Poetics in Hulme, Pound and Stevens.* Lewisburg: Bucknell University Press, 1997.

Rainer, Emig. *W.H. Auden: Towards a Postmodern Poetics.* London: Macmillan, 2000.

Rainey, Lawrence. 'The Price of Modernism: Reconsidering the Publication of *The Waste Land*,' *Critical Quarterly* 31 (1989): 21–47.

Reilly, Catherine. *Scars Upon My Heart.* London: Virago, 1981.

Rice, Thomas Jackson. 'Paradigm Lost: "Grace" and the Arrangement of *Dubliners*,' *Studies in Short Fiction* 1995 Summer 32 (3): 405–21.

Richardson, Angelique, and Chris Willis, eds. *The New Woman in Fiction and in Fact: Fin de Siècle Feminisms.* London: Macmillan, 2001.

Robinson, Roger, ed. *Katherine Mansfiel —In From the Margin.* Baton Rouge: Louisiana State University Press, 1994.

Roe, Sue, and Susan Sellers, eds. *The Cambridge Companion to Virginia Woolf.* Cambridge: Cambridge University Press, 2000.

Romero Salvadó, Francisco J. *The Spanish Civil War.* London: Palgrave, 2005.

Schwartz, Sanford. *The Matrix of Modernism: Pound, Eliot and Early Twentieth-Century Thought.* Princeton: Princeton University Press, 1985.

Scott, Bonnie Kime. *The Gender of Modernism: A Critical Anthology.* Bloomington: Indiana University Press, 1990.

Scott, Bonnie Kime. *Refiguring Modernism.* 2 vols. Bloomington: Indiana University Press, 1995.

Shaw, Valerie. *The Short Story: A Critical Introduction.* London: Longman, 1983.

Shuttleworth, Antony, ed. *And In Our Time: Vision, Revision, and British Writing of the 1930s.* London: Associated University Press, 2003.

Shuttleworth, Antony. 'The Real George Orwell: Dis-simulation in *Homage to Catalonia* and *Coming Up for Air*,' in Antony Shuttleworth, ed. *And In Our Time: Vision, Revision, and British Writing of the 1930s.* London: Associated University Press, 2003, 204–220.

Sillars, Stuart. *Structure and Dissolution in English Writing, 1910–1920.* London: Macmillan, 1999.

Silver, Brenda R. 'Periphrasis and Rape in *A Passage to India*,' *E.M. Forster: New Case Books*. Ed. Jeremy Tambling. London: Macmillan, 1995, 171–94.

Spender, Stephen. *The Struggle of the Modern.* Berkeley: University of California, 1963.

Spender, Stephen. *The Thirties and After: Poetry, Politics, People*. London: Fontana, 1978.

Stallworthy, John, and David Daiches, eds. *The Norton Anthology of English Literature*. 7th ed. vol. 2c. New York: Norton, 2000.

Stott, William. *Documentary Expression and Thirties America*. Oxford: Oxford University Press, 1973.

Sword, Helen. *Engendering Inspiration: Visionary Strategies in Rilke, Lawrence, and H.D.* Ann Arbor: University of Michigan Press, 1995.

Symons, Julian. 'Introduction,' *Homage to Catalonia*. Ed. Peter Davison. London: Penguin, 1989.

Taylor, Georgina. *H.D. and the Public Sphere of Modernist Women Writers, 1913–1946: Talking Women.* Oxford: Clarendon Press, 2001.

Thacker, Andrew. *Moving Through Modernity*. Manchester: Manchester University Press, 2003.

Thorton, Weldon. *D.H. Lawrence: A Study of the Short Fiction.* New York: Twayne, 1993.

Volker, Schulz. 'D.H. Lawrence's Early Masterpiece of Short Fiction: "Odour of Chrysanthemums",' *Studies of Short Fiction* 1991 Summer 28 (3): 363–70.

Westman, Karin E. '"For her generation the newspaper was a book": Media, Mediation, and Oscillation in Virginia Woolf's *Between the Acts*,' *Journal of Modern Literature* 29: 2 (Winter 2006): 1–18.

Wexler, Joyce Piell. *Who Paid for Modernism? Art, Money, and the Fiction of Conrad, Joyce, and Lawrence.* Fayetteville: University of Arkansas Press, 1997.

Willet, John, ed. *Brecht on Theatre*. London: Methuen, 1964.

Williams, Julia McElhattan. '"Fiction with the Texture of History": Elizabeth Bowen's *The Last September*,' *MFS: Modern Fiction Studies* 1995 Summer 41 (2): 219–42.

Williams, Keith and Steven Matthews, eds. *Rewriting the Thirties*. London: Longman, 1997.

Williams, Raymond. *The Politics of Modernism: Against the New Conformists*. London: Verso, 1989.

Willison, Ian R. et al., eds. *Modernist Writers and the Marketplace*. London: Macmillan, 1996.

Wimsatt, W.K. and Cleanth Brooks. *Literary Criticism: A Short History*. Chicago: University of Chicago Press, 1957.

Wright, David. 'Interactive Stories in *Dubliners*,' *Studies in Short Fiction* 1995 Summer 32(3): 285–93.

INDEX